WOLLSTONECRAFT, MILL, AND WOMEN'S HUMAN RIGHTS

EILEEN HUNT BOTTING

Wollstonecraft, Mill, and Women's Human Rights

Yale UNIVERSITY PRESS

NEW HAVEN AND LONDON

Published with assistance from the foundation established in memory of
Philip Hamilton McMillan of the Class of 1894, Yale College.

Yale University Press books may be purchased in quantity for educational,
business, or promotional use. For information, please e-mail sales.press@yale
.edu (U.S. office) or sales@yaleup.co.uk (U.K. office).

Set in Janson Oldstyle type by Newgen North America.
Printed in the United States of America.
Library of Congress Control Number: 2015947730
ISBN: 978-0-300-18615-4 (cloth : alk. paper)

A catalogue record for this book is available from the British Library.

This paper meets the requirements of ANSI/NISO z39.48-1992
(Permanence of Paper).

10 9 8 7 6 5 4 3 2 1

CONTENTS

ACKNOWLEDGMENTS

First, I need to thank Bill Frucht for arranging the thoughtful readers' reports on the book that have encouraged me to develop it into its current form. In addition, I have benefited immensely from the mentoring of Nancy Hirschmann, Virginia Sapiro, Gordon Schochet, Ian Shapiro, Rogers M. Smith, Steven B. Smith, and Sylvana Tomaselli. Chapter 4 is partly based on my research and writing for an article cowritten with my former undergraduate student Sean Kronewitter, "Westernization and Women's Rights: Non-Western European Responses to Mill's *Subjection of Women*, 1869–1908," *Political Theory* 40:4 (August 2012), 464–94, and an article cowritten with Dr. Charlotte Hammond Matthews of the University of Edinburgh, "Overthrowing the Floresta-Wollstonecraft Myth for Latin American Feminism," *Gender and History* 26:1 (April 2014), 64–83. Chapter 5 draws on my work for an article cowritten with my former undergraduate students Christine Carey Wilkerson and Elizabeth N. Kozlow, "Wollstonecraft as an International Feminist Meme," *Journal of Women's History* 26:2 (Summer 2014), 13–38. In both chapters 4 and 5, I built on some of my arguments originally written for the essay "The Personal Is Political: Wollstonecraft's Witty, First-Person, Feminist Voice," in Mary Wollstonecraft, *A Vindication of the Rights of Woman*, ed. Eileen Hunt Botting (New Haven: Yale University Press, 2014), 261–79. In 2008 and 2011, the Kroc Institute for International Peace Studies at the University of Notre Dame provided funding to support the professional translation of a variety of texts used to chronicle Wollstonecraft's and Mill's international reception. The Institute for Scholarship in the Liberal Arts at Notre Dame enabled me to hire a great copy editor, Mary Copeland, and an excellent research assistant, Cameron O'Bannon.

Finally, this book is for my family—the living, the dead, and those yet to be born.

INTRODUCTION
WOMEN'S HUMAN RIGHTS AS INTEGRAL
TO UNIVERSAL HUMAN RIGHTS

Wollstonecraft and Mill: Two Watersheds
for the Idea of Women's Human Rights

The idea of women's human rights is the view that women are entitled to equal rights with men because of the sexes' shared status as human beings. Mary Wollstonecraft first and John Stuart Mill after her were the primary philosophical architects of this view. Wollstonecraft developed a rational theological justification for the idea that women held equal rights alongside men, while Mill built a secular liberal utilitarian foundation for the same argument. Each of these watershed contributions to theories of women's human rights—the first religious, the second secular—is best understood as emerging from a sequential (if often implicit) dialogue. Looking backward, this dialogue moved significantly beyond past traditions of thought concerning the rights of persons, which had been biased toward, and even exclusively focused upon, men. Going forward, their international reception by both Western and non-Western intellectuals ensured that Wollstonecraft and Mill have shaped debates about women's human rights on a global scale. There have been many dozens of thinkers and activists from around the world who helped to form this powerful political concept, in part through a dialogue with these two innovative schools of thought.

In order to argue for the human rights of women, Wollstonecraft, Mill, and their international interlocutors were forced to reconceive the notion of human rights itself. They realized that the idea of human rights could not be universal—that is, apply equally to each and every human being—without the explicit inclusion of women, or "half the human race." Without such universal coverage for men and women alike, the idea of human rights would not be coherent, let alone just. Wollstonecraft's and Mill's joint reconceptualization of human rights undermined the idea of the patriarchal family and its traditional rationalizations: for until the family underwent an egalitarian transformation, human rights would not be available to women. Their shared understanding of universal human rights also threatened to destabilize a range of patriarchal institutions and practices related to marriage, education, law, government, and political economy. Given its global reach—actual and potential—the idea of women's human rights should be understood as a central concept for modern political philosophy. Yet its intellectual history has largely been untold until now.[1]

Defining Women's Human Rights

Before we can understand or even trace the intellectual history of the idea of women's human rights as rooted in Wollstonecraft, Mill, and their global readership, we need to have a grasp of the concept's more recent definition in world politics and international law. The 1948 Universal Declaration of Human Rights recognized "the equal rights of men and women" in its preamble. Yet the declaration's only other specific mention of women, in article 16, strongly associated them with their traditional reproductive roles within marriage and the family: "Men and women of full age, without any limitation due to race, nationality or religion, have the right to marry and to found a family." Second-wave feminists underscored the moral problems with the marginalized and domesticated status of women within appeals to universal human rights after World War II. Women's rights were not typically seen as integral to a general set of human rights to which women were entitled on the basis of their humanity but rather were seen as rights that they possessed on the basis of their gender roles and sexual functions. In her 1966 Statement of Purpose for the National Organization for Women, Betty Friedan called for a renewed attention "to the proposition that women, first and foremost, are human beings, who, like all other people in our society, must have the chance to develop their fullest human potential."[2]

After the adoption of the Convention on the Elimination of All Forms of Discrimination against Women (CEDAW) by the General Assembly of the United Nations in 1979, the idea of women's human rights became a cornerstone of United Nations development programs, state constitutions, and democratic social movements around the globe. Charlotte Bunch contributed to making the idea into a feminist idiom, through her advisory roles in the United Nations and her founding of a research institute on women and global leadership at Rutgers University in 1989. The same year, feminist activists from the Philippines-based GABRIELA women's coalition had inspired her with the slogan "women's rights are human rights." In a 1990 article, Bunch proposed that theorists and policy makers take a more "creative" approach to human rights. The ongoing "feminist transformation of human rights," if more broadly adopted, could challenge the "narrow" legal definition of human rights so that "women's lives" would be recognized as an integral part of the human experience that international law sought to protect.[3]

Held in June 1993, the United Nations' World Conference on Human Rights built on the rising international view that women's rights are a kind of human rights. Participants in the conference produced the Vienna Declaration on Human Rights. The Vienna Declaration represented a milestone for human rights and for feminism because of its definition of the term "human rights of women" for international law. The document used the term "human rights of women" in two interrelated ways. First, it meant women's shared rights with men, such as nourishment, safety, and education. As a corollary, it entailed women's equal access to these human rights, without gender discrimination. Second, it meant women's rights as human beings to be free from "gender-specific abuses" such as "murder, systematic rape, sexual slavery, and forced pregnancy," as was tragically prevalent in "situations of armed conflict."[4]

The first branch of the Vienna Declaration's definition of women's human rights presented those rights as equally shared with men, on the basis of their shared and equal status as human beings. As stated in article 1, "The human rights of women and of the girl-child are an

3

inalienable, integral and indivisible part of universal human rights." This conception of women's human rights was identical to the conception of universal human rights promulgated by the Universal Declaration in 1948. Its rhetorical formulation, however, aimed to remind people that women are human like men and therefore are entitled to share the same basic human rights as men.[5]

An offshoot of this first definition of women's human rights specified a fundamental right to nondiscrimination. Reinforcing CEDAW, the Vienna Declaration called for the "elimination of gender bias in the administration of justice" as one of the human rights to which both women and men were entitled. This universalistic legal principle of nondiscrimination, if implemented, would allow for the practical possibility of equal access to the human rights shared between the sexes. This principle had to be implemented in a way that respected the equality of men and women in order to realize its objective of ensuring their equal access to human rights such as nourishment and education.[6]

The second branch of the Vienna Declaration's definition of women's human rights did not dwell on abstract issues of justice, such as defining equality of rights and access to them, but concentrated rather on concrete issues of injustice. In particular, it focused on remedying the gender-specific injustices women had faced because they had historically been denied both entitlement and access to universal human rights. To address these gender-specific injustices, the universalistic concept of women's human rights had to be applied in a way that recognized the fact that women on the whole had typically faced particular kinds of human rights violations. The Vienna Declaration specified sexual violence as the main and most troubling example of a human rights violation that affected women more than men. Independent of which sex was the victim, such violations of human rights were wrong. Yet the differences in how sexual violence affected men and women were real and thus relevant for future lawmaking. Because they had been disproportionately subjected to sexual violence, women around the globe had an urgent need for new laws and policies that explicitly protected their gender against further violations of their human rights to bodily integrity, sexual choice and expression, personal security, and, most important, life itself.[7] Taken together, the two branches of the Vienna Declaration's definition of women's human rights raise a paradox. How can women's human rights, such as the right not to be raped, be both universal in scope and particular to women? Put another way, how can human rights function as absolute moral standards at the same time as they are tailored to address contingencies of gender, culture, time, and place?

A resolution to this paradox is implicit in the Vienna Declaration's two-branch approach to defining women's human rights. Imagine the two branches of the definition of women's human rights as springing from their roots in the Universal Declaration, especially its preamble's statement of "the equal and inalienable rights of all members of the human family." With this image in mind, the right not to be raped may be categorized under the branch of shared and equal human rights for men and women as well as under the branch of gender-specific human rights for women. Because both kinds of women's human rights are derivative from universal human rights, the right not to be raped is ultimately a universal human right even if particular laws and policies at any given time or place focus on women's special and urgent need for its assurance. The two-part structure of the legal definition of women's human rights suits its application to the concrete complexities of politics and law, including the global problem of discrimination against women and how it intersects with other dangerous prejudices. The internal complexity of the idea also suggests its interest for abstract debates in moral, political, and feminist philosophy, such as the relationship between the universal and the particular, the absolute and the relative, as well as conceptions of equality and difference.[8]

Tracing a Genealogy of Women's Human Rights: Wollstonecraft, Mill, and Beyond

The philosophical roots of this international legal definition of women's human rights can indeed be traced long before the United

Nations' human rights declarations of 1993 and 1948. Through this first book-length comparative study of the political theories of Wollstonecraft (1759–97) and Mill (1806–73), I argue that they represent two watershed moments—the former religious and the latter secular—in the development of this influential modern political concept. The concept of women's human rights grew not from the heavily invoked, revolutionary-era idea of the "rights of man" but rather from the more radical idea of the "rights of woman." The introduction of the concept of the rights of woman amid the late eighteenth-century European and American discourses on "natural rights" and the "rights of man" made the emergent idea of "human rights" universal in scope, applying to each and every human. As Wollstonecraft argued in 1792, it was necessary to revise the constitution of the French republic to include "the rights of woman" in order to realize "JUSTICE for one half of the human race." Without the rights of woman, the rights of man demanded by the French revolutionaries could merely be understood as rights for the male half of the human species.[9]

Her studied and sympathetic attention to the particular, gender-based injustices that faced women of her time led Wollstonecraft to theorize the necessity of including women in any universalistic and egalitarian definition of what she called "the rights of humanity." Her friend Thomas Paine had once used the term "human rights" in his 1792 treatise *The Rights of Man, Part the Second*, but he did not dwell on the issue of the rights of woman. Wollstonecraft's signal contribution to political theory was to systematically explain why any such concept of the "rights of humanity" or "human rights" must refer equally and explicitly to both women and men, girls and boys in order to be universalistic in both its conceptual scope and its potential applications. Other prominent women's rights advocates from the late eighteenth century—such as French revolutionaries Nicolas de Condorcet and Olympe de Gouges as well as the pseudonymous "Sophia" before them in England—had also argued for the equal rights of men and women. Unlike these shorter essays, Wollstonecraft's 1792 book *A Vindication of the Rights of Woman* comprehensively treated the questions of why and how the sexes should have equal rights in all domains of human life. Translated into French, Spanish, German, Dutch, Danish, and Czech, and published in multiple English editions, Wollstonecraft's *Rights of Woman* also decisively impacted the terms of the international philosophical and political debates on women's rights for roughly the first century after its debut in London.[10]

Despite Wollstonecraft's significance as a systematic theorist of why women's rights are integral to universal human rights, philosophical genealogies of the concept of women's human rights have typically reached only as far back as Mill's 1869 book *The Subjection of Women*. As the first major secular philosopher of women's human rights, Mill exerted an expansive influence in the twentieth century—especially on liberal political theorists such as John Rawls, Susan Okin, and Martha Nussbaum—but his influence meant that the history of the idea was often cut short. I begin with Wollstonecraft, because her *Rights of Woman* was the first internationally renowned philosophical treatise to analytically address women's rights among the radical political questions raised by the French Revolution. Prior to Mill, Wollstonecraft was the most significant feminist political philosopher and icon in the Atlantic world and its colonies, as much for as despite her scandalous reputation as a sexual radical. Mill's *Subjection of Women* was published in twenty-six non-English editions, seventeen countries, twelve European languages, and three non-European languages between 1869 and 1928. The global popularity of *The Subjection of Women* gave it even greater power than the *Rights of Woman* to inform both Western and non-Western thinkers' approaches to defending the human rights of women.[11]

By approaching the question of the evolution of women's human rights through the genre of philosophical genealogy, I follow Friedrich Nietzsche's *On the Genealogy of Morals* (1887) in method and intent. Nietzsche sketched the development of the modern Western ideas of good and evil through their transformations in ancient Greek, Christian, and modern European culture. He did not aim to provide a comprehensive, uncritical, or dispassionate narrative of the evolution of Western morality. Rather, he sought to tell a conceptual story of how these ideas arose and were transformed by larger cultural and political trends such as religion and democracy. Moreover, he sketched the development of these values into order to spur the questioning of them. Similarly, my objective is to reveal the major contours of the philosophical development and reception of women's human rights. By connecting the intellectual history of the past with the politics of the present, such a genealogy instigates moral debate on the idea in question.

In any philosophical genealogy written in the spirit of Nietzsche, the author ought to acknowledge her own normative philosophical commitments. This honesty of perspective allows for the story (in this case, the origins and development of women's human rights) to unfold in a way that more fully engages the issues it raises, including those raised by such normative commitments. Some of my commitments lie with the feminist liberal tradition. Feminist liberalism is a family of philosophical approaches to the problem of women's subjection that prioritize women's and gender issues (including women's rights to equal educational, employment, and political opportunities alongside men) among its other liberal democratic political commitments (such as legitimate representative government and social justice for the poor and marginalized). Feminist liberalism has been critical of liberalism, because the latter alone does not always fulfill its own egalitarian principles of justice with respect to women, in theory or in practice.[12]

At the same time as Marxism, psychoanalysis, and existentialism inspired a variety of feminist philosophical alternatives to the school of Wollstonecraft and Mill, feminist liberalism came to be widely critiqued over the course of the twentieth century. Wollstonecraft and Mill became scapegoats for such criticism, functioning as one-dimensional caricatures of feminist liberalism for feminists and non-feminists alike. The stridency on the feminist side was especially strong. For both radical feminists such as Zillah Eisenstein and conservative feminists such as Elizabeth Fox-Genovese, "liberal feminism" was a negative yet apt epithet for the tradition, as exemplified by Wollstonecraft's *Rights of Woman*. From both the right and the left, the pejorative use of the term "liberal feminist" neatly captured the despised individualistic, rationalistic, and bourgeois aspects of Wollstonecraft's and Mill's political thought.[13]

Such critiques have assumed, however, that Wollstonecraft, Mill, and their followers are primarily liberals and secondarily feminists. Paying attention to their defining contributions to the idea of women's human rights allows us to develop a counterinterpretation of their legacies for feminism today. Wollstonecraft and Mill exercised a critical style of feminist inquiry into the value of liberal ideas for women, which ultimately put feminism first and liberalism second. Liberalism had to meet certain feminist standards of justice—such as the actual guarantee of equal human rights for the sexes—in order to realize its own basic moral principles. In Nussbaum's formulation, these liberal principles could be stated most generally as (1) recognizing the "equal dignity of persons," (2) respecting the power of "moral choice" within each person, and (3) ensuring the consequent right of each person to fair treatment by society at large. Nussbaum further argued that feminist criticism had the potential to transform liberalism in a way that made it "more deeply consistent with its own most foundational ideas."[14]

Fundamentally, I also share Okin's feminist liberal conception of the integral place of women's rights within a universal and egalitarian conception of human rights. As Okin wrote in 1998, five years after the Vienna Declaration, "The male bias of human rights thinking and its priorities had to change in order for women's rights to be fully recognized as human rights." By male bias, she meant the historic tendency for male-dominated societies to perpetuate legal and cultural norms that discriminate in favor of men against women. Similarly to Mill in chapter 1 of his *Subjection of Women*, she acknowledged the practical necessity of confronting the fact of male bias in public opinion about women's rights. As Mill conceded in the opening pages of his argument, "I am willing to accept the unfavorable

9

conditions which the prejudice assigns to me." He consequently admitted that the "burthen of proof" was upon him to demonstrate women's desert of equal rights with men, and that society would be better off for granting them. More than a century later, Okin followed a similar strategy in her women's human rights advocacy. The male-biased presumption against women's rights had to be exposed, analyzed, and proven to be logically inconsistent with any concept of universal human rights, before public opinion could change.[15]

Although male bias posed a serious obstacle to the recognition of women's rights as human rights, it was hardly the only prejudice to which human rights discourse was prone. Cultural biases, rooted in racism, nationalism, and classism, often intersected with sexism. Together, such prejudices produced even more complex, and often seemingly insurmountable, barriers to broad understanding of women's rights as a kind of human rights. For example, Wollstonecraft and Mill regularly appealed to a Western European standard of women's progress that presumed the comparatively lesser status of women in non–Western European cultures, particularly among Muslim and Hindu peoples. Although Wollstonecraft and Mill argued for the human rights of women and men in a universal sense, their Eurocentric prejudices compromised the global scope of their abstract definitions of women's human rights when applied in rhetorical practice.

Looking back at the problem of cultural bias in Wollstonecraft and Mill, I share the contemporary postcolonial feminist theorist Inderpal Grewal's ethical concerns with such Western-biased uses of the idea of women's human rights. In 1999, Grewal set forth a postcolonial model for assessing the moral ambiguities of the concept of women's human rights, particularly as it applies to non-Western cultures. Grewal contended that the Vienna Declaration masked the imperial dimension of the idea of women's human rights with its appealing language of universal human values. Although she supported the idea that feminism ought to be international in its scope and goals, she was skeptical of the view that the United Nations' "human rights regime" was actually representative of the interests and needs of women in the developing world. Rather, the United Nations' human rights declarations were a product of complex geopolitical systems that reified inequalities of power across national, class, ethnic, religious, and gender lines. The result was an approach to women's human rights that privileged the perspectives and interests of the West against those of the rest of the world, most especially the postcolonial and developing world. Focusing on India, Grewal assessed how universalistic human rights discourse did not address the particular—culturally rooted, religiously based, nationally driven, and economically sustained—problems that faced women of her ancestral nation. Instead, universalistic human rights discourse had the tendency to treat women's problems homogenously, and to use an implicitly or explicitly Western liberal standard of justice in attempts to address abuses of them.[16]

This book brings together Okin's concern with confronting male bias and Grewal's concern with tackling cultural bias in the definition of women's human rights. My primary aim is to explain how a revised and internationalized theory of women's human rights, grown out of Wollstonecraft and Mill but stripped of their Eurocentric biases, is a valuable contribution to thinking about universal human rights today. I understand this theory of women's human rights to be a foundational plank of feminist liberalism.

Indeed, contemporary feminist liberals have connected their egalitarian theories of justice to the tradition rooted in Wollstonecraft and Mill. More important, they have seen the enduring relevance of this school of thought for addressing grave problems of global justice today. I follow Amartya Sen, Nussbaum, and their philosophical mentor Rawls in understanding global justice as the quest for social justice—or the realization of human rights, as well as fair and nondiscriminatory access to other public goods—at the international or transnational level. Sen, for example, has recently treated the *Rights of Woman* as a philosophical antecedent for his social justice theory, especially the idea that women across the world would be empowered by their societies to be "active agents of change" if they were granted the basic freedom and rights necessary for their own self-development.[17]

I have written this genealogy in the spirit of Sen's recovery of Wollstonecraft as a foundation for theorizing global justice in a cosmopolitan way. By cosmopolitan, I mean attempts to think globally that are respectful to both a core set of universal human values and relational differences within and across cultures. The Wollstonecraftian strand of cosmopolitanism prioritizes universal human rights, especially the basic right to agency itself, yet subsequently examines how gender and other cultural differences affect the differential and unjust treatment of women within and across societies. The interrogation of such injustices paves the way for further allegations, or aspirational claims, of women's need for human rights in law, policy, and culture. According to Sen, such allegations derive their creative force from their imaginative character. By alleging a human right for women that does not yet exist in practice, an advocate may open up new vistas of thought on what human rights could and should be in the future. For Sen as for Bunch before him, such creative, feminist transformations of human rights depend upon far-seeing and often courageous political demands on behalf of women's "agency and well-being."[18]

Feminist theory has become known for its diversity of approaches to conceptualizing and understanding the thorny problems of social justice that face women. Even with the plentiful divisions within contemporary feminist theory, the widely accepted twentieth-century social scientific distinction between gender and sex has produced an important conceptual overlap across many of its schools of thought. This gender-sex distinction draws a line between socially constructed gender roles and the biologically based sexual differences that manifest across individuals in the human species. Gender roles are assigned, performed, and sometimes subverted within social contexts, and are often culturally specific. Sexual differences are understood as rooted in the physiology of the body and its genetics. In the words of the physical anthropologist Agustín Fuentes, "Sex is a biological state that is measured via chromosomal content and a variety of physiological and developmental measures. Gender is the roles, expectations and perceptions that a given society has for the sexes." The upshot of this distinction is that gender roles are understood as products of human society, its cultures, and its economic and political systems, and as such, may be distinguished from sex understood in biological or genetic terms.[19]

Teasing out the ways that gender roles are symbolically and institutionally associated with sex within human cultures, yet are not in fact dependent on sex, has become a core theoretical project of feminism. One of the most influential examples of this project was Wollstonecraft's rejection of Jean-Jacques Rousseau's thesis that girls are by nature inclined to play with dolls and admire their looks in the mirror. For her, this was a classic case of a male theorist who mistook the effects of a male-dominated culture for its causes. Breaking a new path for male feminist philosophers, Mill made the related point that those who believe "the inequality of rights between men and women has no other source than the law of the strongest" conveniently ignored that the rule of law had institutionalized such relations of domination. He pointedly asked: "But was there ever any domination which did not appear natural to those who possessed it?"[20]

This genealogy of women's human rights builds on the gender-sex distinction, conceptualizing gender alongside race, ethnicity, class, religion, and nationality as identity traits that are sculpted within human cultures. Although I interpret Wollstonecraft's and Mill's feminist theories of human development as approaching remarkably close to the contemporary social scientific distinction between gender and sex, I also examine how Wollstonecraft and Mill were not entirely thorough in exposing the cultural contingencies that fashioned religion, class, and nationality. This tendency in their political theories informed their—sometimes unreflective, sometimes purposive, but always paradoxical and troubling—perpetuation of their British culture's prevalent stereotypes of non-Western, non-Christian peoples, especially Muslims and Hindus, in their arguments for women's human rights. Although Wollstonecraft and Mill technically understood that male bias was a kind of artificial cultural bias that could be gradually transformed through public criticism, they did not subject their Eurocentric prejudices to the same rigorous critique. For this reason, I draw a distinction between male bias and cultural bias in my analysis of their writings, while acknowledging that they, strictly speaking, categorized the former as a subset of the latter in their respective political theories.

By looking at an intellectually and culturally diverse array of responses to Wollstonecraft and Mill, we see how a range of political thinkers have responded to their arguments for women's human rights as well as their rhetorical reliance on negative cultural stereotypes. Mill's liberal utilitarianism made his arguments easy to adapt in other cultures and religions, as it did not make metaphysical demands on his readers. On the other hand, it was the resonance of Wollstonecraft's brand of rational (and radical) Christian dissent that made her arguments and rhetoric for women's human rights immediately influential in the early feminist abolitionist movement, especially among Unitarians in Britain and Quakers in the United States. Her metaphysical and religious orientation did not lend itself to political and cultural adaptation beyond the transatlantic popularity of rational dissenting Protestantism in the first half of the nineteenth century, however.

Mill thus eclipsed Wollstonecraft as a philosophical source for women's human rights arguments at the turn of the twentieth century, as evidenced by his spirited global reception on the woman question from political magazines in Meiji Japan to parliaments from New Zealand to the Southern Cone. By the time an international group of political representatives collaborated to produce the Universal Declaration of Human Rights in 1948, the language of human rights had been secularized. This genealogy outlines how the creative and critical adoption of Mill's liberal utilitarianism by a variety of intellectuals from around the globe aided the secularization of the idea of universal human rights. It also illustrates some of the enduring ethical problems with this secular trend in human rights discourse—

including pervasive cultural insensitivity to non–Western European religious practices and prejudicial Western assumptions about the backwardness of such religions on gender issues.[21]

To better grapple with these ethical issues surrounding the cultural biases of women's human rights advocates, I attend to the social scientific distinction between "insider" and "outsider" perspectives on cultures. Following the work of Brooke Ackerly, I take the insider perspective to be a point of view held by a researcher who studies the community or culture to which she at least partly affiliates herself. The outsider perspective is the obverse: a point of view held by a researcher who studies a community or culture to which she does not affiliate herself. Affiliation may be internal (holding at least some beliefs of the group) and/or external (expressing outward signs of belonging at least to the margins of the group). Building on the feminist standpoint theory of Patricia Hill Collins, Ackerly has advanced a third category, what she terms the "multi-sited critic," a point of view that bridges these insider and outsider perspectives. The multi-sited critic is a researcher who self-identifies as bridging several cultural sites and self-consciously uses a variety of insider and outsider perspectives in studying the value of the practices of these groups and their belief systems. The difficulty of achieving this multisited or multisided perspective in practice does not compromise its value as a normative ideal to which people may aspire in both their private lives and their public work.[22]

Throughout, I often read Wollstonecraft as embodying the insider perspective of a woman of faith who has faced patriarchal injustice partly due to her Christian culture, yet enacted an immanent and personally compelling critique of this oppression from within her community. I also tend to read Mill as a kind of outsider social scientist. As a man, he stood outside the direct experience of patriarchal oppression by virtue of his gender, but witnessed the suffering it caused the women in his life and felt the pain it indirectly brought upon him. Mill sought to comparatively study the global phenomenon of patriarchy in order to diagnose its pathologies and prescribe its social remedies, so as to remove it as an obstacle to happiness. On the other hand, both Wollstonecraft and Mill spoke to the ethical questions of why, when, and how people should strive to bridge these insider and outsider perspectives in human rights advocacy. They advanced reasons for achieving, partly or fully, a multisited point of view on how different cultures influence the moral formulation and political dissemination of women's human rights.

One final methodological caveat: this book provides an international philosophical genealogy of the concept of women's human rights, not a definitive causal story about how Wollstonecraft and Mill drove the development of this idea beyond philosophy and in its institutionalization in law and politics. The latter cannot be demonstrated with any certainty, but the former can be sketched—historically and philosophically—in a way that I hope will be productive and informative for scholars in humanistic and social scientific disciplines. This genealogy is comparative on two levels: first, it identifies and analyzes the important similarities and differences between Wollstonecraft's theory of women's human rights and Mill's; second, it looks at a range of non–Western European responses to these watershed theories as a way of illustrating how a robust cross-cultural and international dialogue has shaped the reception of the idea of women's human rights since the nineteenth century.

Especially through its international reception, feminist liberalism has been able to shed a crude Eurocentrism in favor of a cosmopolitan yet culturally sensitive ethic of humanistic regard for the welfare of women. Non–Western European feminist thinkers have revised and internationalized Wollstonecraft's and Mill's theories of women's human rights, by critically engaging their books as well as their life stories from the nineteenth century forward. Such cross-cultural dialogues on women's human rights have contributed to the ongoing philosophical reconciliation of feminism with liberalism. As Nussbaum argued, in the conclusion of her *Women and Human Development* (2000), the goal of a globally oriented feminist liberalism is not to strip human communities of their cultural and religious traditions but rather to find ways of fairly balancing the demands of cultural affiliation, religion, and universal human rights.[23]

Overview and Chapter Summary

The first chapter opens with a genealogy of the philosophical idea of rights and its limited applications to women from the late medieval era through the early nineteenth century. Against this intellectual background, we better understand why Wollstonecraft turned to a universalistic, rational Christian metaphysics and ethics, and why Mill turned to a liberal, rule utilitarianism, to justify the integral place of women in any coherent conception of the rights of humans. Chapter 2 proceeds to comparatively evaluate Wollstonecraft's religious and Mill's secular foundations for justifying women's human rights, displaying each of their real limitations as much as their strengths. Although contemporary liberals have taken nonfoundationalist, or purely political, approaches to justifying human rights in response to what Rawls called "the fact of pluralism," I argue that the respective foundationalist approaches of Wollstonecraft and Mill remain politically salient in different ways for defending women's human rights in conditions of cultural pluralism. Chapter 3 explains why their dramatically different theories of rights fit into their strikingly similar virtue theories of human development, and their resultant backing for state-mandated universal primary education (UPE). I consider the moral problem that their consequentialist arguments for the societal benefits of female education may reinforce the gender biases that they seek to undercut. Chapter 4 focuses on the related problem of cultural bias for women's human rights arguments. Wollstonecraft and Mill established a contradictory rhetorical model for making women's human rights claims in the sense that it reduced particular non-Western women to cultural stereotypes rather than respecting them as distinct individuals and peoples worthy of human rights in the first place. However, rhetorical analysis of the arguments of three early non–Western European respondents to the *Rights of*

Woman and *The Subjection of Women* demonstrates how it is possible for feminist liberals to achieve a partial yet sufficiently ethical transcendence of such cultural biases. Chapter 5 concludes the book by resolving the paradox evoked by Wollstonecraft's and Mill's uses of autobiography as a literary mode of women's human rights advocacy. How can autobiography, as a genre predicated upon the subjective biases of the author, serve as a vehicle for making nondiscriminatory claims for universal human rights? First, Wollstonecraft, Mill, and their international readership modeled how autobiography may provide a stirring emotional and intersubjective basis for women's human rights advocacy, even inspiring cross-cultural solidarity for the cause. Second, they represented how writing, reading, and responding to autobiography may serve as forms of public resistance to reductive or merely instrumental treatments of the human subject, due to the genre's basic assumption of the intrinsic value of individual human lives.[24]

Chapter 1 outlines the place of women in the evolution of rights discourse in Western political thought prior to Wollstonecraft and Mill. I begin this brief history of Western ideas of rights with the late medieval philosophies of the Franciscan theologians John Duns Scotus and William of Ockham and the Renaissance-era work of the Spanish Jesuit and Scholastic theologian, Francisco Suárez. I examine the growth of interest in the moral and political status of women in early modern theories of rights, freedom, and power, especially in the social contract tradition of Thomas Hobbes, John Locke, Jean-Jacques Rousseau, and Immanuel Kant, but also in the appropriations of Stoicism by Hugo Grotius and Rousseau. After tracing the gendered development of political discourses on the "rights of man" and the "rights of woman" in the wake of the French Revolution, I explain how the deficiencies of past theories of rights—above all, their male bias and sidelining of women—led Wollstonecraft and Mill to develop two alternative foundations for a truly inclusive concept of human rights. While Wollstonecraft drew from her mentor Richard Price's dissenting Christian theology to forge a new metaphysical and deontological grounding for women's human rights,

Mill revised classical utilitarianism into a liberal utilitarianism that placed women's human rights on a wholly secular foundation.

Chapter 2 delves further into the question of the moral foundations for human rights, and the strengths and weaknesses of Wollstonecraft's and Mill's respective answers to it. Although Wollstonecraft's capacious metaphysics built a big tent under which all humanity could find coverage for their rights, its explicitly Christian framework suited it more for persuading people who shared those same or similar theological beliefs. In short, Wollstonecraft's theory of human rights fell short of realizing its universalistic ethics in practice. Mill faced the opposite problem: his liberal theory of human rights was wholly secular and utilitarian, requiring a comparatively minimal set of moral beliefs from its adherents. The resultant issue was the instrumental, and thus insecure, status of rights within his utilitarian ethics and political theory. Mill's designation of utility as the sole grounding for morality made his conception of rights instrumental to its good consequences, especially the free and full development of individuals. His theory of rights fell short of securing human rights in any absolute or final sense, because the value of rights was always determined in relation to the rule that the free and full development of individuals should be fostered to ensure the greatest happiness for all. Despite their different flaws, these two accounts of human rights both fit Charles Beitz's definition of "naturalistic" foundations for human rights: for Wollstonecraft and Mill, all human beings held equal rights "by virtue of their humanity," or what makes them human. Although Wollstonecraft's theory is grounded on her rational theology, it is naturalistic in the sense that it depends upon her conception of the human being as made in God's rational image. By contrast, Mill's theory is secular (in that it contains no appeal to theology, religion, or the supernatural) and nonmetaphysical (in that it rejects the *a priori* approach of metaphysics in favor of an *a posteriori*, empirical approach to defining a conception of the human being in relation to a utilitarian conception of happiness). Mill's theory nonetheless fits Beitz's definition of a naturalistic account of human rights insofar as it relies upon a conception of the human being as a "progressive being," capable of free and full self-development toward happiness.[25]

Partly because of their flaws, such foundationalist approaches are not as prominent as nonfoundationalist approaches to justifying a universalistic conception of human rights in contemporary liberal political theory. Most famously represented by the later Rawls and his philosophical followers such as Beitz, nonfoundationalist liberal theories take a purely political approach to justifying human rights by way of a hypothetical or actual international political consensus or legal practice. Such a purely political approach does not appeal to comprehensive doctrines, such as metaphysical or religious ideas, or other robust and morally demanding conceptions of human development, happiness, or the good life. In contrast, Wollstonecraft's rational theology and Mill's liberal utilitarianism justified their respectively metaphysical and nonmetaphysical theories of universal human rights by way of their robust normative conceptions of the human being.

Despite their joint reliance on "comprehensive" and thus contestable conceptions of humanity, the foundationalist approaches of Wollstonecraft and Mill nonetheless remain politically relevant. Their respectively religious and secular justifications of universal human rights have implications for the practical question of how to ethically advocate for women's human rights in a way that is respectful to cultural differences yet also enables genuine reform on behalf of the well-being of women. This is especially the case when women's human rights are not yet recognized in culture or law but must be alleged and defended in order to be institutionalized in the future. The joint reliance by Wollstonecraft and Mill on thick moral conceptions of the human being endowed their political theories with strong yet inclusive normative standards by which they could judge the value of extant or proposed laws, policies, and cultural practices for women's and human development, as individuals or in groups. This option of appealing to a strong normative standard of humanity itself is crucial for debates on women's human rights that often hinge on supposedly intractable conflicts between state sovereignty, individual freedom, and traditional cultural practices. A basic and broad "concept of a person" can serve as a principled yet practical point of moral orientation by which women's human rights advocates may judge resolutions to these conflicts that are both ethical and persuasive. To test and compare the moral and practical value of Wollstonecraft's and Mill's naturalistic accounts of human rights in matters of political reform, I examine how their theories apply to the question of reconciling women's human rights with the practice of religious polygamy in nineteenth-century Mormon Utah and in contemporary Islam.[26]

Chapter 3 compares Wollstonecraft's and Mill's theories of human development, particularly their views on the relevance of sex and gender to education. I situate Wollstonecraft and Mill within a modern liberal tradition of virtue ethics, which posits a virtuous yet varied range of development outcomes as best or most happy for human beings. Despite the differences in their philosophical foundations for women's human rights, Wollstonecraft and Mill agreed that girls have the same fundamental right as boys to receive an education that would nurture the development of their core human capabilities. Both prescribed a state mandate for UPE as a necessary practical step toward transforming the pernicious, male-biased gender norms that had stunted women's self-development as well as human development as a whole.

Given their concern for persuading governments to pay their obligation to provide girls and boys the same access to an education in the broadest and most virtuous sense, it is not politically surprising that Wollstonecraft and Mill dwelled on the extrinsic social benefits of such an education rather than solely on its intrinsic benefits for the children. Ethically, however, such consequentialist arguments for women's right to education had the countervailing rhetorical effect of construing girls and their education as mere instruments to broader social and political ends. This rhetorical strategy obscured the principle of equal respect for human individuals that is the cornerstone of both Wollstonecraft's and Mill's abstract foundations for universal human rights. By emphasizing how the education of women would make men and society happier, Wollstonecraft and Mill reinforced the prevalent gender stereotype of women as passive or selfless servants of their fathers, husbands, and children. Ironically, their consequentialist arguments for the public benefits of UPE did not escape gender bias so much as perpetuate it, despite their philosophical intentions to the contrary. To avoid such a pernicious feedback loop, reformers ought to balance or even counteract appeals to the public utility of UPE with regular reminders of its intrinsic value for individual girls and women.

Chapter 4 confronts the place of Western prejudices within Wollstonecraft's and Mill's narratives of women's progress. Despite their repeated defenses of a common human nature that united the sexes, Wollstonecraft and Mill in their adaptations of Enlightenment philosophies of history made their theories of women's human rights less universalistic because of their Eurocentric biases. Following philosophers such as Voltaire and Adam Smith, Wollstonecraft and Mill assumed a Western European model of human economic and cultural development. Like Lord Kames and Antoine-Leonard Thomas, they condemned the low status of women in non-Western, non-Christian cultures and argued for the advancement of women based on such prejudiced Eurocentric comparisons with supposedly backward Muslims and Hindus. Although Wollstonecraft and Mill put strong feminist twists on these Western Eurocentric theories of human progress, they did not escape their cultural biases.[27]

The critical examination of the place of cultural bias in their political theories leads us to a more general ethical question: May one advocate a global standard of human rights without an imperial mindset that imposes one's own cultural biases upon others? Through an international genealogy of the reception of Wollstonecraft and Mill in the nineteenth and early twentieth centuries, I reveal that some of their earliest interlocutors also faced the problem of cultural bias. Some replicated an Orientalist idiom for feminism and liberalism, while others confronted, challenged, and ultimately subverted this trend. Three nineteenth-century non–Western European feminist liberals—Maria Tsebrikova of Russia, Martina Barros Borgoño of

Chile, and Elvira López of Argentina—emerge from this reception history as examples of the practical possibility of achieving a partial yet sufficiently ethical transcendence of cultural bias in women's human rights advocacy. Tsebrikova, Borgoño, and López overcame a tendency toward perpetuation of cultural bias within feminist liberalism through their self-reflective adoption of "rooted," or culturally attuned, cosmopolitan perspectives in crafting universalistic arguments for women's human rights. The comparative study of their reception of Wollstonecraft and Mill suggests that feminist liberalism may be reformulated in light of their and other non–Western European intellectuals' concern with making culturally sensitive claims for the rights of women worldwide.[28]

Chapter 5 returns to the fundamental commitment of Wollstonecraft and Mill to the universal human right to education, by exploring how it prompted them to affirm the power of literacy and literature for women's human rights advocacy. In their literary writings, Wollstonecraft and Mill incorporated the experiences of the women they loved (such as Mary's friend Fanny Blood and John's wife, Harriet Taylor) into their personal narratives, making them function as biographies as much as autobiographies. Such literary works as Wollstonecraft's novel *Mary, a Fiction* (1788) and Mill's *Autobiography* (1873) are thus better understood as (auto)biographies. Wollstonecraft and Mill can be read as contributing to the development of a modern genre: the literature of human rights.

Building on testimony and witness of women's struggles for recognition of their human status, their (auto)biographical writings developed two narrative frameworks for advocating the human rights of women: Wollstonecraft's stories of heroic womanhood and Mill's stories of spiritual marriage. These narratives proved to have an international impact. Wollstonecraft's first-wave feminist, and often religious, readers from the United States and across Europe hailed her as a "voice in the wilderness"—a feminist political prophet who cleared the way for their formal organization of the women's rights cause. Mill's representation of his spiritual marriage with Harriet Taylor had an even more global reach, becoming an emotional touchstone for translators of *The Subjection of Women* from late nineteenth-century Maharashtra and Prague to twentieth-century Japan and South Korea.[29]

Despite their success in inspiring men and women from different cultures to care about rectifying the social and political inequality of the sexes, Wollstonecraft's and Mill's (auto)biographical writings pose a series of philosophical questions for women's human rights advocates. May one use subjective human stories as evidence to legitimate universal human rights claims? If so, then how can such stories avoid being exploitative of the individuals whose lives and deaths originally inspired them? By underscoring the necessary overlap between biography and autobiography, Wollstonecraft and Mill broke down the apparent divide between "self" and "other." Not solely subjective, their (auto)biographies wove their personal experiences of love and friendship into larger intersubjective stories about the intrinsic value of human lives. Hence Wollstonecraft and Mill cleared the way for writers of the literature of human rights to use testimony and witness of the real joys and sorrows of human persons, without reducing their subjects to mere means to a broader political end.

By reading, writing, and speaking about self, other, and their relationships to each other, one gains literacy in the skills necessary for a narrative practice of human rights advocacy. This narrative practice produces sensitive and compelling human stories, which have the emotional power to move people to act on their duty to respect, provide, or allege the rights of self and others. As suggested by Wollstonecraft's and Mill's vibrant global reception, such a concrete, passionate, and literary approach to advocating for women's human rights may productively work in tandem with different abstract rational justifications for universal human rights. This practical and narrative mode of human rights advocacy has been made into history by ordinary people, whose lives, work, and stories show the centrality of individuals and other nonstate actors to the sustenance of the human rights tradition, past and present.[30]

Contemporary feminist political theorists such as Ackerly have argued that Third World and non-Western feminisms are not only compatible with but have provided a grounding for international women's human rights activism. Building on the visionary ideas of postcolonial feminism, they have demonstrated that the study of women's activism and work in the developing world was (and is) part of the process of forging a humane, solidaristic, yet culturally sensitive account of feminist social justice for women in a globalized political economy. *Wollstonecraft, Mill, and Women's Human Rights* is one further contribution to this tradition of feminist thinking in which liberalism's Western biases are critically assessed, but with the aim of a cross-cultural dialogue that pushes forward a more rooted cosmopolitan understanding of the human rights of women worldwide, and how they play out in particular cultures and religious traditions.[31]

A PHILOSOPHICAL GENEALOGY
OF WOMEN'S HUMAN RIGHTS

Entering the Labyrinth: The Debate on the Origin of Human Rights

The circuitous quality of intellectual histories of universal human rights seems to be unavoidable. Entering the debate on the origins of the modern idea of rights is much like stepping into the fantastical labyrinthine library imagined by Argentinian author Jorge Luis Borges: one is forced to retrace one's steps, and the steps of scholars past, in a futile attempt to find the elusive founding text to which the apparently infinite collection of books on human rights refers back. I begin, like most historians of rights, in late Enlightenment-era Europe, then turn back to the late medieval era and the Renaissance, traveling through neo-Stoic thought and the social contract tradition, only to arrive again at the American and French Revolutions and their legacies for the globalizing political thought of the nineteenth century. By focusing on the marginalized place of women in theories of rights before Mary Wollstonecraft and John Stuart Mill, we can better perceive the pivotal philosophical role that the inclusion of women plays in postrevolutionary theories of universal human rights. When studied against the background of previous theories of rights and their real deficiencies in relation to women, the innovativeness of Wollstonecraft's religious and Mill's secular approaches to justifying women's human rights shines in high resolution.[1]

As Jack Donnelly has argued, the idea of human rights originates in the West. He begins his history of the idea of universal human rights amid "the rise of modern markets and modern states and the rise of political claims of equality and toleration" in Europe. Richard Tuck, Brian Tierney, and Annabel Brett have pushed further back into the Western tradition, to the Roman Catholic theologians of the late medieval era, to find the earliest known theories of subjective rights. Subjective rights are those rights that belong to an individual human

26

subject or agent; for the medieval theologians, these primarily included individual rights to property and the simple use of nature for survival. The Protestant and neo-Stoic school of Hugo Grotius has been identified as another important strain in the development of the modern concept of the rights of individuals, especially in the international realm. The English and European social contract tradition, beginning with Thomas Hobbes and extending through Immanuel Kant, has also been commonly cited as a source for contemporary theories of human rights.[2]

Moral cognates of rights, such as dignity and respect, have been integral to non-Western cultures and religions, Confucianism, Hinduism, and Islam, from the earliest historical records. According to Micheline Ishay and Paul Gordon Lauren, this ancient overlap in moral norms across world religions and cultures provides a historical basis for the international community's more recent institutionalization of universal human rights laws. Political theorists as various as Mary Ann Glendon, George Kateb, Amartya Sen, and Martha Nussbaum have used this "overlapping consensus" of intercultural moral norms as a starting point for arguing that an idea of human dignity is the historic basis for contemporary theories and laws concerning universal human rights.[3]

These vexed philosophical questions of establishing the moral foundation for rights, and understanding the relationship of rights to other moral concepts, such as sentience, dignity, respect, or equality, are the topic of chapter 2. Here, I focus on the equally challenging question of the historical origins of the modern ethical-political idea of subjective rights, especially for women. Since the European Enlightenment, subjective rights have become a dominant political concept. In the wake of the social contract tradition, they have been commonly construed as moral entitlements of human beings, like nourishment, freedom, education, and citizenship, which enable their survival and development. Subjective rights have been conceptualized as grounded in the will, or agency, of human beings, whether or not they have been theorized as derivative from an objective source of moral authority, such as natural law or positive law.[4]

In a complex adoption of social contract theory, the early nineteenth-century German idealist philosopher G. W. F. Hegel built his relational idea of individual rights on a thin conception of the human subject. This human subject had a will, by which he could distinguish himself from both internal and external natural forces. Conscious of his own freedom of will, he could identify himself as separate from his bodily desires or the physical obstacles to the satisfaction of his desires. His claims to rights, for Hegel as well as many rights theorists since, were an expression of his subjective will, the practical human need for recognition and respect of one's individuality in relation to others, and acknowledgment of his legal status.[5]

Driven by the desires and needs of individual human beings, subjective rights are meant to be directed toward the legitimate use of nature, property, freedom, or other forms of personal or political power. Defining the moral bounds of the individual's use of subjective rights in relationship to others is the ethical-political problem that has preoccupied liberal and democratic political theories from their origins in Grotius (1625) and Hobbes (1642) to the present. This idea of subjective rights has its roots in the West, after 1200. Whether one begins with late medieval Catholic theology, Protestant variants of Stoicism, the social contract tradition, or the democratic revolutions of the late eighteenth century, subjective rights have their philosophical origins in the religious and political debates of the British Isles, the Continental European powers, and their Atlantic colonies.

That said, we should recall Amartya Sen's important distinction between rights and the cognate moral concepts that support them. Pointing to the ancient tradition of "conscious theorizing of tolerance and freedom" in Asian cultures, Sen argued that the "basic ideas underlying freedom and rights" are not exclusively Western. Indeed, the cross-cultural prevalence of these "underlying" moral ideas contributed to the widespread appropriation of the concept of subjective rights in non–Western European cultures after the French Revolution. William Theodore de Bary and Tu Weiming have illustrated this phenomenon with examples of modern Chinese fusions of rights with Confucianism, such as China's input into the 1948 Universal Declaration. According to de Bary, such intercultural exchanges and revisions of ideas mean that "human rights [are] still in the process of formation."[6]

Attention to the idea of women's human rights allows us to see how human rights gradually became an international and intercultural, as well as a philosophically universalistic, political concept. As David Armitage and Jennifer Pitts have shown, with their historical studies of the rise of modern forms of imperialism and internationalism, there was a global turn—for better and for worse—in British and European political thought at the turn of the nineteenth century. Political thought became globalized in its perspectives, as well as in its reception and influence, as much through as despite the growth of Western imperialism. Feminist historians have long noted that this trend was especially salient for the global diffusion of women's rights discourse. At the turn of the nineteenth century, consideration of the moral and political status of women and slaves compelled political theorists to expand their definitions of rights-bearing subjects. The resultant rise of abolitionist and women's rights discourses paralleled, if not propelled, the global turn in political thought, as exemplified in the work of Wollstonecraft and Mill.[7]

The Rise of the Rights of Woman in the Western Enlightenment

Before the essays of French revolutionaries Nicolas de Condorcet and Olympe de Gouges on women's rights in 1790–91, philosophers debated the superiority or inferiority of women to men in the European *querelle des femmes*, but they did not typically express their views in the language of rights. This querelle was the lively intellectual debate on the question of the equality of the sexes that animated aristocratic courts and salons as well as Roman Catholic convents in Europe and its Latin American colonies after Venetian-born Christine de Pizan completed her landmark feminist treatise, *The Book of the City of Ladies*, in France in 1405. Most of this querelle, however, revolved around the concept of equality and did not invoke the related idea of rights until the mid-eighteenth century. In 1739 London, "Sophia, a Person of Quality" published a long essay entitled "Woman Not Inferior to Man." Its provocative subtitle invoked the concept of the "natural right of the fair sex to a perfect equality of power, dignity, and esteem, with the men." Sophia used the Enlightenment-era discourse of "natural rights," arising from seventeenth-century treatises by Frenchman François Poulain de la Barre and Englishman John Locke, to demand from men "our right of sharing with them in public action."[8]

Sophia's essay, thought by some to have been written by the English bluestocking Lady Mary Wortley Montagu, continued to have an impressive national and international reception into the 1830s, from Britain to France to Brazil. It may have even influenced Wollstonecraft, given the parallel between its subtitle, "Vindication of the Natural Rights of the Fair-Sex," and the title of her 1792 *Vindication of the Rights of Woman*. But by that point, a new public discourse on the "rights of man" and the "rights of woman" had emerged in the wake of the American and French Revolutions. It was the discourse on rights spurred by the French Revolution, and the debate over it in Britain, that served as the immediate and pressing political backdrop for Wollstonecraft's extended philosophical argument for the extension of equal "civil and political rights" to the degraded "half of the human species."[9]

Eighteenth-century rights discourse—which became prominent in Britain, America, and France—promoted the individual and, more often, the group rights of male political subjects or citizens in challenge to the prevalence of absolute monarchy in early modern Europe. On an abstract level, these rights were variously conceptualized as basic powers, liberties, wants, needs, and entitlements of human beings. In particular legal systems, these rights were institutionalized for particular groups, such as land-owning men, so that they enjoyed protection for their property as well as political opportunities to participate in government and lawmaking. Philosophers infrequently dwelled on the question of how rights applied to female humans, until rights became the most salient political issue in the

North Atlantic world in the wake of the American Revolution in the 1770s and the buildup to the French Revolution in the 1780s.[10]

In eighteenth-century British political thought, rights such as freedom of conscience were often paired with duties such as religious tolerance. In such moral pairings, rights were understood as correlative, or reflexive and relational. Such correlative rights served as a kind of practical shorthand for abstract moral principles that defined ethical human relationships and obligations to one another within political communities. As condensed and concretized versions of abstract moral principles that ought to govern human relationships, rights unsurprisingly came to be summarized in lists and preserved in public, political documents. The English Bill of Rights, produced by the Glorious Revolution of 1688–89, illustrates the trend toward a public, itemized, interpersonal, and political understanding of rights. Rather than focusing on or even significantly expanding the rights of individuals, the bill set forth a list of rules for legitimate relationships between the government powers of Parliament and the king. The related 1689 Act of Toleration made a selective form of religious toleration (benefiting most religious groups besides Roman Catholics, nontrinitarians, and atheists) mandatory for England and its colonies.[11]

Particularly within eighteenth-century Protestant and dissenting Christian theologies, philosophers conceived rights as rooted in a rational human nature as designed by the divine Creator. Thinkers such as Kant and Wollstonecraft understood rights as a product of the human subjective mental capacity to use reason to construct abstract principles of ethical conduct. For Wollstonecraft and her theological mentor, the Reverend Richard Price, these principles derived from the universal, rational, moral law of God. Humans typically had access to God's law via reason once this mental faculty was sufficiently developed through education. As necessary, adults could teach the content of the moral law to children or other persons without sufficiently developed rational faculties. For Kant, on the other hand, the epistemological divide between the noumenal and the phenomenal realms meant that the human mind could not know for certain whether these universal moral principles derived from God's moral laws. Despite their differences over epistemology and the possibility of knowing the divine basis of rights, both Kant and Wollstonecraft contributed to the deontological school of thought on human rights. Deontological conceptions of rights are derived from a set of moral rules or universally applicable duties (such as the Kantian ethical principle to respect human beings as ends in themselves), rather than justified in terms of their actual or expected consequences.[12]

Sentience, suffering, and sympathy also emerged as a defining set of capacities of human beings that grounded late eighteenth-century arguments for rights. David Hume, Jean-Jacques Rousseau, and Jeremy Bentham began with the human subjective experience of pain and pleasure as the starting point for enacting ethical relationships, including rights and duties. The personal experience or sympathetic witness of pain encouraged human beings to develop an intersubjective (or overlapping subjective) consensus on the human right to relief of suffering and the corresponding duty to provide such relief. By the late eighteenth century, human subjective (and intersubjective) constructs of rational or sympathetic regard for self and other(s) came to be seen as the basis for defining the rights and duties of individuals in modern political communities.[13]

The Philosophical Origins of Subjective Rights for Women

The idea of subjective rights—or rights belonging to and exercised by the individual human subject or agent—extends further back into European religion and politics, however. As Richard Tuck's work on medieval and Renaissance political thought has shown, the concept of subjective rights has a complex historical development within the Catholic theological tradition of John Duns Scotus, William of Ockham, and Francisco Suárez, among others. In these theological debates, subjective rights were conceived as natural rights, or rights that obtained in the natural condition of humans prior to the Fall of humanity. In response to the thirteenth- and fourteenth-century church's heated debate over the radical Franciscan commitment to a life of poverty without private property, Scotus and Ockham developed arguments for a natural right to "simple use," or a reasonable consumption of nature's bounty, for purposes of survival. However, neither theologian applied these arguments for the natural right to simple use of nature beyond his philosophical ruminations on the life of prelapsarian man. Moreover, Scotus and Ockham primarily had Adam in mind. Although Ockham occasionally discussed Adam and Eve's mutual natural rights to the simple use of nature before the Fall, it was Eve's marital relationship to Adam that was the context for such hypotheses. In other words, Eve had rights only insofar as she was cleaved to Adam as his wife. In addition, Ockham claimed that, after the Fall, Adam's and other men's "power" rightfully extended to the personal appropriation of "temporal things," including "rational beings" such as "women and children." Despite her auspicious beginnings as a free agent in the form of the inquisitive Eve, postlapsarian woman became a mere thing that man had a right to own and dominate.[14]

According to Tuck, this late medieval debate over the meaning of "jus" (right) and "dominium" (property) contributed to the Renaissance-era conception of subjective rights. The turn of the seventeenth-century Spanish Jesuit philosopher Suárez further developed the idea of rights as belonging to and exercised by the human subject. The exercise of rights was a robust expression of the individual will. Suárez even spoke of "human rights" and applied the idea to women, if only in a limited way. He defended "a maiden's right to her own freedom" before marriage, paying heed to the Roman Catholic culture's patriarchal view of female chastity as a precondition for a woman's entry into marriage. Yet he described it as "her" right and freedom. By implication, her freedom to be a maiden and to enjoy bodily integrity was not the right of her father or suitors to give or take away but rather a right that she possessed and exercised as a female human, which other human subjects (including men in power) were morally obligated to respect. Although Suárez said nothing about women's natural right to abstinence (or other forms of sexual freedom) in marriage, his defense of a maiden's right to maintain her chastity is a signal moment for feminist ethics. He at least implied a natural right for a maiden to be free from sexual coercion or violence as a girl child. He also implied a natural right to a maiden's control of the sexual functioning of her body, at least in the negative sense—a significant power in an age when female mortality via maternity and venereal disease was high. Suárez's emphasis on rights as an exercise of human will or power, even in the case of a chaste maiden, was an important precursor to the seventeenth-century Protestant rights theories of such thinkers as Grotius, Hobbes, and Locke.[15]

Partly influenced by Roman Stoicism as well as Jesuit Scholastics such as Suárez, Grotius was a Dutch theorist of natural law and natural rights who put the freedom of the individual human will at the center of his ethics and political theory. In his 1625 treatise *The Rights of War and Peace*, he argued that both women and men had a right to use deathly force to defend their chastity against the threat of rape, on the grounds of the inalienable natural right to self-preservation that belongs to and may be justly exercised by all human persons. Although suicide was generally prohibited according to his Protestant moral theology, Grotius made an exception for women to commit suicide to protect their chastity if it was the only option available for self-defense against such heinous physical violation. This extreme example of female self-assertion against male sexual violence highlights the importance of the expression of the human will for guaranteeing moral outcomes in his Christian ethical system. By freely choosing to kill herself to protect her chastity, a woman willed what was moral at great earthly cost to her, but with greater heavenly reward for adhering to God's moral law even unto death. As in the case of Suárez's defense of the right of a maiden to maintain her chastity before marriage, Grotius's defense of the right of a woman to kill herself to maintain her chastity revolves around the idea that women can and should exercise their God-given wills in order to freely realize Christian virtue. On the other hand, both of these examples conceive of women's moral agency primarily in terms of preserving their chastity and only extend a narrow conception of natural rights to women. Most disturbingly, the Grotian case required a woman to die as a consequence of exercising her natural right to protect her chastity. The very act of using the right extinguished the possibility of enacting rights further.[16]

Grotius drew from Cicero the case of the woman who must kill herself to preserve her honor. Other Roman and Stoic sources shaped his ethics and politics, and within them, his theory of natural rights and its limited applications to women. Although Grotius cited the early Christian Roman thinker Lactantius to establish that "what is unlawful for Women is as much unlawful for Men, and one and the same Obligation is thought to lie equally on both," he also made moral and social distinctions between the sexes on the grounds of their different sexual natures and functions. He quoted the fourth-century Roman historian Ammianus Marcellinus to support the view of women as generally childlike in reason and thus fundamentally unequal to men in mental capabilities. Therefore women, on the whole, required adult male guidance in intellectual and ethical matters. Despite the universality of the natural moral law and its equal applicability to the sexes, women did not function as equal moral agents alongside men but rather functioned as dependent creatures needy of protection and guidance from men in times of war and peace. Along these lines, Grotius typically construed women's worth not as intrinsically rooted in their nature as persons but rather as extrinsically related to their reproductive and sexual functions as mothers and wives. In war, women had a natural right to be secure from male violence because of the broader social need to protect female reproductive powers for a nation's own self-perpetuation. In peace, the sexes had a common right to monogamous marriage, the criminalization of polygamy, and the restriction of divorce to cases of adultery, because such contractual legal arrangements established a kind of equilibrium between them despite their sexual inequality. Such marital laws prevented the sexual exploitation of women by men at the same time as they established a legitimate outlet for overpowering male heterosexual desire (which, according to Grotius, made celibacy unrealistic for most men). He thus based his handful of arguments for women's rights on the extrinsic value of women's sexual attractiveness and reproductive powers for men and for maintaining peace in society at large. Because he predicated his notion of women's rights upon the sexual functioning of women and its value for others, especially men, these arguments exposed the limits of Grotian theory for conceptualizing women's rights in any noninstrumental and nonpatriarchal sense, whether in domestic or international politics.[17]

Like Suárez and Grotius before him, Hobbes in his *De Cive* (1642) and *Leviathan* (1651) gave a striking example of how women could wield natural rights—but took the concept of women's freedom in a far more radical direction. Hobbes theorized a right of mothers in the state of nature prior to the establishment of government, or any kind of positive law. He posited that infants in the state of nature were fully dependent on their mothers for nourishment and other aspects of survival. Given that the children could not defend themselves, mothers thus had the right to choose to "expose" or to "care for" their offspring. Hobbes's conception of mother right was tied to his definition of power as the "present means to obtain some apparent good" and his definition of freedom as "the absence of Opposition." Women in the state of nature took "the right of Dominion over the Child" to its logical extreme when they no longer perceived the care of the dependent child to be worthwhile, and there was no obstacle to the act of infanticide. This violent conception of a female natural right set Hobbes apart from other early theorists of women's natural rights. But it also opened the door to imagining a more vigorous set of rights for women, particularly in their natural state.[18]

Not until the mid- to late seventeenth century, particularly in the aftermath of the English Civil Wars over religious freedom, did a Protestant theory of the rights of human subjects emerge in full force. Focused on the individual rights to private property and religious conscience, this Protestant political discourse sought to propel reform of Catholic absolutist monarchical government. Locke's *Second Treatise of Government* (1690) was the paradigmatic work on the issue. It reflected many of the political trends embodied in the Glorious Revolution of 1688–89, including the English Bill of Rights that institutionalized the Protestant succession, constitutional monarchy, and stronger legislative powers of Parliament. In addition to these political rights, Locke also outlined the natural rights of individual human agents, inside and outside government. Locke's theory of natural rights echoed the debates of Scotus and Ockham, who had puzzled over the questions of individual rights to consumption and property in a prelapsarian, or natural, state. On the other hand, Locke's emphasis on personal entitlement to the work of one's hands—at least in the state of nature before government—paid homage to the late seventeenth-century Protestant equation of subjective rights with the right to own and build private property.[19]

Likely inspired by Hobbes, Locke addressed the powers of women in the family within the context of the state of nature. He assigned women equal "parental power" to care for the children, so the mother and father shared authority over their offspring in the state of nature. The mother and father also had equal freedom to leave each other once their children were grown. There were no further moral duties to bind them together in the shared project of child rearing, and no positive laws or government to legally inscribe them within the bonds of marriage.[20]

Although Locke did not use the term "right" in direct relation to women, his arguments for these equal parental and spousal powers and freedoms in the state of nature implied that women held some natural rights alongside men, at least beyond the patriarchal restrictions of positive law. As with the brief accounts of women's natural rights by Suárez, Grotius, and Hobbes, Locke's consideration of women's natural freedoms and powers focused on their sexual roles. As Susan Okin demonstrated, this early modern trend of conceptualizing women's natural rights, freedoms, or powers in terms of their sexual functions was the latest iteration of the deep patriarchal dimension of Western political thought, extending back to ancient Greece.[21]

For the bulk of the eighteenth century, rights-bearing subjects were typically assumed, in theory and practice, to be adult white male landowners. Even a progressive thinker like Locke, who sought to restore the rights of the people against tyrannical government, stopped short of extending the full slate of rights to children, adult females, or slaves taken in a defensive war. Since he reserved most of his speculations about women's powers and freedoms to the state of nature before the institution of government, he avoided the question of whether women should be political subjects in his ideal state, a limited constitutional monarchy. In private correspondence with Mrs. Mary Clarke in 1684, Locke acknowledged that girls had the same capability for mental improvement as he would later outline for boys in his published treatise *Some Thoughts on Education* (1693).[22]

Although Wollstonecraft built on Locke's educational principles to argue for boys' and girls' equal right to free public coeducation, such an egalitarian conception of the sexes' learning capabilities was hardly the norm in the late eighteenth century. Even Kant's radical, *a priori*, metaphysical view of the absolute moral equality of humans as rational beings, bound by universal duties from which they derived their universal rights, did not keep him from espousing a patriarchal view of women's ethical and mental potential. In his *Observations on the Feeling of the Beautiful and the Sublime* (1764), Kant bluntly stated that women could not act morally, or according to a rational grasp of universal principles of duty. In his *Metaphysics of Morals* (1797), he elaborated the political implications of this view of sex inequality by arguing that women could not be "active," self-governing citizens of a republic, because, like children, they were excluded by nature from autonomous conduct. Patriarchal prejudice had clearly proven to be a persistent, though adaptable, feature of modern theories of rights, including the fundamental rights to education and political participation.[23]

Modern Western Patriarchalisms

In his groundbreaking book *Patriarchalism in Political Thought* (1975), Gordon Schochet made the influential case that there were varieties of patriarchalism in early modern British and European political thought. Most famously defended by Robert Filmer, the seventeenth-century patriarchalism of the divine right of kings posed absolute monarchs as the legitimate heirs of the power bequeathed to Adam by God to control and dominate nature, as well as Eve. What was left sexually ambiguous was the status of queens, or female monarchs, whose legitimacy as heirs of Adam's power was generally undisputed. The conflation of paternal power with monarchical power meant that political patriarchalism, in cases such as Queen Elizabeth I and Queen Anne, occasionally manifested in history as political matriarchalism.[24]

Filmer's brand of patriarchalism, and its legitimation of absolute monarchies through a genealogy of power rooted in Genesis, gave way to a new political and philosophical order after the Wars of Religion in Europe and the British Isles. According to Schochet, the political conflicts and ideological debates of the Glorious Revolution led to the transformation of patriarchalism in the eighteenth century. Eighteenth-century patriarchalism was focused less on the legitimation of monarchical power and more on the inclusion of new classes of men in powers of governance. The issue of the expansion of the male political classes, amid the rise of republican discourses in early eighteenth-century Britain and its Atlantic colonies, precipitated a more overt concern with the problem of women's relationship to politics. This concern was often directed toward explicitly patriarchal arguments for the formal exclusion of women from otherwise egalitarian visions of a new republican political order.[25]

The extension of natural rights arguments to other groups, including African slaves and women, became more prominent around the time of the American and French Revolutions and the rise of British abolitionism. As suggested by Wollstonecraft's repeated symbolic invocations of the 1789 fall of the Bastille in Paris, the liberation of the masses through political rebellion became a model for the liberation of people oppressed by their social status. Yet the masculine gender of rights was consolidated and reinforced in the transatlantic public sphere at precisely the moment when the idea of rights became more than a tool of white male landowners' power. The late medieval, Renaissance, and early Enlightenment "natural rights" of God's human creatures, which were generally patriarchal in implication or application, openly became "the rights of man." Philosophically growing in the seventeenth century but politically dominating Europe and America in the late eighteenth century, the rights of man doctrine was for white, middle-class, tax-paying, property-owning male subjects who wished to enjoy the powers of self-governing republican citizens.[26]

There is some explicit evidence of white middle-class men's jealous defense of their growing rights against the prospect of sharing them with other historically marginalized groups, including women. In response to his spouse Abigail Adams's March 1776 request for him to "remember the ladies" in the crafting of the new constitution for revolutionary America, congressional delegate John Adams wrote: "As to your extraordinary Code of Laws, I cannot help but laugh. We have been told that our Struggle has loosened the bands of Government everywhere. That Children and Apprentices were disobedient—that schools and Colledges were grown turbulent—that Indians slighted their Guardians and Negroes grew insolent to their Masters. But your Letter was the first Intimation that another Tribe more numerous and powerfull than all the rest were grown discontented. . . . Depend upon it, We know better than to repeal our Masculine systems." With less irony and more anxiety than Adams, the Genevan philosopher Jean-Jacques Rousseau also had posed elaborate arguments against the inclusion of women in the "masculine systems" of modern republicanism in his widely read literary and political writings from the 1750s and 1760s. Rousseau asserted that the arbitrary sexual domination of women over men in the domestic realm was reason to not permit them formal political power. In April 1776, Adams likewise concluded, in his reply to his wife, that he hoped General George Washington would not allow the "Despotism of the Petticoat" to engender a new form of political tyranny on American soil, so soon after the colonies' rebellion from Britain.[27]

The confluence of social contract ideas and neo-Stoic ideas in Rousseau's political thought reinforced the patriarchal biases in his theory of republicanism as the best, or only legitimate, state. Indebted to Hobbes and Locke, Rousseau's version of social contract theory was distinctive for giving explicit reasons why women should not be rights-bearing citizens in his ideal republican regime. His theory of republicanism required a robust practice of sex-role differentiation, such that men were formal citizens in the public realm and women focused on the rearing of future male citizens and female denizens in the domestic sphere. Any mixing of the sexes in politics would undermine the stability of society and government. To prevent this outcome, Rousseau followed the ancient Romans in prescribing the disenfranchisement of women from republican civil rights. While he proclaimed that popular sovereignty was the basis for legitimate, or republican, government, Rousseau narrowly defined the sovereign lawmakers as the adult men of the community. According to Carole Pateman, Rousseau rationalized a fraternal social contract in which men bonded together as autonomous citizens while women stood on the outside of government, without real access to freedom, power, or rights.[28]

Despite his harsh criticisms of Grotius, Rousseau's appropriation of Stoicism also proved to be discriminatory toward women, when read in conjunction with his social contract theory. The virtue of human passivity in the face of misfortune was a theme of Seneca that ran through Rousseau's literary writings, but in a way that undercut the place of female agency in his ethics and politics. Stoic acceptance of one's negative circumstances may be empowering to a man otherwise endowed with civil and political rights, as in the case of the lowly Swiss tutor St. Preux's choice to live under the watchful eye of the aristocratic Wolmar in Rousseau's novel *Julie* (1761). For a woman without such rights, a Stoic resignation to fate could possibly extinguish her freedom altogether, as when Julie unhappily obeyed her father in entering a loveless arranged marriage to the much older Wolmar, instead of eloping to England with her true love, St. Preux. In a kind of Stoic epiphany, Julie came to see her choice as not tragic but actually liberating for its fulfillment of patrimonial duty, despite her lingering feelings for St. Preux: "Tied to a husband's destiny, or rather to a father's intentions by an indissoluble bond, I enter upon a new career which is to end only with death." Alongside his fraternal social contract theory, Rousseau's neo-Stoic storytelling not only permitted but also encouraged women's passivity under patriarchal rule.[29]

Indebted to the philosophical ideas of Rousseau and his *Social Contract* (1762), which formally excluded women from an otherwise radical vision of popular sovereignty, the 1789 French *Declaration of the Rights of Man and Citizen* embodied the overt masculinization of rights ideology in the revolutionary era. At the same time, it helped to trigger an international discourse on the rights of man in which women played a leading and subversive role. During the early 1790s, female political theorists such as Wollstonecraft and de Gouges publicly questioned the masculine biases of the rights of man doctrine.

Wollstonecraft's treatise *A Vindication of the Rights of Men*—the first published response to Irishman Edmund Burke's *Reflections on the Revolution in France* in late 1790—contained the seeds of her philosophy of women's human rights. Against Burke's conservative critique of the political dangers of the revolutionary rights of man doctrine, Wollstonecraft suggested that the real danger lay in not expanding the concept to include women: "Who will pretend to say, that there is as much happiness diffused on this globe as it is capable of affording?" She then strongly implied that the education of women's rational capacities was part of the "recognition" of the "full force" of the "*native* unalienable rights of men." Human happiness and "social virtue" would be maximized for every person "if she could gain the strength that she is able to acquire." In a few short sentences, Wollstonecraft synthesized the basic principles of her theory of women's human rights: (1) women must be granted rights because they are entitled to them on the basis of their humanity; (2) the right to education is fundamental because it enables the development of women's ability to successfully use other civil and political rights; and (3) the granting of rights without distinction of sex is a precondition for the well-being and virtue of humanity as a whole.[30]

On a rhetorical level, Wollstonecraft's explicit switch to the feminine pronoun "she" was a telling critique of the male bias of the rights of man discourse that she sought to supplant with her universalistic philosophy of human rights. By moving from the masculine language of the "rights of men" to a specifically feminine pronoun, Wollstonecraft underscored the special and urgent need for civic recognition of women's human rights, especially to education. Using a similar rhetorical technique, de Gouges's 1791 Parisian pamphlet "Declaration of the Rights of Woman and Citizen" uncovered the patriarchal bias of the 1789 *Declaration*, by rewriting the list of French republican rights with the female sex included.

From the Rights of Man to the Rights of Woman

Some of the earliest extensions of the revolutionary-era rights of man doctrine to women are found in political essays of the French republican tradition: Condorcet's 1790 essay "On the Admission of Women to the Rights of Citizenship" and, a year later, de Gouges's aforementioned "Declaration" asked for women to be granted the same civil and political rights as men in the new French republic. Their arguments began with the premise that republican citizenship rights ought to extend to all adults, not simply men.

Joan Scott has illuminated how early French feminist activists such as de Gouges played on the paradoxical character of women's rights discourse within modern patriarchal republicanism. Through their robust involvement in the liberal stage of the Revolution from 1789 to 1792, Frenchwomen signaled the disconnection between the idea of natural, individual rights and the exclusion of half the human species from them. As the ex-bishop and French revolutionary Charles Maurice de Talleyrand-Périgord had observed in his 1791 *Rapport sur l'instruction publique*, "To see one half the human race excluded by the other from all participation of government, was a political phenomenon that, according to abstract principles, it was impossible to explain." This paradox, or tension between abstract principles of justice and the patriarchal culture in which women were bound, was the inspiration for Wollstonecraft's *Rights of Woman*, which she pointedly dedicated to Talleyrand-Périgord in the hope that he and his new republic might push past it.[31]

Wollstonecraft's 1792 *Rights of Woman* shaped a new, international political rhetoric and public discourse on rights. It was quickly translated into French and published in Paris and Lyon in the same year. In 1793, a Parisian reviewer argued that Wollstonecraft's book put in theoretical form what had transpired in the early stage of the Revolution in the form of women's highly visible participation in republican politics: "So many Frenchwomen have already fulfilled the wishes of Mrs. W! Did they not work arduously in the excavation of the Champ de Mars? How many came armed for the defense of their country?" Seen from the French republican perspective, Wollstonecraft's treatise illustrated what Hegel would later describe as philosophy's tendency to articulate what recently has passed: "The owl of Minerva begins its flight only with the onset of dusk."[32]

Wollstonecraft's book may have captured the political spirit of the immediate past, but it also directed the trajectory of women's rights discourse across Britain, Europe, and the United States. Janet Todd's estimate that fifteen hundred to three thousand copies of the *Rights of Woman* were sold between 1792 and 1797 may be low, as Susan Branson has discovered that fifteen hundred copies of the book were printed in Philadelphia alone in 1794. At the turn of the nineteenth century, there were more copies of the *Rights of Woman* in American libraries than of Paine's *Rights of Man*. In addition to two further editions in London and several reprintings in Boston and Philadelphia, the book was published in Dublin in the 1790s.[33]

The *Rights of Woman* also spread across Continental Europe. Selections from the French edition were translated for *Diario de Madrid* in September 1792, despite the repressive character of the Spanish monarchy and its censorship policies. This review and translation may have influenced other Spanish articles on women's education in the 1790s. In 1793–94, George Salzmann—the Schnepfanthal educator whose children's stories Wollstonecraft had translated into

English in 1790—arranged the publication of the first German edition of the *Rights of Woman*. His lengthy introduction to the book presented many of Wollstonecraft's ideas as friendly to his own progressive ideas on children's coeducation, especially through outdoor play. Salzmann distanced himself from Wollstonecraft's stronger feminist arguments, however, by emphasizing the need for a benevolent paternalism in education and focusing on the instrumental value of women's education for the well-being of husbands. His German edition of the *Rights of Woman* was translated into Dutch in 1796 and into Danish in 1801. Accented with a satin binding and pink ribbon, the Danish edition delicately affirmed Salzmann's conservative reading of the book's compatibility with traditional gender roles.[34]

It was the popularity of Wollstonecraft's *Rights of Woman* in 1790s America that marked a tipping point toward the enthusiastic public embrace of the idea of equal rights for the sexes. The September 1792 issue of Philadelphia's *Lady's Magazine* devoted nine pages to excerpts and analysis of Wollstonecraft's book. The editor's introduction to this piece proudly announced: "This lady is known to the world, by her answer to Mr. Burke, and we now behold her employing her pen on behalf of her own sex." In his 1793 Fourth of July oration, New Jersey congressman Elias Boudinot took note of a striking shift in political discourse: "The Rights of Woman are now heard as familiar terms in every part of the United States." Wollstonecraft's book had an almost immediate impact on the formation and spread of women's rights discourse in America.[35]

Prior to 1792, the idea of women's rights had been bandied about in Anglo-American public discourse in a more satirical than serious fashion. As with John Adams's 1776 letter to Abigail Adams, a 1791 poem in the *United States Chronicle* poked fun at the idea that women would even want the "Rights of Man" that Thomas Paine defended, since they already enjoyed absolute sexual power over their husbands:

> But have not women greater rights than these;
> Do they not rule and govern as they please?

> The servile men of every age and nation,
> Are always slaves to female legislation.

Several of the earliest responses to the *Rights of Woman*, especially in London, were similarly indisposed to taking the issue of sex equality seriously. Thomas Taylor, the Cambridge Platonist, penned a parodic *Vindication of the Rights of Brutes* in 1792. He used crude sexual humor to suggest that extending rights to women was as silly and perverse as attributing rights to elephants, by envisioning a future egalitarian society in which women freely chose to breed with rights-bearing pachyderms. Another satirical pamphlet in London that year thanked "Mrs. Mary with the hard German name" for her ideas on "the general rights of girls," and exclaimed "Oh! Mr. Paine, what do we not owe you" on the matter of "the general rights of boys." In October 1792, a Philadelphia newspaper published an article entitled "The Rights of Woman," which directly scorned Paine for ignoring the rights of woman but indirectly derided Wollstonecraft's egalitarian conception of rights. The pseudonymous Susannah Staunch instead declared a satirical list of rights of wives—including retaliatory adultery and an "unquestionable and uncontrollable right in the kitchen, the laundry, and the dairy." Such humorous gendering of Anglo-American rights discourse, with Paine often associated with the rights of men and Wollstonecraft often linked to the rights of women, belied the cultural resistance to a truly egalitarian conception of human rights.[36]

Wollstonecraft's Christian Metaphysical Foundation for the Rights of Women

Even as secularization began to shape the cultures of the North Atlantic states, philosophical and rhetorical appeals to the God-given nature of rights were common in the eighteenth century. As in the natural religion of Thomas Jefferson's *Declaration of Independence* (1776), sometimes God and nature were equated or equivocated in Enlightenment thought. In that foundational document of the American Revolution, he appealed to the rights of the American people over and against the laws of the British Empire, and framed the former's rights as grounded on "the laws of nature and of Nature's God." The three dominant schools of thought on natural rights in the late eighteenth century—Protestant Christianity, social contract theory, and Enlightenment-era appropriations of Stoicism—to various degrees built on this premise, that the natural rights of human beings were dictates of reason and as such derived from God's natural law of morality.[37]

Wollstonecraft dove straight into these debates on the basis of rights as a young professional writer and translator in London in the early 1790s. Born in 1759, to a middle-class Anglican family in East London, she was privately tutored and mentored by several Protestant intellectuals in her youth: John Arden, a dissenter and scientific lecturer whose daughter Jane befriended Wollstonecraft in Yorkshire in their mid-teens; Mr. Clare, a clergyman who served as her informal teacher in north London in her late teens; and the Calvinist turned unitarian Reverend James Burgh and his wife, Hannah Harding, who assisted her in establishing a coeducational day school on Newington Green in north London in her mid-twenties. Around 1784, Wollstonecraft met the Reverend Dr. Price, a rational dissenter and abolitionist preaching at the Newington Green church. Although she continued to attend Anglican services, she soon theorized the foundation of human rights similarly to this dissenting minister. Given that she was raised Anglican, found her teachers among Protestant ministers, and wrote extensively on theology as an adult, it is not surprising that Wollstonecraft took a broadly Protestant Christian approach to theorizing a theological and metaphysical foundation for women's human rights.[38]

Although social contract and neo-Stoic ideas have been identified in her writings, Wollstonecraft is not typically categorized as belonging to either of these schools on natural rights. Her extensive critique of Rousseau in her *Rights of Woman* provides ample evidence of her dislike of his brand of social contract theory. The 1755 *Second Discourse*'s model of the "state of nature" was an "unsound" starting point for political theory, since it was "reared on a false hypothesis." There was no evidence for Rousseau's (or other theorists') fanciful claims about human beings before society and government. Perhaps because of her skepticism of the imagined divide between nature and society proposed by Rousseau, she did not regularly appeal to the concept of "natural rights." Instead, she preferred such terms as "rights of humanity," "civil and political rights," "sacred rights," "rights and duties," "rights of men," and "rights of woman." Her favored terms defined human rights not in relation to what was supposedly natural but rather to what actually established people as rights-bearing subjects: their humanity, the laws of their governments, and morality itself.[39]

Further distancing herself from the social contract tradition, Wollstonecraft only mentioned the concept of the "social compact" four times in her writings—referring to either current forms of constitutional mixed government (Britain and France) or a future "truly equitable" form of republicanism in which the sexes were equal contributors to civic virtue because "women were educated by the same pursuits as men." At the beginning of the *Rights of Men*, her single abstract description of the "social compact" merely represented her ideal republican state as one that guaranteed "the birthright of man": "such a degree of liberty, civil and religious, as is compatible with the liberty of every other individual with whom he is united in a social compact." Unlike Hobbes, Locke, Rousseau, and Kant, Wollstonecraft never employed contract theory to explain the reasons for the formation of societies, governments, or systems of international law.[40]

As for Enlightenment-era appropriations of Stoic ideas, Wollstonecraft at times seemed to embrace their value for women, especially those who fared badly in society. In an anonymous 1790 review of Catherine Macaulay's *Letters on Education* signed "M" and subsequently attributed to Wollstonecraft, the "doctrines of the Stoics" were praised as deserving of "respect." Beyond this tenuous evidence of Wollstonecraft's approval of Stoicism, Richard Vernon has cited the *Rights of Woman*'s dramatic representation of the bereft widow as the best mother as more conclusive proof of her Stoic brand of feminism. Wollstonecraft pictured a young woman of virtue who, in the wake of her husband's death, chose to focus on her children rather than pursue the awakening of new sexual love: "She is left a widow, perhaps, without a sufficient provision; but she is not desolate! The pang of nature is felt; but after time has softened sorrow into melancholy resignation, her heart turns to her children with redoubled fondness, and anxious to provide for them, affection gives a sacred heroic cast to her maternal duties." At first glance, the Wollstonecraftian widow's melancholy yet moral state might suggest her Stoic disposition in the face of personal tragedy. Yet her "heroic" fulfillment of her duties to her children despite her sadness at the loss of her husband and her competing feelings for another man was also broadly compatible with Protestant Christian ethics. Even Vernon, who has made the strongest case for Wollstonecraft's Stoicism, has conceded that these ideas would have been filtered through her reception of the rational Christian theology of her mentor Price.[41]

Wollstonecraft's apparent Stoicism might be better explained in terms of currents in late eighteenth-century Protestant Christian ethics, especially the kind that Kant systematized on a purely rational plane in his moral philosophy. Like Kant's theory of the dutiful reasons for ethical conduct in his *Groundwork for the Metaphysics of Morals* (1785), Wollstonecraft's story of the widow made it clear that morality depends not on happiness but rather on the intention to fulfill obligations. Despite this basic commonality, Wollstonecraft never took the stronger Kantian position that the autonomous, or duty-oriented, performance of moral rules required the outright rejection of heteronomous, or happiness-producing, motives. On the other hand, she agreed with Kant that happiness could be a by-product of making moral choices. The widow ultimately experienced happiness in her devotion to the care of her children, even given the loss of her spouse and the opportunity for a second marriage. As Wollstonecraft imagined, "I see her surrounded by her children, reaping the reward of her care." The emotional authenticity of Wollstonecraft's widow can thus be contrasted with Rousseau's Julie, whose Stoic denial of her unhappiness in her arranged marriage to Wolmar only led to her death-bed revelation of her eternal love for St. Preux. In a letter intended for her lover that her husband found after her death, Julie disclosed the truth that she always loved St. Preux the most: "Nay, I leave thee not, I go to await thee. . . . Only too happy to pay with my life the right to love thee still without crime, and to tell thee so one more time." The Wollstonecraftian widow, by contrast, partook of worldly love plus the promise of otherworldly joy: "Her children have her love, and her brightest hopes are beyond the grave, where her imagination often strays." Her rational control of her passions allowed her to emotionally flourish in this world as a prelude to eternal happiness in the next life.[42]

Indeed, Wollstonecraft presumed neither a Stoic nor a Kantian tension between reason and the passions in her ethical system. Instead, she followed the British empiricist Hobbes in understanding the passions as "necessary auxiliaries of reason." "Auxiliaries," in the eighteenth-century English lexicon, were helpers or assistants (sometimes referring to military assistance but originally referring to intellectual relationships, such as the productive role of mathematics for physics). The passions, especially the primary "impulse" to self-preservation, were thus the helpers or assistants for the proper development of human reason. For Wollstonecraft, as for Hobbes, the development of human reason was not open-ended or morally neutral but rather aimed toward the realization of a circumscribed set of human goods. The passions assisted reason's development such that adult humans came to understand the value of their rational "struggle" with passion as constitutive of the goods that defined their lives as ones worth living and preserving. Even if it was difficult to negotiate the "game" of life—partly because of the impulses of passion—a person could rationally grasp the most important (and often unexpected) moral lessons from the process of playing the game. Reason was not only transformed in this cooperative relationship with the passions but also strengthened in the process. To put this point into sharp relief, Wollstonecraft offered the hard case of the widow, whose long-term and genuine happiness depended upon reasonably controlling her grief and finding comfort and pleasure in enacting her duty to her children.[43]

Given their male biases and general sidelining of women, Christian sources for natural rights theories were as problematic for Wollstonecraft's philosophical purposes as neo-Stoic and social contract theories. Just as Wollstonecraft rejected the conceptual divide between the state of nature and the social contract, she also rejected scriptural accounts of an original state, such as the story of Adam and Eve, as productive for ethics or politics. Such origin stories were empirically unverifiable and thus prone to distorting the facts of the human condition. This was especially true in the case of understanding the relationship between the sexes, as the story of Adam and Eve had been repeatedly used to defend women's subordination to men, even by great minds such as the poet John Milton. According to Wollstonecraft's feminist biblical hermeneutics, "Man, from the remotest antiquity, found it convenient to exert his strength to subjugate his companion" through "inventions" such as "Moses' poetical story" about Eve being made from Adam's rib.

Rather than rely on scriptural accounts or conjectural stories about the origins and progress of humanity, Wollstonecraft established a few "first principles" by which humans and their rights might be rationally understood from a metaphysical/ethical perspective. In the opening chapters of the *Rights of Woman*, Wollstonecraft defined rights as "the privilege of moral beings." Moral beings are human beings, who are designed by God to achieve "pre-eminence over the brute creation" and to acquire "virtue" and "knowledge" through the exercise of "reason." She argued that women might "procure" rights through the "exercise of reason." By using reason to gauge moral action toward others, women would "obtain the sober pleasures that arise from equality." She insisted that such "sober pleasures" were secondary to the primary reason for women's understanding of themselves as rights-bearing subjects: women's "first duty is to themselves as rational creatures." The subjective rights of women were therefore derivative from their duties, especially the duty to develop their moral and intellectual potential as rational creatures of God.[44]

Responding to the deficiencies of Christian, neo-Stoic, and social contract theories of natural rights for securing freedom and well-being for women, Wollstonecraft thus developed an alternative theological and philosophical foundation for the full inclusion of women in the rights of humanity. In crafting a universalistic and egalitarian understanding of human rights, she drew on a variety of schools of thought within the rational Christian dissenter tradition. Dissenting Christians were the non-Anglican Protestants in England who had gained the right to practice their alternative forms of Christianity under the Toleration Act of 1689.

Wollstonecraft's intellectual exposure to rational Christian dissent of the sort espoused by Price took place between 1784 and 1786, when she heard his sermons at the Newington Green church. Her first publications on issues such as female education, marriage, and family—*Thoughts on the Education of Daughters* (1787), *Mary, a Fiction* (1788), and *Original Stories from Real Life* (1788)—show the deep Augustinian influence of Anglican Christianity on her early political thought. Yet these major writings before the French Revolution also indicate her growing engagement with the alternative school of religious and political thought represented by rational Christian dissenters such as Burgh and Price. It was Wollstonecraft's two *Vindications*, published in 1790 and 1792, that reflected her full adoption of the Pricean approach to grounding human rights on a rational theological foundation.[45]

Price was the son of a Presbyterian minister. His Newington Green church was founded as a Presbyterian church in 1708. In the late eighteenth century, this church became more strongly associated with the broader dissenting Christian movement from trinitarian to unitarian theology. Price's own theological views on the trinity moved in this direction. He considered himself an Arian: he viewed Jesus not as cosubstantial with God but rather as a creature made by God before his physical incarnation. For this reason, he thought Jesus should not be worshipped, because worship ought to be reserved for God.[46]

Wollstonecraft, by the time she wrote the *Rights of Men*, seems to have pushed beyond Price's Arianism toward a Socinian, or unitarian, view of God. Rebuffing Burke's hypocritical combination of elitism and Christianity, she implied that the Irish statesman respected Jesus for his regal "lineage" from David, whereas her devotion to "the carpenter's son" depended only on his appointment by "Divine authority." Like other late eighteenth-century Socinians such as Joseph Priestley, Wollstonecraft revered Jesus as a mortal man (a "carpenter's son") who was chosen by the one God to serve as the greatest moral exemplar for humanity. Her antitrinitarian theology did not make her any less devoutly Christian, however. In the *Rights of Men*, she proclaimed a deep personal and emotional bond with the one God of the Old and New Testaments, alongside a piety toward the moral example of Jesus, in a way that revealed the resilience of orthodox elements of her Protestant faith.[47]

On matters of moral theology, Price and Wollstonecraft argued against voluntarism and empiricism in favor of rationalism. Voluntarists, such as Ockham, had argued that the moral law was an expression of God's will. Empiricists, such as Hobbes, had argued that there was no stable enforcement of the laws of nature (beyond the constant right to practice self-defense) until government and positive law were established by the will of the absolute sovereign. Both schools presumed that morality was an expression of the will of a sovereign ruler, divine or mortal. Both Price and Wollstonecraft rejected these schools of thought on the grounds that they made morality arbitrary. Wollstonecraft critically read Burke's defense of political institutions as sources of moral authority along these lines: "Nature and Reason, according to your system, are all to give place to authority; and the gods, as Shakespeare makes a frantic wretch exclaim, seem to kill us for their sport, as men do flies." If moral rules were merely expressions of divine or personal will, then morality could be reduced to the subjective volitional whims of the Creator or human rulers.[48]

Instead, Price and Wollstonecraft took a rationalistic approach to conceptualizing God and humanity's relationships to the moral law.

For both of them, the moral law is objective, because it is rational and has this ontological property independently of God's will. If the moral law was merely an expression of God's will, then morality could be reduced to the whims of an all-powerful sovereign Creator who failed to subject himself to the rules of reason. To avoid this pitfall of theological voluntarism, Price and Wollstonecraft set forth a two-part rationalistic account of the basis of morality that pertained to both God and humankind: (1) the moral law exists independently of God's will but as part of his nature as the supreme rational being, and (2) the moral law is universal in its application to all humans, who may grasp it via reason because they are made in the image of God. As Wollstonecraft explained in theological terms in the *Rights of Men*, "I FEAR God! I bend with awful reverence when I inquire on what my fear is built—I fear that sublime power, whose motive for creating me must have been wise and good; and I submit to the moral laws which my reason deduces from this view of my dependence on him.—It is not his power that I fear—it is not to an arbitrary will, but to an unerring reason I submit.—Submit—yes . . . to the law that regulates his just resolves." Price's and Wollstonecraft's theological and metaphysical definition of the moral law as part of God's essence, but independent of his will, had roots in Thomas Aquinas. It also had Enlightenment Protestant expressions among rights theorists such as Locke.[49]

This idea of the moral law as grounded on reason, independently of any being's will, gave the idea of human rights the possibility of an objective and universal foundation. Following Price, Wollstonecraft in her *Rights of Men* posited a theological and metaphysical account of the grounding of "sacred rights" on the "eternal foundation of right." This foundation was found in "the immutable attributes of God": first and foremost, the reason which God and his human creatures shared. In his 1767 theological *Dissertations*, Price had defended a conception of God as rational, providential, and caring: "A God without a Providence is undoubtedly a contradiction. Nothing is plainer than that a Being of perfect reason will in every instance take such care of the universe as perfect reason requires." Wollstonecraft likewise opened her *Rights of Woman* with a similar theodicy: "Firmly persuaded that no evil exists in the world that God did not design to take place, I build my belief on the perfection of God." For Wollstonecraft as well as Price, the realization of the "sacred rights" of humanity was part of God's rational and benevolent providential plan for the development of human potential within creation.[50]

For Price and Wollstonecraft, human beings had moral rights and moral duties—in short, ethical relationships with one another—because they had access, via reason, to understanding the universal principles of morality. These principles were part of God's nature as the supreme rational being, but they were principles to which God voluntarily subjected his will. Humans, too, had a choice: a choice to direct their freedom of will and rationality to the understanding and application of these principles in their interactions with each other. As Wollstonecraft argued in the *Rights of Men*, "The more man discovers the nature of his mind and body, the more clearly he is convinced, that to act according to the dictates of reason is to conform to the law of God." The human subject's freedom of will, combined with her rationality, empowered her to enact the moral duties derived from the objective and universal law of God, and the rights derived from such duties.[51]

Both Price and Wollstonecraft thus reserved a robust place for freedom of the will in their accounts of moral theology, ethics, and human rights. Rational Christian dissenters typically emphasized the freedom of the will's legitimate expression in the civil and political rights to freedom of conscience and religious toleration. This English nonconformist tradition grew in power after the Toleration Act of 1689, which had permitted non-Anglican Protestants to establish churches such as the one on Newington Green.[52]

Price had developed a strong human rights theory while preaching in various capacities at Newington Green since 1758. He supported the abolition of chattel slavery and backed the American and the French Revolutions. In 1776, he argued that among the "inalienable rights of human nature" was the right to exercise free will through participating in the social compact; through such willful popular participation, governments would finally be rendered legitimate in their powers. Furthermore, the practice of moral liberty, religious liberty, and civil liberty raised human beings above the level of "a poor and abject animal." Price defined moral liberty as the exercise of free will and reason in order to put God's moral law into action. Moral liberty, for Price as for Wollstonecraft, was the rational self-governance of individual human beings according to universal principles of morality. This concept of moral liberty undergirded their ideal conceptions of citizenship as participation in a self-governing republic with a popular legislative assembly. Although they thought that moral liberty was an important component of civil and political liberty, it was not a precondition for one's entitlement to civil and political rights. The case of chattel slavery illustrated this point: the slave was not allowed to be either physically or morally free but still deserved to be granted her liberty so that she could learn to be free physically, morally, civilly, and politically.[53]

Wollstonecraft's rational theological approach to universal human rights built on Price but extended the argument explicitly and systematically to women. While Price repeatedly referenced the "inalienable rights of humanity" in his sermons and political writings, he never seems to have made a public, recorded plea for women's human rights. His abolitionist arguments against human slavery only implied women's human right to be free from slavery. Wollstonecraft, on the other hand, began to specifically and systematically argue for women's human rights alongside the abolition of slavery in her earliest political treatise, the 1790 *Rights of Men*.

Before penning the *Rights of Men*, Wollstonecraft did not often use the language of rights in the sense of subjective, or individually held and exercised, rights. The influence of Price at Newington Green seems to have triggered a shift in Wollstonecraft's conception of rights. As a student, teacher, and theorist, she long had an interest in the issue of female education—but she had not previously framed education as a right of each and every human individual. In her early publications, she conceptualized education as a moral duty of adults to be performed in relation to their children; on the obverse side, it was a moral duty of children to follow their parents' instruction to ensure their own development toward consistent practice of God's moral law. By the time she composed the *Rights of Men*, Wollstonecraft had begun to theorize an egalitarian view of universal human rights—beginning with education and leading to republican political participation. Her view followed Price in its grounding in the theology of rational dissent. Her specific application of the concept of subjective rights to women, however, was a philosophical milestone in the realization of the concept's universalistic and egalitarian potential.

Mill's Secular Alternative to Religious and Metaphysical Theories of Rights

It was also in this late eighteenth-century intellectual context that classical utilitarian thought, as set forth by Jeremy Bentham and James Mill, began to be developed. Utilitarianism—or the view that happiness is the only good, and suffering the only bad, and right action is that which maximizes this good understood in this way—was a philosophical expression of the secularization of high culture in the late Enlightenment. John Stuart Mill, born in 1806 in the Pentonville neighborhood of London, was a product of this secular utilitarian school of thought, beginning with his earliest education by his father, James. James Mill was raised Presbyterian but wholly rejected religion as an adult, not only because of his personal lack of faith but also because of his broader ethical conviction that religion was the primary cause of suffering. Utilitarianism posed the competing objective of reducing pain by promoting the greatest pleasure for the greatest number of people and other sentient beings. Debunking religion was one step that both Bentham and James Mill adopted as part of the diffusion of happiness around the globe.[54]

Bentham had famously declared the idea of natural rights as "nonsense on stilts." Viewed from his wholly sensory and empirical utilitarian perspective on happiness, religion was nonsense. Consequently, any religious or other metaphysical justifications of rights were doubly absurd: propped up by shoddy arguments, natural rights were destined to fall down from their lofty heights once subjected to rigorous scientific scrutiny. Although he agreed with Bentham that metaphysical foundations for rights were nonsense, John Stuart Mill did not abandon the project of justifying rights on alternative grounds. Rather, his philosophical convictions about the nature of morality and rights brought him to the conclusion that enslaved people and women (including enslaved women) have rights. These rights he called "moral rights" to distinguish them from the "legal" or positive rights that typically had been granted only to men in power, and often with the purpose of oppressing groups such as slaves and women. His nearly lifelong political concern for advancing the rights of women and other historically oppressed groups such as African slaves encouraged him as a philosopher to move in this radical direction. Mill accordingly developed an abstract rational justification for the moral rights of humans, which rested upon a secular and nonmetaphysical (meaning *a posteriori* and empirical) utilitarian conception of the individual human being as a "progressive being." Such a progressive being was capable of and entitled to liberty and free and full self-development toward the happiness of herself and other sentient beings. In order to realize such free development toward happiness for each and all, humans needed to have their moral rights to freedom and self-development enshrined in and ensured by law. Hence, Mill made a case for the institutionalization of moral rights as legal rights, so that legal rights could be a force for the happiness of humanity and sentient life as a whole. Mill's conception of moral or human rights thus served as a nonmetaphysical and rationally justified normative standard according to which the law and other man-made institutions ought to be critically judged and ultimately reformed.[55]

Attention to Mill's biography (and autobiography) is instructive for understanding the roots of his nonmetaphysical approach to justifying human rights. James Mill raised his son John Stuart in a deliberately secular way, educating him at home and apart from any religious schools or universities. Although he was baptized and occasionally sent to services at a local Anglican parish as a young child, John Stuart later recalled, "I have *never* believed in Christianity as a religion." In correspondence with his friends and fellow intellectuals Auguste Comte and Thomas Carlyle, Mill represented himself as exceptional for his utterly secular upbringing and consistent lack of faith.[56]

In contrast to his fellow Londoner Wollstonecraft—who died about nine years before he was born in 1806—Mill received a training in moral philosophy that was entirely secular. Written in several versions between 1853 and 1870, his *Autobiography* famously chronicled his "unusual and remarkable" education. Most distinctively, Mill noted, "I was brought up from the first without any religious belief."[57]

From 1810 to 1813, Mill's family lived near Newington Green. Unlike Wollstonecraft's exposure to the abstract metaphysics of rational dissent at Price's church on the green, Mill's education was deliberately situated on entirely scientific and empirical grounds. Between the ages of four and seven, Mill took daily walks with his father, James, from the green to the countryside. During these earliest remembered encounters with nature, he was expected to present accounts of "what I had read the day before." James Mill focused his young son's attention on learning from the historical examples of great "men of energy and resource in unusual circumstances." Among these great men was James himself, whose views on "civilization, government, morality, [and] mental cultivation" John Stuart was expected to restate "in his own words." Religion was treated as a subspecies of history, with a focus on the exemplary history of Protestant reformers—such as John Knox and the Quakers—who had challenged clerical and aristocratic power. The remainder of John Stuart's unusually early and intensive intellectual education concerned classical languages, mathematics, experimental natural science, logic, and, most important, the modern empirical "science" of political economy.[58]

As foundations for human knowledge, James Mill had rejected both revealed religion and natural religion, including deism. He taught

John Stuart that "concerning the origin of things nothing whatever can be known." The question "'Who made me?' cannot be answered, because we have no experience or authentic information from which to answer it"; furthermore, it raises the question "Who made God?" Faced with such unanswerable questions, arguments about the origins of the universe failed to provide foundational evidence for either religious or scientific worldviews. At a very young age, John Stuart adopted his father James's secular philosophical approach to epistemology: if "nothing could be known" about the remote origins of the universe, then more immediate and material grounds for understanding oneself and nature must be sought.[59]

This alternative empirical grounding for human knowledge, including morality, was Bentham's utilitarian philosophy. John Stuart described his father as "the earliest Englishman of any great mark, who thoroughly understood, and in the main adopted, Bentham's general views of ethics, government, and law." James Mill's "standard of morals" was utilitarian in Bentham's sense, by "taking as the exclusive test of right and wrong, the tendency of actions to produce pleasure or pain."[60]

John Stuart recalled that as early as the age of seven he also had a close personal relationship to Bentham. In the winter of his fifteenth year, John Stuart's worldview was transformed by reading Dumont's *Traité de législation* (1802), a redaction of Bentham's *Introduction to the Principles of Morals and Legislation* (1789). Dumont's treatise, as guided by Bentham's principles, demystified religion and other metaphysical views (including the ideas of natural law and right reason) as "dogmatism in disguise."[61]

John Stuart, from that point onward, understood Bentham's "principle of utility" as the only certain and systematic foundation for a modern, scientific, and thus secular approach to ethics, economics, and politics: "The 'principle of utility,' understood as Bentham understood it, and applied in the manner in which he applied it through these three volumes, fell exactly into its place as the keystone which held together the detached and fragmentary component parts of my knowledge and beliefs. It gave unity to my conception of things. I now had opinions; a creed, a doctrine, a philosophy; in one among the best senses of the word, a religion." Bentham's utilitarianism gave the young Mill a secular creed or philosophical orientation that inspired him with a kind of religious zeal to "to be a reformer of the world." If the happiness of humans and other animals could be calculated from their experience of pleasure and their avoidance of pain, the planned realization of broadly beneficial laws and policies seemed within practical reach. Mill devoted the next five years to such projects, in writing, debate, and leadership of the Utilitarian Society of young male intellectuals who shared his expectation that the systematic application of principles of utilitarian political economy could reform the world. During this time, he identified his "own happiness" with that of the realization of the greatest good for all in every sphere of life.[62]

Then, in the fall of 1826, the twenty-year-old Mill faced what he later called the "crisis in my mental history." He asked himself: If "all your objects in life were realized" would you be happy? "An irrepressible self-consciousness distinctly answered, 'No!'" He described this devastating psychological experience in terms of the loss of *all* foundations, including the philosophical architecture of utilitarianism: "The whole foundation on which my life was constructed fell down."[63]

The consequence of this loss was Mill's rebuilding of his sense of self and his philosophy upon restructured utilitarian foundations. He began by theorizing the defects in both his own early education and the Benthamite utilitarian outlook, particularly their lack of personal affect: "My education, I thought, had failed to create those feelings in sufficient strength to resist the dissolving influence of analysis." Without the subjective emotional sympathies and pleasures that could make his commitment to utilitarianism meaningful *for him*, he was like a "well-equipped ship" without a "sail." He had the goal, the greatest aggregate pleasure for humanity, but not the motive, his own sense of pleasure in life, or even a sense of the subjective value of his own life. Mill's mental crisis taught him that defining one's life by a telos, or ultimate goal, is not enough. One needs a grounding or a centering point, which can only be one's subjective sense of self and its value. From this psychological grounding, one may set sail toward a goal, without losing a greater sense of purpose upon arrival. The journey was not over with the accomplishment; rather, the process of self-development continued with the new set of experiences waiting on the horizon.[64]

His fresh connection with his "irrepressible self-consciousness" motivated John Stuart to develop his own utilitarian moral philosophy, which put the value of the human individual's self-development at its core. He still believed that happiness was the "test of all rules of conduct, and the end of life," but that it was "only to be attained by not making it the direct end." He made an inward turn to contemplating and valuing "the internal culture of the individual" more than external and material signs of human well-being. Such contemplation of one's self, and human selfhood in general, was the source of "real, permanent happiness." This inward turn did not require a "turning away" from "the common feelings and common destiny of human beings" but rather required a "greatly increased interest in" such common human experiences. The latter insight came from his reading of the poetry of William Wordsworth, which Mill felt was an expression of the poet's own "spontaneous overflow of powerful feeling" in the face of the natural beauty of everyday human life. Johann Wolfgang von Goethe's conception of the best education as cultivating the complex and many-sided character of individuals was another inspiration for the young Mill in his time of recovery.[65]

His discovery of this indirect route to personal happiness allowed Mill to conceive a general view of self-development as the indirect route to the greatest happiness for the greatest number. Self-development of individuals was the necessary first step toward the end of realizing the greatest happiness for all. The aggregate beneficial effects of a law or policy were not sufficient grounds for meeting Mill's revised utilitarian test of morality. In his primary test of the morality of the law or policy, the benefits for individual self-development had to be articulated. This new formulation of utilitarianism was liberal, or oriented toward the reciprocal protection of the liberty of individuals in ethical and political relation to others' liberty. His liberal utilitarianism understood the conditions for individual liberty and free and full self-development as necessary for generating an authentic global utility.

Two of Mill's major political writings fleshed out the process by which this liberal utilitarian approach to promoting happiness could be put into practice. *On Liberty* (1859) presented the first step as the recognition of the "principle" of individuality, or the view that spontaneous self-development was "the chief ingredient of individual and social progress." Once individuality was articulated in "civilization, instruction, education, [and] culture" as "a necessary part and condition of all those things," its realization could be understood as the indirect, though morally correct, path to the greatest happiness of the whole.[66]

In *On Liberty* and *The Subjection of Women* (1869), Mill identified education as the primary practical tool by which an aesthetic and moral appreciation of individuality could be cultivated in people over time and across generations. Properly understood in the broadest sense, education was not merely socialization or social control. Rather, it was a long-term process of realizing the rich range of capabilities of human beings, first as individuals, and secondly as a species. According to Mill's liberal utilitarian principles, it was especially crucial for education to cultivate the individuality of women in addition to inculcating men's appreciation for women's virtuous yet varied self-development. Without nurturing a culture in which individuality would thrive among women as much as men, society would miss out on "doubling the mass of mental faculties available for the higher service of humanity."[67]

Less difficult than such deep cultural reform in the long run, but perhaps as complicated in the short term, the next step was to reform the law. For this task, Mill assigned "one very simple principle": the view that moral rightness was acting so that the consequences of one's action maximized happiness (or minimized suffering). In the domain of law, he advocated that legislators and jurists use this harm principle as a conceptual device for assigning the appropriate "legal penalties" to those who, whether individually or collectively, enacted harm upon others. Consequently, only the harmful conduct by the individual that "concerns others" could be subject to legal scrutiny and rightful punishment. The liberal political import of the harm principle was to demarcate a legal space within which the individual could experience an expansive self-regarding liberty, conducive to his or her free and full self-development, without "encroaching on the rights of others." Individual human rights, including women's rights to education and suffrage, ought to be legislated according to thoughtful applications of the harm principle, since its aim was to encourage the flourishing of an other-regarding ethic of individual freedom under the law. The last, long-term, and most visionary step of this twofold, educational and lawmaking, process was letting people spontaneously self-develop according to established moral and legal rules of their "rights as human beings" so that a virtuous happiness for all might prevail.[68]

Around the same time that Mill discovered these indirect routes to personal and global happiness, he was becoming practically and philosophically engaged with the question of women's rights and related issues such as sexual education concerning contraception. In 1823, the young Mill was arrested for distributing pamphlets on birth control. In the *Autobiography*, he dated his interest in the issue of women's rights to his second decade of life, when he critically responded to his father James Mill's *Essay on Government* (1820). He dissented from the elder Mill's claim that "women may consistently with good government, be excluded from the suffrage, because their interest is the same with that of men." Mill insisted that his father could not escape the charge that this abstract point about representation—which assumed homogenous interests across a group—had problematic implications for ethics and politics, especially in the age of suffrage reform. In his *Autobiography*, Mill favorably recounted how William Thompson's 1825 "*Appeal* in behalf of women" pitted its arguments against his father's assumption that married women's interests were identical to their husbands' interests. New England suffragist John Neal later recalled how he debated John Stuart Mill in London on the issue of women's rights in the late 1820s, in the wake of the public discussion of James Mill's failure to adequately address women's rights.[69]

John Stuart's early pondering of the woman question was also indebted to Bentham. In his *Autobiography*, Mill reported that on the "important point" of women's suffrage, Bentham was "wholly on our side." By addressing the woman question as part of their philosophical calculus of how to maximize happiness for all sentient beings, James Mill and Bentham set the stage for John Stuart's more robust philosophical and political engagement of the issue over the course of his career.[70]

The young Mill's deepening concern with the woman question has usually been linked to his profound intellectual relationship with the female friend who would eventually become his beloved wife, Harriet Taylor. The pair exchanged their unpublished essays on marriage in 1831 or early 1832. In these tantalizingly short works of philosophical prose, Taylor and Mill set forth their distinctive views on reform of marriage and the social status of women. As Alice Rossi argued in her edition of the couple's writings on the equality of the sexes, Taylor was more in the school of the Unitarian Radicals of 1830s London, whose keen interest in using rationalistic theology for advancing women's rights extended from Wollstonecraft to Harriet Martineau; Mill, on the other hand, was shaped by the Philosophical Radicals of Britain, in taking a secular, utilitarian, and Romantic approach to the issue of realizing women's equality with men.[71]

Taylor's essay shows her to be the more radical feminist of the two at the time. Mill's essay defended a Romantic vision of a more equal form of marriage, in which the wife inspired the husband intellectually as well as through the beauty of the domestic environment she created for them. As he poetically opined, "The great occupation of woman should be to *beautify* life: to cultivate, for her own sake and that of those who surround her, all her faculties of mind, soul, and body; all her powers of enjoyment, and powers of giving enjoyment; and to diffuse beauty, elegance, and grace, everywhere." Mill's essay concluded with worries about protecting women outside such beautiful and enjoyable marriages, especially against the forces of public opinion that judged their sex quite harshly for assertions of independence. To his credit, he endorsed an equal right to divorce so that women would not be "forcibly united to one of those who *make* the opinion."[72]

Taylor's response delved deeper into an assessment of patriarchal power relations. She critiqued the gendered divide between public and private, which placed men in civil and political roles outside the home and women predominantly within the private space of the family. Even liberals with radical leanings like Mill understood women's roles as focused on caring for others, as when he claimed women's "great occupation" is to "beautify" life for everyone. Taylor ironically remarked, as Wollstonecraft had done, on the similarity of the plight of prostitutes and wives: "Women are educated for one single object, to gain their living by marrying—(some poor souls get it without the churchgoing. It's the same way—they do not seem to be a bit worse than their honoured sisters)." Taylor's essay also defended women's "most entire equality with men, as to all rights and privileges, civil and political." She emphasized the rights to divorce, to be single and childless, and to have careers outside the home, on the grounds that recognition of such rights would open the door for further social reforms that would promote the equality of the sexes in society and law. Poignantly, the friends privately exchanged these manuscripts on marriage during the early days of their platonic relationship. Both in their mid-twenties, Mill was single, but Taylor was married to her first husband, John, and raising their three young children.[73]

Mill's early criticism of his father's assumption of the homogeneity of spousal interests within marriage led him to publically challenge the view that male heads of families could adequately represent the interests of women in politics. The logic of the "indirect route" to happiness could be applied to this case of justifying women's rights within utilitarianism. Male heads of household cannot be substituted for their wives, as though they held equivalent functions in the calculus of utility; rather, individual wives may differ from their husbands in the subjective assessment of their own and their family's interests.

Harriet Taylor's differences of opinion from her "upright, brave, and honorable" first husband were a poignant case in point; John Taylor's interests were not the same as Harriet's, despite his "steady and affectionate" friendship with her. Mill reasoned that all adult individuals, including women, must be allowed political conditions under which they can represent their subjective perception of their interests, such as via the right to vote. The self-development and individual human rights of women, therefore, were preconditions for the good of the whole political community.[74]

Beyond his inspiration by Bentham, his father, and his future wife, Mill was aware of Wollstonecraft's work on women's rights, too. In 1843, his friend and correspondent Auguste Comte—the French positivist philosopher—wrote to him about his youthful fascination with her work in the late 1790s. Comte expressed how she played a role in his early philosophical engagement of the relationship between the sexes: "All thinkers who seriously like women as something more than pretty playthings have nowadays passed through a similar phase, I believe. In my turn, I well recall the time when the strange book of Miss Mary Wollstonecraft—written before she married Godwin—influenced me strongly." Mill and Comte's ensuing correspondence on the woman question was later published in 1860s St. Petersburg and 1870s Paris, stirring further feminist debates.[75]

Despite his early interest in Wollstonecraft's philosophy of sex equality, Comte later positioned himself against the Wollstonecraftian school of thought on the common humanity and rights of the sexes. In his 1843 letters to Mill, Comte instead posited a "natural hierarchy" of men over women that translated into separate and unequal social roles for the sexes. He went so far as to claim that women—by virtue of their "organic" sexual inferiority—were in a "state of radical childhood" and thus incapable of management roles, inside or outside the household.[76]

Mill's epistolary response to Comte illustrated the impact of the past decade of theoretical discussions with Taylor on marriage and the sources of female subordination. Mill deflated Comte's claim of a female incapacity for management by pointing out women's comparative strength in running households, and even industries, in England. Via a comparison of Western European women with the Russian serfs, Mill argued that women's secondary status to men was a product of socialization: "The servitude of women, although milder [than that of the serfs], is a servitude without respite, encompassing all of their activities, which discharges them, much more completely than was ever true for the serfs, from all essential planning for the future and from all active direction of their own conduct with respect to society but even in the way of individual interest." By 1843, Mill was clearly developing a more comprehensive political theory of how society imposed inequality on the sexes. His reflection on the moral psychology of women's oppression opened the door to his deliberation on the necessity of social and economic reforms, especially educational and workplace opportunities, to unlock women from their ascribed position of total subordination.[77]

While Mill never cited Wollstoneraft as a source for his work, we know that his intellectual partner Taylor read the *Rights of Woman*. She also shared the book with her adolescent daughter, the future women's suffragist Helen Taylor, in the early 1840s. Harriet Taylor's brand of feminist liberalism had much in common with Wollstonecraft's ideas, as well as the growing organized feminist movement in the 1840s United States. Taylor's 1851 essay "The Enfranchisement of Women," published in London's *Westminster Review*, paid homage to the recent, path-breaking women's rights conventions in Seneca Falls, New York, and Worcester, Massachusetts. Taylor made a strong public demand for women's formal political incorporation as an essential aspect of social justice, nationally and internationally. Recalling the language of Wollstonecraft's appeal to Talleyrand-Périgord, Taylor pointedly asked: "For with what truth or rationality could the suffrage be termed universal, while half the human species remain excluded from it?" In an undated, cowritten essay from this period, Taylor and Mill together answered the question with even more rhetorical and philosophical force: "THE RIGHTS OF WOMEN are no other than the rights of human beings." This may be the first direct formulation of the proposition that women's rights are human rights—and it was a joint production, like so much in the couple's life together. For example, it was Taylor's early advocacy on behalf of the women's suffrage cause that launched Mill's leadership roles, as an author and politician, amid the international flourishing of feminist activism in the 1860s.[78]

Both Mill and Taylor were in all likelihood philosophically indebted to the ideas of Wollstonecraft, who was the most famous (and infamous) women's rights advocate in the world in the mid-nineteenth century. Other feminist authors such as Sophia, Madame de Staël, Frances Wright, Martineau, and Margaret Fuller enjoyed international receptions, particularly in the Atlantic world, but none was so strongly associated with the concept of women's rights as Wollstonecraft. All too transparent in its honest biographical treatment of Wollstonecraft's premarital sexual relationships, her husband William Godwin's well-meaning *Memoirs of the Author of A Vindication of the Rights of Woman* (1798) continued to be scandalous in Victorian Britain. It may have been Wollstonecraft's special infamy as a fallen woman in her homeland that made Mill and Taylor reluctant to overtly relate their feminist liberal ideas to their predecessor. Regardless, Mill quickly eclipsed Wollstonecraft as the best-known feminist political philosopher around the globe, with the publication of *The Subjection of Women* in six languages, eight countries, and twelve editions or printings in 1869 alone.[79]

Another reason for Mill's silence with regard to Wollstonecraft might be the fundamental difference in their approaches to defining and justifying women's human rights. Wollstonecraft's rational Christian metaphysics stood in stark contrast to Mill's practical and secular liberal utilitarianism. Despite their relative proximity in time and place, they erected two alternative foundations for women's human rights. Chapter 2 comparatively assesses the strengths and weaknesses of each of their theories of rights for addressing feminist questions of justice, then and now.

two
FOUNDATIONS OF UNIVERSAL HUMAN RIGHTS
WOLLSTONECRAFT'S RATIONAL THEOLOGY
AND MILL'S LIBERAL UTILITARIANISM

The Problem of Foundations, Revisited

Natural rights theories—from the late medieval era to the late eighteenth century—had sidelined women for the most part. As shown in chapter 1, these theories had limited value for understanding women as rights-bearing subjects. The era of the French Revolution saw the rise of new theories of rights that conceived of women as moral, social, and political equals alongside men. Most notably, Mary Wollstonecraft revised the rational dissenting Protestant theology of her mentor Richard Price so that it explicitly justified the inclusion of women in the "rights of humanity." Moreover, she theorized rights in deontological terms, like her contemporary Immanuel Kant, to fortify their status in ethics and politics. As correlates of moral duties prescribed by God's rational and universal moral law, human rights were moral absolutes for Wollstonecraft. In this respect she anticipated the liberal philosopher Ronald Dworkin's view of "rights as trumps," in the sense that she ascribed to rights the power to override any competing ethical or political demands. In an alternative approach, John Stuart Mill sought to correct classical utilitarianism's neglect of individual rights while accepting its secular frame and grounding of utility. Unlike Jeremy Bentham's dismissal of the idea of justifying rights independently of positive law as "nonsense on stilts," Mill's liberal utilitarianism aimed to institutionalize in law the rationally justified moral rights of women and other historically oppressed groups as an indirect yet necessary step toward realizing the greatest happiness of all.[1]

Each of these revisions of earlier philosophies of rights came with their own problems. Wollstonecraft faced a dilemma born of the fact of religious pluralism. In its theoretical justification, her capacious metaphysics staked a big tent under which all members of humanity could be assured coverage for their rights. In rhetorical practice, however, the Christian elements of her system of thought made it more persuasive than not to people who shared those same or similar theological beliefs. Mill confronted a different problem, since the moral beliefs required for persuading people to accept his secular utilitarian approach to grounding human rights were minimalistic in comparison to Wollstonecraft's metaphysics. Mill's main issue was rather one related to the justification of rights: namely, the insecure status of rights within his liberal utilitarianism. Because he followed Bentham in understanding utility as the sole foundation for morality, Mill conceptualized rights as instruments for promoting the utility of the whole. Rights could not function as trumps for Mill. Rights could only serve as tools for realizing the greatest happiness through the indirect route of encouraging the free and full self-development of each and every individual. Although he sought to improve upon the classical utilitarian neglect of individual rights, his liberal utilitarianism nonetheless returned to the same moral problem that plagued his father, James, and Bentham. Can the good of any given individual be rightly sacrificed for the greatest happiness of the greatest number? Wollstonecraft could answer this question with a definitive no, because of her deontological grounding for human rights and theological view of the intrinsic worth of human creatures. While the secular Mill escaped Wollstonecraft's demanding metaphysics and theological biases, he failed to defend individual human rights in any absolute sense that would unconditionally protect people from personal sacrifice for the sake of the happiness of the majority. Whether such sacrifice was supererogatory—arising from a heroic sense of duty—or forced upon the individual from without, Mill's theory of rights could not completely rule out the moral validity of such an extreme utilitarian demand. As John Rawls argued, utility could potentially trump rights even in Mill's liberal revision of classical utilitarianism.[2]

Despite their different flaws and foundations, Wollstonecraft's and Mill's alternative justifications of human rights are examples of what Charles Beitz calls "naturalistic" theories of rights, which are predicated on conceptions of the nature of the human being. Both Wollstonecraft's rational theology and Mill's liberal utilitarianism offer "naturalistic" theories of rights in the sense that they posit that all human beings hold equal rights "by virtue of their humanity," or what makes them human. The definition of the human person thus becomes crucial for both Wollstonecraft's and Mill's theories of universal human rights. In particular, their explicit inclusion of women in their respective definitions of the human gave Wollstonecraft and Mill each a basis for the idea of women's human rights. From Wollstonecraft's religious and metaphysical perspective, women's human rights were grounded in women's natures as human creatures made in the rational image of God. Regardless of sex, humans were equally subject to their divine Creator's universal, rational moral law. As moral equals, men and women were obliged to put the rational moral law of their divine Creator into practice through the dutiful respect of each other's human rights. From Mill's secular perspective, women's human rights were based on a conception of utility that was nonmetaphysical (meaning *a posteriori* and empirical) yet abstract and normative (specifically, eudaimonic or virtue oriented). Mill followed Bentham and Auguste Comte in rejecting the type of abstractions found in metaphysical and ontological philosophies in favor of proceeding with phenomenal and experiential data as the basis for the explanation of facts about the natural world. He thought that he had abstracted from the empirical study of sentient life a conception of utility that had strong, though nonmetaphysical, normative implications. His conception of utility revised classical utilitarianism by positing a eudaimonic or virtue-oriented conception of happiness as the normative end point of its ethical system. In Mill's liberal utilitarianism, the virtuous happiness of each individual human being, especially his or her robust sense of personal agency and self-development, would be maximized if the equality of the sexes was recognized in culture and law through the institutionalization of human rights for women and men alike. Although his naturalistic account of the human being derived from empirical observation rather than metaphysical speculation, it was a normative ideal in the sense that it posited a thick moral conception of virtuous happiness as the goal of individual human development.[3]

From a contemporary liberal philosophical perspective, each of these views of the foundations of universal human rights is problematic for similar and different reasons. Similarly, Wollstonecraft's and Mill's theories today encounter the problem of foundations itself. Since Rawls made his turn toward a political liberalism that explicitly avoids appeals to any comprehensive doctrines (such as metaphysical or religious views, or other robust normative conceptions of human development, happiness, or the good life), a number of liberal thinkers have followed suit with nonfoundationalist approaches to justifying human rights. Such Rawlsian nonfoundationalist theories define human rights without relying on deep, demanding, or divisive moral doctrines. The purpose of these "purely political" definitions of human rights is to establish a broad yet thin consensus upon which a stable international conception of rights can be built. This consensus is historically rooted in legal practices of human rights but may also be projected into the future, as in the case of Rawls's hypothesis of an international league of liberal and decent peoples bound together by established human rights norms. Rawlsian approaches tend to proceed from the analysis of the ongoing public articulation and understanding of human rights in politics and law in the wake of the 1789 *Declaration of the Rights of Man and Citizen* and especially the 1948 Universal Declaration. For example, Beitz and Jack Donnelly have based their normative arguments about the appropriate scope and content of human rights upon the international legal consensus that has snowballed since 1948, rather than appealing to potentially divisive naturalistic foundations for rights as do Wollstonecraft's rational theology and Mill's liberal utilitarianism.[4]

By a nonfoundationalist approach to human rights, Donnelly means that he takes human rights as socially constructed "givens" from a particular historical and legal context. He begins his narrative of the evolution of universal human rights with the 1789 French *Declaration*, which established equal rights for most men in the revolutionary republic. Since then, national and international laws and policies concerning the rights of humans have broadened, ever so gradually, to include blacks, women, and other marginalized groups.[5]

The problem with Donnelly's nonfoundationalist approach is that it fails to address the practical need (and historic practice) of appeals to naturalistic foundations for rights in a time prior to the institutionalization of such rights for marginalized groups. By 1789, women's human rights had only been barely and murkily conceptualized in European political thought. As Olympe de Gouges and Wollstonecraft demonstrated, the idea of the rights of woman was so visionary that just to change the gender of a pronoun or a noun in the dominant rhetoric of the rights of man was a radical move.

Yet de Gouges and Wollstonecraft both had to do more than change pronouns from masculine to feminine. Confronted with the fact of their social and political marginalization in even postrevolutionary republicanism, they felt pressed to appeal to a conception of the common humanity of the sexes in order to persuade men in power that women were in fact worthy of the same civil and political rights as men possessed. De Gouges grounded her arguments on the idea of human rights that grew out of the Rousseauian tradition of natural religion, while Wollstonecraft employed the Anglophone discourse of rational dissenting Christianity to make the case for women's human rights. Regardless of their belief (or possible nonbelief) in such foundations, their philosophical and rhetorical appeals to kinds of natural or metaphysical bases for women's human rights (such as their respective conceptions of the human being) were politically necessary in their contexts.

Rawlsian nonfoundationalist approaches take for granted a cultural and legal institutionalization of human rights that Wollstonecraft and even Mill could not presume, especially in the case of women. Back then, the idea of women's rights was just that—an idea, and a laughable one even in the wake of the French Revolution. In order for one to take rights as a "given," those rights need to be recognized as a "societal given," in culture and law. There is an important distinction between having rights and having those rights recognized and respected by other people or protected by state power. Wollstonecraft and Mill understood this distinction and the problems it raised for human rights advocacy. They were faced with the struggle of convincing people that women were humans with the same rights as men, and as such were deserving of popular recognition and legal protection of their rights like men. It made sense to them that they had to provide a solid moral foundation for this radical view, to give it philosophical validity. As masterful rhetoricians poised to fight a battle for the losing side, Wollstonecraft and Mill also knew that the coherence of their arguments for the foundations of universal human rights had implications for their persuasiveness in the public sphere. Their simple and elegant logic was in many ways their most powerful weapon in the rhetorical and political battle for the public recognition and legal institutionalization of women's human rights.

Neither Wollstonecraft nor Mill had the luxury of starting with the given of universal human rights; rather, each had to construct an argument for the establishment of rights as legal and cultural givens for all humans. Pablo Gilabert has defended the ongoing relevance of such foundationalist (or what he calls "humanist," and what Beitz calls "naturalistic") arguments as "working in tandem" with contemporary Rawlsian nonfoundationalist, or purely political, human rights approaches. Foundationalist arguments for human rights may productively work in tandem with such nonfoundationalist arguments in the sense that the former are better equipped to advance human rights prior to their cultural and legal institutionalization, while the latter are better suited for the articulation of human rights within positive law and official public policy. First, foundationalist arguments establish an abstract yet robust normative standard by which the deficiencies of current institutions, in culture and law, may be judged with respect to rights. In the words of Gilabert, a "humanist perspective is crucial to recognize the significance of institutions, frame their shape and impact, and explain why their creation or transformation is needed." In addition to such critical assessment of current institutions, foundationalist arguments enable a visionary perspective from which new or unrealized human rights might be imagined and demanded for "enjoyment" in the future. Alongside

Amartya Sen, Gilabert conceives of such foundationalist arguments for human rights as critical tools for "alleging" or advocating how new or unrealized rights ought to be prospectively specified and ultimately realized in law and policy. The justification of human rights via humanistic/naturalistic foundations therefore has important practical implications for persuasive allegation and subsequent dissemination of human rights.[6]

Wollstonecraft and Mill thus began with foundationalist approaches to the abstract rational justification of universal human rights. Their respective theological and secular methodologies continue to be relevant to contemporary politics, particularly because of their persuasive powers for audiences in different cultural contexts. Although Wollstonecraft's particular brand of theological argument for women's human rights is not as salient today, other religious variants of this type of metaphysical foundationalism have become important. Non-Western cultures, animated by religions such as Islam, Confucianism, and Hinduism, seek to incorporate the language of women's human rights into their systems of religious and political beliefs. Some Western religious women have looked back to Wollstonecraft and other early women's rights advocates as sources for their own bridging of feminism with Judaism, Christianity, and other world religions.[7]

But it is Mill's secular liberal utilitarian foundation for human rights that continues to wield the most influence today, in both a negative and a positive sense. Positively, it has helped to produce a global idiom for arguing for women's human rights in universalistic terms that do not necessarily privilege any particular religion and are easily adaptable in a variety of legal and political systems. Mill's humanistic/naturalistic approach derived human rights from a secular yet normatively rich account of human individuality and its potential for virtuous yet varied moral development. His abstract definition of individual rights by way of a secular account of human nature allowed Mill to use rights claims as a critical tool for judging the insufficiency of current schemes of justice. Such political criticism, in turn, should generate positive claims for specific rights that society ought to institutionalize for women in order to realize justice for the "disqualified half of the human race."[8]

Negatively, the political influence of the Millian approach has been matched with its practical failures. First, secular naturalistic conceptions of human rights do not necessarily address the cultural preference of many humans for their deeply held religious beliefs to resonate with their principled political conception of the equal dignity of human beings. Second, liberal utilitarian foundations for human rights might also express (often latent) secular biases, especially for Western models of economic and civilizational progress. Both of these dimensions of Millian liberal utilitarianism may impede the nuanced and ethical application of universalistic women's human rights arguments in situations of religious or other forms of cultural difference.

In what follows, I set forth analyses of Wollstonecraft's theological and Mill's secular approaches to justifying women's human rights arguments, expounding their strengths as much as their weaknesses. Despite their flaws, Wollstonecraft's and Mill's foundationalist approaches to justifying human rights remain salient in different ways for liberal and feminist approaches to advocating for human rights. In particular, they offer distinct yet often complementary models for how to ethically and persuasively allege and defend women's human rights in situations of religious or cultural conflict, by attending to those religious and other cultural differences in one's approach to human rights advocacy. To test and compare their value for human rights advocacy, I assess the advantages and disadvantages of both approaches in the context of historic and contemporary debates on religious polygamy considered as a women's human rights issue.

Wollstonecraft's Theological and Deontological Foundation for Universal Human Rights

Two puzzles confront any reader who wishes to understand Wollstonecraft's theory of rights. First, one finds a preponderance of references to duties, both general and specific, over references to specific conceptions of rights, across Wollstonecraft's corpus of writings. In the *Rights of Woman* alone, Wollstonecraft used the term "rights" thirty-two times but employed the term "duties" about three times as often. This trend seems curious for a book that declares on its cover to be a vindication of the rights—not the duties—of woman.[9]

Second, readers notice Wollstonecraft's tendency to make consequentialist arguments for the benefits of granting rights to women. Wollstonecraft frequently discussed the extrinsic, social benefits of granting civil and political rights to women, often for men: "Would men but generously snap our chains . . . they would find us more observant daughters, more affectionate sisters, more faithful wives, more reasonable mothers—in a word, better citizens." As for the intrinsic, personal benefits of human rights for individuals, Wollstonecraft reverently spoke of the "sober pleasures" of thinking and acting as a rational moral agent and rights bearer. While these consequentialist forms of argument are not in themselves problematic, they seem to stand in tension with her overall concern with moral duty. If human beings have God-given duties to respect each other's human rights, then the performance of duty would matter far more than the consequences of performance. In other words, the obligation to provide human rights to others obtains independently of the intrinsic or extrinsic consequences of the act of provision. Yet Wollstonecraft often ostensibly argued the reverse: in particular, that the public benefits of granting rights to women are what justify their provision. On this reading, she paradoxically appears to defend rights for women on condition of their generating benefits for society at large, especially the men who currently run it.[10]

A common resolution to these twin puzzles can be found via a deontological and theological reading of Wollstonecraft's theory of human rights. Understanding Wollstonecraft's deontological (or duty-based) justification for human rights better accounts for her rhetorical and philosophical emphasis on the concept of duty, even in treatises that aim to vindicate the rights of men and the rights of women. By deontological, I mean the definition of moral rightness (what is absolutely right) as logically and ethically prior to the moral good (what is contingently beneficial). Deontological conceptions of human rights are grounded on an idea of their moral rightness, first and foremost. Human rights are thus seen as derivative from an abstract, rational, universal, and obligatory moral rule or principle. In other words, people ought to recognize and respect human rights because it is their moral duty to do so.

Following Kant, such deontological theories of rights are typically justified in strict opposition to consequences. Under the Kantian view, one ought to recognize and respect rights because it is morally right to do so in an absolute and universal sense, not because they produce good social outcomes. Furthermore, one is morally obliged to recognize and respect rights even when the practice of such rights might produce bad social outcomes. Wollstonecraft shared the Kantian deontological conception of human rights as primarily defined by their absolute (and rational) moral rightness. Her mentor Price has been called a Kantian moral philosopher; I also situate Wollstonecraft within a family of Kantian approaches to ethics.[11]

Wollstonecraft distinguished herself from Kant and other strict deontological theorists, however, in her regular recourse to consequentialist arguments for the intrinsic and extrinsic benefits of granting human rights to individuals. At the same time, she agreed with Kant that rights are justified not in terms of their consequences but rather in terms of their derivation from universal, rational moral duties. And yet, both Wollstonecraft and Kant recognized that happiness and other beneficial consequences may be by-products of performing duties and respecting the corresponding rights of oneself and others. Although the performance of duty does not necessarily lead to happiness, and the expectation of happy consequences does not morally justify the performance of duty in the first place, the exercise of duty may be pleasurable (as in Wollstonecraft's aforementioned "sober pleasures" of thinking and acting as a rational being). Although Kant is often starkly caricatured as rejecting any relationship between morality and happiness, his *Groundwork for the Metaphysics of Morals* (1785) opened with the example of a man with painful gout who chose to take care of his health rather than indulge his love of rich food, not because it relieved pain or increased pleasure, but because it was the right and rational thing to do. His consequent experience of health brought him a happiness that was a by-product of performing this self-regarding duty for the right reasons.[12]

Given their broad agreement on the relationship between morality and happiness, the key difference between their systems of deontological ethics was that Kant's metaphysical approach to defining duties and corresponding rights was *a priori* yet nontheological, whereas Wollstonecraft's was *a priori* yet theological. In Kant's epistemology, the human mind constructed its rational understanding of reality and morality without reference to the noumenal realm (which includes the fundamentally incomprehensible God's-eye point of view). Because she did not make such an epistemological distinction between the noumenal and the phenomenological, Wollstonecraft's metaphysical theory of rights could and did ground itself on theological principles. Her theologically informed metaphysics also allowed her to define humanity in broader terms than Kant's strictly *a priori*, nonempirical, nontheological, metaphysical approach to defining humans as rational and moral beings.[13]

Wollstonecraft's rational theology, as set forth in her two *Vindications*, provided the grounding for several levels of her theory of human rights. First, it provided Wollstonecraft with an *a priori*, metaphysical conception of the human being: humans are creatures of God, endowed with reason and the potential to use it to mentally access and put into practice the divine moral law. Second, this conception of the human being served as the starting point for her perfectionistic account of human development. Wollstonecraft understood the ultimate purpose of human life as the learning and practice of moral virtue in social and political relationships. Third, and most important for her ethical system, was her theological conception of the rationality and benevolence of God's providential plan for human development. Wollstonecraft affirmed this view of providence in chapter 1 of the *Rights of Woman*: "Firmly persuaded that no evil exists in the world that God did not design to take place, I build my belief on the perfection of God. Rousseau exerts himself to prove that all *was* right originally: a crowd of authors that all *is* now right: and I, that all will *be* right." This belief or article of faith, which Wollstonecraft professed at the time she wrote her two *Vindications*, provided a psychological basis or motive for the human pursuit of rational and virtuous self-development in society.[14]

Wollstonecraft's rational theology, especially its premise of a benevolent and rational providential plan for human development, seamlessly accommodated the beneficial consequences of rights into her moral and political philosophy. Her broadly metaphysical/ethical view of human development allowed her to define human rights primarily as morally right and secondarily as personally and socially beneficial. Her consequentialist arguments for women's human rights were therefore supplemental to her fundamental deontological justification for them. These dual, rank-ordered justifications of human rights rested on her metaphysical conception of humanity's purpose within God's creation. As Wollstonecraft wrote in the *Rights of Woman*, "The grand end of [human] exertions should be to unfold their own faculties, and acquire the dignity of conscious virtue." This theologically informed ethical framework encouraged her to articulate how the recognition and respect of human rights generate benefits for people that are rational, right, and good for the development of the human species in both the short and long term.[15]

As with the Kantian view, Wollstonecraft's deontological conception of human rights was correlative: "Rights and duties are inseparable." Within this correlative account of rights, duty remained foundational. While all rights derived from duties, not all duties entailed rights. Moreover, for Kant as for Wollstonecraft, only rational beings had duties and therefore held rights. As she wrote to Talleyrand-Périgord in the dedication to the *Rights of Woman*, "a duty" cannot "be binding which is not founded on reason." A rational being would only recognize a duty as binding if it was rational and universally applicable to all rational beings; furthermore, any rights derived from such a duty would belong only to rational beings.[16]

Moving far beyond Kant, Wollstonecraft pushed this correlative and rational account of the relationship between duties and rights in an explicitly feminist direction, by addressing the practical asymmetry between empowered male rights bearers and disempowered female rights claimers. Near the end of the *Rights of Woman*, she argued that men have no basis for expecting women to perform any duties without acknowledging their rights. If "women have not any inherent rights to claim," then "by the same rule, their duties vanish, for rights and duties are inseparable." For Wollstonecraft, the concept of duty defined what our relational obligations are to others, as moral and rational equals governed by the same moral rules. These obligations included our duty to respect other people's rights regardless of their social status (a step that Kant, disappointingly, did not take to its logical conclusion, particularly in the case of women).[17]

In the *Rights of Woman*, Wollstonecraft upheld rights as "the privilege of moral beings" but underscored that holding such privilege required the exercise of the duty to respect oneself. She particularly stressed to her female readership, who had often been degraded by the limited options for self-development afforded by patriarchal society, that their "first duty is to themselves as rational creatures." The fundamental recognition and self-respect of one's ontological status as a moral, rational, and equal human being, capable of rational assessment of one's moral relationships with other human beings, was a psychological precondition for three dimensions of Wollstonecraftian ethics. First, it allowed one to understand oneself as a duty-bearing and rights-bearing subject. Second, it enabled understanding of one's rights and duties as bearing on other people's rights and duties. Third and ultimately, it promoted the exercise and realization of human rights and duties on a broader social and political scale.[18]

Wollstonecraft's view of humans as "moral beings," whose "first duty" was to respect themselves as such, parallels Kantian ethics. In his second formulation of the categorical imperative (or conception of universal duty), Kant set forth an influential view of humans as "rational beings," who are moral ends in themselves and not mere means to other ends. As such moral ends in themselves, humans hold and are obligated to reciprocally respect "the rights of human beings." In her reading of Kant's ethics, Onora O'Neill has argued that the primary content of his categorical imperative is this abstract ethical principle that humans ought to respect themselves and others as moral equals. It is this ethical principle that also stands at the core of Wollstonecraft's deontological theory of human rights and duties. In her *Rights of Men*, we find a negative formulation of this principle according to her Pricean moral theology: "Every thing looks like a means, nothing like an end, or point of rest, when we can say, now let us sit down and enjoy the present moment." Wollstonecraft went on to argue that if people consider themselves only in terms of their material needs or means, rather than as rational beings striving to follow the moral law, then they will exit this life without the "conscious dignity" of moral virtue.[19]

As we have seen, Wollstonecraft's rational theology furnished a view of human beings on a purely metaphysical level, as moral ends in themselves. At the same time, her theologically informed metaphysics opened up a wider perspective on humans, not solely as rational beings, but also as embodied, affective, yet rational creatures capable of both morality and happiness. Ensconced within her broader metaperspective on the nature of humanity, her view of the human-rights-bearing subject as embodied, affective, and rational was both empirically grounded and normatively rich. It was an account of sentient human bodies and their moral relationship to other sentient bodies in the divinely created natural world. For example, her practical theory of physical education began with empirical observation of girls as they are embodied, and then proceeded to the normative question of how they ought to experience embodiment: "If girls were allowed to take sufficient exercise," then they would exhibit a bodily and mental self-confidence that would thwart essentialist explanations of their supposed natural "imbecility."[20]

For Wollstonecraft, the affective capacities of humans, in particular their sympathy for other creatures' feelings, worked with reason to produce appropriate moral judgments, including rights claims. In her first *Vindication*, Wollstonecraft described her personal experience of "reverence" of the "rights of men" as a process in which she drew on both her mind and her body: "Sacred rights! for which

I acquire a more profound respect, the more I look into my own mind; and, professing these heterodox opinions, I still preserve my bowels; my heart is human, beats quick with human sympathies— and I FEAR God!" Abstract contemplation of human rights and their grounding in God's moral law led her to sense her own embodiment as a human and capacity for heartfelt sympathy with other human beings.[21]

With this empirically grounded yet normatively rich approach to defining the human being in the natural world, Wollstonecraft situated the fact of human embodiment within her broader metaphysical/ethical system. Unlike Kant, who has been criticized by feminist philosophers for positing an "idealized" conception of a rational male agent at the core of his ethical theory, Wollstonecraft advanced an approach to ethics that remained abstract yet resisted such a built-in sex bias. Her philosophical anthropology of human beings and their rights specifically accounted for biological sex differences across the species. Girls and women, for example, had a right to education concerning reproduction, pregnancy, childbirth, and infant care. They might have faced the physical challenge of biological motherhood and the consequentially "grand" duty to intensively care for their dependent offspring "in their infancy" despite their own vulnerability while recovering from childbirth. The capacity for biological motherhood entailed women's human right to know what to expect from such a physical and moral challenge, should it be posed.[22]

At the most abstract level, Wollstonecraft's view of human rights bearers was purely metaphysical and theological: it was an account of human beings as rational and moral beings, subject to following God's moral law via the faculty of reason. As shown in chapter 1, this view had its roots in Price's rational theology, especially the universalism of his moral theology. From this religious context, Wollstonecraft crafted her own metaphysical vision of reality that was, at least in theory, open to accommodating a variety of theological positions within it. She made it clear in her two *Vindications* that the orthodox Christian ontological claim that Jesus was God was not a necessary premise for her account of human rights. She alluded to what was likely her own Socinian view of Jesus as a man—not God or even a preincarnational creature of God—who was the greatest human exemplar of morality.[23]

The presentation in the *Vindications* of Jesus as a moral exemplar is now widely recognized as compatible with a variety of world religions, including Judaism, Islam, Hinduism, and Buddhism, which acknowledge him as such. Indeed, Christian denominations since the nineteenth century, including orthodox sects, have often emphasized the "human" or "embodied" Christ alongside other dimensions of his nature. The theological generality of Wollstonecraft's metaphysical outlook made her argument for universal human rights potentially appealing to people from a variety of faith perspectives, especially within monotheistic traditions. Theoretically, her account of human rights was a big tent under which all people, religious or not, could find shelter. And yet, its rational dissenting Christian framework made it in rhetorical practice more persuasive to those who shared at least some of Wollstonecraft's religious belief system, as the conclusion of this chapter explores with the example of her feminist followers in nineteenth-century Mormon Utah.[24]

Viewed from the vantage of either the empirically grounded or the most abstract metaphysical level of her thought, her conception of the human being allowed Wollstonecraft to apply the concept of subjective rights to each and every human due to his or her potential for rational agency. Her privileging of rationality as the defining trait of human beings understood as moral beings made her ethics vulnerable to several criticisms, however. Like Locke and Kant, Wollstonecraft appeared to idealize an adult rational human being as the model for her moral agent who bears rights and duties. Unlike in Locke and Kant, this agent was not an idealized male, nor was it an idealized disembodied being. Nevertheless, like Locke and Kant, Wollstonecraft in her presumption of the human agent's potential for rational autonomy might lead one to think that her moral theory cannot accommodate a place for either the cognitively disabled or the uneducated. Are persons who are not yet capable of exercising reason—because they lack education—and persons who cannot develop those capacities—due to disability—not entitled to rights? In fact, her distinction between the potential to use reason and the actual practice of reason enabled her theory of human rights to cover these cases. For Wollstonecraft, the potential for reason, not the actual use of reason, strongly but not exclusively defined the nature of humanity. For example, Wollstonecraft lamented that the mind of a woman of her time was "scarcely raised by her employments above the animal kingdom." Despite their irrationality, the women of her day were nonetheless human because they had the potential to "acquire the qualities that ennoble a rational being." Even if women did not develop their reason sufficiently to rise "above the animal kingdom," they retained their moral status as human creatures made in the image of their rational God. Her metaphysical perspective on human beings and their purpose in the universe allowed Wollstonecraft to categorize even the most "degraded" people, women and slaves, as fully human despite society's attempts to dehumanize them. Her 1798 novel *Maria, or the Wrongs of Woman* illustrated this point with the first-person testimony of a female servant, Jemima, who worked in an asylum where another woman, Maria, had been imprisoned by her husband. Recalling her destitute teenage years as a household servant, Jemima explained to Maria how her abusive family treated her like a "creature of another species." Raped by her master at the age of sixteen, she was expelled from his home while pregnant, leaving her only the guilty and desperate choice to drink a potion for abortion. Nevertheless, such abuse and impoverishment could not actually strip Jemima of her moral status as a human being. Indeed, Jemima overcame her feeling of estrangement from the "human race" by fulfilling her moral duty to aid another woman in need. Using her powers of reason to strategize a way out of the asylum for both of them, she not only helped Maria escape but also heroically reunited her friend with her infant daughter.[25]

Beyond the potential for reason, Wollstonecraft had an expansive understanding of the variety of capabilities that define the human experience, such as sympathy, love, play, and bodily integrity. This complex view of the physical joys and freedoms of embodied human life was captured in her Rousseau-inspired account of child development: "Every young creature requires almost continual exercise, and the infancy of children . . . should be passed in harmless gambols, that exercise the feet and hands, without requiring very minute directions from the head, or the constant attention of a nurse." According to this wide-ranging conception of human development, a cognitively disabled child might actualize her love of play and bodily integrity alongside other human capabilities even if reason never manifested in her adult self.[26]

Although Wollstonecraft could find shelter for nonrational and uneducated people under the big tent of human rights, her insistence that reason is the basis of human morality made her theory of education open to the charge of paternalism. If a girl lacks reason, and yet reason is necessary for directly accessing the law of God, then the girl is dependent upon the moral judgment of her rational superiors to instruct her about right and wrong. In accepting such paternalism as a necessary part of educating a child toward the autonomy of adulthood, Wollstonecraft ran the risk of reinforcing the very patterns of male domination that her egalitarian theory of rights sought to undercut. Her answer to this problem was practical: establishing a free public system of "national education" that treated boys and girls identically from age five through nine. If children were treated as equals in primary school, then they would be equally subject to paternalism. Such equitable paternalism was fully justified only insofar as it limited itself to developing reason and other human capabilities such as play during childhood and adolescence, so that the girls and boys would grow up to become self-governing and mutually respectful adults.[27]

Wollstonecraft's capacious metaphysical/ethical system enabled the emergent Enlightenment-era conception of human rights to become universal. All humans, viewed from Wollstonecraft's broad metaphysical perspective, have the potential to use reason to grasp the moral law; therefore all humans have the rights that derive from the moral law. These rights are universal in another sense: they are morally universal, insofar as they apply in all times and places, regardless of what positive law, culture, or religion says about particular people's eligibility for claiming them. Humans hold these rights even if their societies do not recognize and respect them as holding them.

Wollstonecraft, as a human rights advocate, was faced with the political predicament that arises from the application of such an abstract and universalistic moral view. She neatly summarized this predicament as "asserting the rights which women in common with men ought to contend for" in the hostile context of a patriarchal society that educated women to be subordinate to men, and encouraged men to treat women as their subordinates. Speaking as a voice in the wilderness, she had no choice but to cultivate the sympathy of men in power—"O ye men of understanding!"—in the hope that they might grant at least some of the rights (such as equality of education) to which women had claim as humans. One of her rhetorical strategies was to supplement her abstract, duty-based demands for human rights with pragmatic appeals to the beneficial consequences that men would reap from extending such rights to women.[28]

Wollstonecraft preceded Sen in treating the "allegation" of rights as a moral step toward justice, regardless of the "feasibility" of the "fulfillment" of rights claims. For Sen as for Wollstonecraft, this step is ethically valuable no matter whether people are actually granted such rights in law or policy, but it might also prompt the beneficial consequence of their establishment in the short or long run. The allegation of women's human rights has moral value independent of the consequences of asserting such rights. Even if women were never given the same education as men, it would always be morally right to provide an argument for their right to education. Conversely, if women were given the same education as men, the beneficial consequences would indicate to Wollstonecraft the working of divine providence in the world to direct human development toward its proper ends of reason, virtue, and knowledge. Despite appearances to the contrary, Wollstonecraft's rational theology allowed her deontological justification for human rights to be consistently supplemented with consequentialist (as well as pragmatic) reasoning for the establishment of such rights.[29]

Mill's Complex Consequentialist Foundation for Universal Human Rights

Much as in the case of Wollstonecraft, a set of puzzles faces any interpreter of Mill's theory of rights. First, scholars have noted the relatively diminished place of rights in Mill's political philosophy as compared to ideas such as individuality, liberty, and self-control. Although Mill used the term "rights" or "moral right" twenty-one times in his *Subjection of Women*, the concept of individuality more frequently appeared in this extended defense of the free and full self-development of women. On the face of it, this is an unexpected rhetorical pattern for a book that aims to justify women's provision of "equal rights" with men in order to overcome their historically subjected status.[30]

Second, many a reader of Mill's *On Liberty* (1859) and *Utilitarianism* (1861) has reasonably wondered whether the texts have incompatible objectives. Mill's favorite work, *On Liberty* sought to establish "one very simple principle" by which the liberty of the individual is secured from unjustified interference by law and government. According to the harm principle, the only reason for placing "legal penalties" upon the actions of an individual is "to prevent harm to others." *Utilitarianism*, first published as a series of essays in *Fraser's Magazine*, aimed to defend utilitarianism against some common criticisms, including the charge that its "Greatest Happiness Principle" undermined justice by prioritizing the utility of the greatest number over individual rights. Such critics asked how, if utility is taken to be "the foundation of morals," can utilitarianism serve as a basis for securing rights and liberties for the individual? Rights cannot function as trumps if their beneficial consequences determine their value, for then the utility of the greatest number could legitimately override the rights of the individual. In this light, it seems that utilitarianism—whether

Bentham's classical formulation or Mill's liberal revision—is at best a shoddy foundation for either positive rights already enshrined in law or alleged rights that have yet to be instituted.[31]

The solution to these two puzzles lies in understanding how Mill's liberal revision of classical utilitarianism relied upon the "principle" of "the free development of individuality" set forth in the opening paragraphs of chapter 3 of *On Liberty.* Just as Wollstonecraft's more frequent references to duties than to rights can be explained by her deontological conception of morality, Mill's relative lack of "rights talk" can be explained by the foundational place of individuality in his moral and political philosophy. As he argued in *On Liberty,* "It is only the cultivation of individuality which produces, or can produce, well-developed human beings." Whereas for Wollstonecraft we claim rights as moral absolutes, for Mill we claim rights pragmatically as tools for the realization of individuality. In Mill's liberal utilitarianism, the "principle" of individuality established a "rule of conduct" by which the greatest happiness of the greatest number was best achieved through the indirect route of respecting the liberty, free and full self-development, and equal rights of individuals. If Mill can be thus understood as an indirect utilitarian who maximizes utility via the principle of individuality, then his version of utilitarianism succeeds in providing a more secure foundation for human rights than the classical formulation of Bentham. In addition, Mill's indirect utilitarianism steered clear of the metaphysical speculations and theological demands of Wollstonecraft's deontology, rendering it more useful for human rights advocacy from a secular and empirical perspective. Both Mill's definition of the good as happiness and his definition of the right as the maximization of the good were nonmetaphysical claims in the sense that they are grounded on his secular, *a posteriori*, empirical conception of utility. In the tradition of David Hume and other British empiricists, Mill sought to define morality by way of sensory experience and empirical observation of the natural world. He abstracted from these experiences and observations the idea of utility as the maximization of pleasure and the minimization of pain for all sentient life via the principle of individuality. Though abstract and richly normative, Mill's empirically grounded conception of utility is not metaphysical because it is not based on supernatural ideas or *a priori* reasoning.[32]

Unlike Wollstonecraft, who favored deontology, Mill continued in the utilitarian tradition of justifying morality in terms of the consequences of actions (making individuals free and happy), not in terms of intentions (individual attempts to do the right thing). His *Utilitarianism* began with a consequentialist critique of Kant's metaphysical, *a priori*, and nonempirical ethics. According to Mill, the Kantian categorical imperative generated universal moral rules for rational beings (such as "don't lie") that are impractical due to their abstract, strictly deontological form. In contrast, a utilitarian would productively judge such rules as right or wrong in terms of their projected consequences. For example, a Kantian would legislate that every rational being, including herself, ought always to tell the truth. Yet a utilitarian would helpfully evaluate the morality of this rule by judging its potentially "outrageously immoral" social consequences. For example, take Kant's own hypothetical case of the duty to respond truthfully to a murderer at the door who wishes to confirm that her intended victim is inside your home. Mill would argue that an "outrageously immoral" consequence could be to enable the murderer's crime. Contra Kant, Mill held that consequentialist reasoning is a necessary facet of determining the right thing to do, and utility is the ultimate standard by which such reasoning is done. If the consequences of truth telling will cause suffering or enable wrongdoing, then lying (or at least opaqueness) is in those cases justified for Mill. Furthermore, any rule of morality against lying ought to be nuanced in light of these outcomes. Mill was not claiming that Kant's moral theory indirectly requires consequentialist reasoning but rather claiming that Kantian ethics fails to generate "actual duties of morality" precisely because it does not engage in moral assessment of outcomes.[33]

Having rejected Kantian deontology, Mill turned to his refinement of the idea of utility. He followed Bentham in taking utility to be the "ultimate appeal," or deciding principle, "on all ethical questions." From his secular and empirical perspective, there was no advantage to invoking "the idea of abstract right"—such as a Kantian categorical imperative or a Wollstonecraftian moral law—"as a thing independent of utility." In addition, Mill shared Bentham's general hedonistic view of utility as the greatest happiness (or pleasure) for the greatest number of sentient beings. Bentham and Mill held that "the whole sentient creation," including nonhuman animals, is capable of pain and pleasure. While humans, as rational animals, gauge the maximization of utility on behalf of all sentient life, their calculations ought to include nonhuman animals in the effort to reduce pain and increase pleasure globally, "so far as the nature of things admits." Because animals, like children, "require being taken care of by others," they "must be protected against their own actions as well as against external injury." Putting this inclusive principle of benevolent paternalism into practice, Mill advocated for the "rights of animals" to be conferred by humans to prevent "any practice" that "causes more pain to animals than gives pleasure to man."[34]

Despite his fundamental hedonistic concern with increasing the pleasure and decreasing the pain of the whole sentient creation, Mill privileged the well-being of human individuals in his "theory of life." Chapter 2 of *Utilitarianism* sets forth his reasoning for the "elevated" moral status of human individuals over nonhuman animals: the benevolent calculation of utility for all creatures depends upon the free and full self-development of people into rational, self-governing, yet other-regarding adults. To clarify why human individuals held an elevated place in his liberal utilitarianism, Mill gave the concept of utility more specific meaning beyond the generic greatest happiness principle. In chapter 1 of *On Liberty*, Mill defined utility "in the largest sense, grounded on the permanent interests of man as a progressive being." In the next sentence, he identified these interests to be "individual spontaneity" and freedom from unnecessary "external control" so that spontaneous self-development is possible. His use of the masculine noun "man" was generic, not gender specific. He later stated in chapter 3 of *On Liberty* that the principle of individuality applied to "all human existence." In fact, until individuals of both sexes had an equal opportunity for free and full self-development, the principle would apply in practice "to man, and still more the woman," because females historically had been subjected to the tyrannical force of custom to a greater degree than males.[35]

In chapter 2 of *Utilitarianism*, Mill further refined the definition of utility with his distinction between the higher and the lower pleasures. The higher pleasures were "mental," or "derived from the higher faculties" of the mind, and thus were "preferable in kind" to the lower, or merely "sensual" or "bodily," pleasures. He famously summed up the practical difference between these kinds of pleasure by saying, "It is better to be a human being dissatisfied than a pig satisfied; better to be Socrates dissatisfied than a fool satisfied." Although the higher, Socratic pleasures may not be felt at the same intensity, duration, or quantity as the lower, swinish pleasures, it was rational to prefer the former to the latter once one experienced the qualitative difference. The moral goal of Mill's liberal revision of utilitarianism was not a crude and brutish hedonism but rather a process of dignifying humans as progressive beings who are capable of rational preference of the higher pleasures over the lower pleasures.[36]

Mill proceeded to reformulate Bentham's greatest happiness principle so that it employed the distinction between the higher and the lower pleasures: "According to the Greatest Happiness Principle . . . the ultimate end, with reference to and for the sake of which all other things are desirable (whether we are considering our own good or that of other people), is an existence exempt as far as possible from pain, and as rich as possible in enjoyments, both in point of quantity and quality; the test of quality, and the rule for measuring it against quantity, being the preference felt by those who, in their opportunities of experience, to which must be added their habits of self-consciousness and self-observation, are best furnished with the means of comparison." This, his second and more precise definition of the governing principle of his liberal utilitarianism, made it clear that the greatest happiness was measured not only by how many sentient beings felt pleasure but also in terms of the quality of the pleasure felt, and the quantity of such pleasure felt by individuals. The "test of quality" ought to be performed by people with the "experience" and "habits" of mind requisite for comparing, judging, and ranking pleasures in qualitative terms. The "verdict" of such "competent judges" of the higher pleasures would contribute to the development of subsidiary "rules and precepts for human conduct" that, when followed, would lead people on the indirect path to realizing the greatest quality and quantity of happiness for the whole sentient creation.[37]

As Rawls argued in *A Theory of Justice* (1971), Mill's refined definition of utility presumed "circumstances of liberty" for women and men to choose a way of life befitting a progressive being. According to Rawls, these Millian circumstances of liberty included an education toward individual freedom, legal protection of equal rights, and living under free institutions of government. In chapter 3 of *On Liberty*, Mill gave a trio of reasons why free institutions were necessary for realizing the "permanent interests" of humans as progressive beings. First, free institutions (such as representative government or the option of public schools) provided the political and cultural infrastructure for the development of human capabilities on the broadest scale. Second, the experience of participating in free institutions gave individuals an opportunity to develop rational preferences for liberty and self-control and to make good choices accordingly. Third, people in all times in history have rationally preferred freedom to subjection. Rawls concluded that Mill believed "a considerable degree of liberty is a precondition of the rational pursuit of value," or the pursuit of utility properly understood. In this way, Mill's normative commitment to liberty guided and animated his indirect pursuit of the permanent interests of progressive beings—namely, spontaneity and freedom from unnecessary external control. Rawls went on to show, however, that Mill's arguments for free institutions did not "justify an equal liberty for all," although they "might justify many if not most of the equal liberties." He concluded that the basic utilitarian requirement to maximize happiness on the greatest scale meant that "it is liable to find that the denial of liberty for some is justified in the name of this single end." Although he admired the force of Mill's reasoning for the necessity of free institutions in order to realize utility "in the largest sense," he did not think it sufficient to justify the equal rights of individuals. Having rejected Mill and other forms of utilitarianism as viable options for justifying equal rights, Rawls turned to the social contract tradition as a resource for his liberal theory of justice.[38]

Mill understood his indirect and therefore complex form of consequentialism to be the best available approach to reconcile utilitarianism with a secular though "sacred," or paramount, commitment to equal rights. Although in theory utility could trump rights, the definition of utility in terms of the permanent interests of man as a progressive being made the freedom of individuals a paramount moral value. Assuming this value could be inculcated in people and institutionalized in law, equal rights would eventually prevail in practice. Although he remained vulnerable to the abstract philosophical criticism that his liberal revision of utilitarianism failed to justify equal rights as trumps, Mill thought that his theory of rights—when pragmatically applied in culture and law—would secure rights sufficiently for guaranteeing norms of justice for individuals. Indeed, his *Utilitarianism* went so far as to say that "a right residing in the individual" was "essential" to "justice," which was "the chief part, and incomparably the most sacred and binding part, of all morality." By establishing such rights in culture and law, a society protected "the most vital of all interests." Competent judges of the higher pleasures, like Mill himself, had concluded over time and through experience that reciprocal respect for rights improves both the quality and the quantity of the happiness of the whole.[39]

Rawls's critique of Mill raises the question of whether Mill should be understood as an act utilitarian or a rule utilitarian. These two versions of utilitarianism are products of twentieth-century moral philosophy and thus can only be read back upon Mill's thought. This anachronistic application of rule utilitarianism and act utilitarianism to interpret the case of Mill might explain why there is not yet a scholarly consensus on which school he best fits. Because of the supremacy of utility over other standards of right in his political theory,

Mill has often been interpreted as an act utilitarian. On this reading, he followed Bentham in defining the morality of each and every act in terms of its maximization of pleasure and minimization of pain for the greatest number of sentient beings. Although Mill appealed to the principle of individuality as a rule of conduct to establish a place for equal rights in his utilitarianism, he plainly stated that utility is the ultimate appeal for deciding right from wrong, including the scope of rights. The latter view of utility could be described as act utilitarian. It is famously suspect for its allowance of what Derek Parfit called the "repugnant conclusion" that the overall quality of life may be sacrificed for the more equal, yet minimalistic, distribution of utility across a larger population. If rights are understood as instrumental to utility, then the minimization of rights could be justified in the name of a more equal though minimal distribution of utility overall. The even spread of utility would thereby justify the erosion of the quality of life for all, including their access to rights.[40]

To avoid these grave problems, Mill's complex consequentialism defined utilitarian moral outcomes by way of a variety of intermediary practical rules for social behavior: first and foremost, the principle of individuality, whereby the "person's own character" and not "the traditions or customs of other people" were the "rule of conduct." Mill argued that following this principle or rule of conduct was "the principal ingredient of human happiness, and quite the chief ingredient of individual and social progress." Ideally, culture should be shaped in a way that encouraged people to develop according to this principle, such that they grew in diverse and eccentric ways, displaying a range of talents and capabilities within society. A related practical rule, more narrowly tailored by Mill for the domain of law, was the harm principle. This "one very simple principle" defined wrong in terms of "interfering with the liberty of action" of any individual except when such interference would "prevent harm to others." Mill's harm principle strove to draw a bright line between individual behavior that could be subject to legal penalties versus individual behavior that would be merely subject to disapprobation in the court of public opinion or condemnation by one's own conscience. If an action unnecessarily interfered with the self-regarding actions of another individual, then it was both wrong and subject to legal penalties. If an action refrained from such interference, then it was not wrong and was not subject to legal penalties, and was at least right in the thin sense of allowing individuals freedom from direct harm. For Mill, "tastes and modes of life" that were primarily self-regarding (such as choosing to drink alcohol at a restaurant) should be informally regulated by public opinion and/or conscience and not be subjected to legal penalties. Hence, Mill's harm principle, though focused on the question of determining fair legal regulation of the individual by the state, helped to demarcate an alternative cultural space in which respect for individuality served as the prevailing rule of conduct. Although one's free and full self-development might be appropriately reigned in by public opinion or personal conscience, one's behavior could not rightfully be punished by the state except to prevent harm to others.[41]

Such cultural and legal noninterference in the self-regarding actions of the individual might also generate right outcomes in the thick sense, especially if practiced on a broad scale and for the long run. Nancy Hirschmann has argued that Mill's complex consequentialism posited a thick conception of positive liberty (freedom to be self-sovereigns) as at least one moral by-product of a thin conception of negative liberty (freedom from unnecessary interference). For Bentham as for Mill, the consequences always determined the morality of the act. Yet Mill's principle of individuality (and its legal cognate, the harm principle) established constraints on the set of utilitarian outcomes that were both moral and beneficial. Following these practical rules of social conduct and legal regulation would enable us to take the indirect yet individually oriented route to realize the permanent interests of humans as progressive beings, by asking us to prioritize the value of the individual's self-development in our calculations of what is good and bad for sentient life. The moral result should be the realization of self-sovereignty, or virtuous individual self-development across the human species, for the benefit of all sentient creation.[42]

In this light, Mill's indirect utilitarianism looks more like rule utilitarianism than act utilitarianism. According to J. O. Urmson's groundbreaking interpretation, Mill understood the moral rightness of any given action to be determined by its accordance to a rule (or what Mill often called a "secondary principle"). Mill provided a list of such rules in chapter 5 of *Utilitarianism,* including "the moral rules which forbid mankind to hurt one another," such as "breach of friendship" and "breach of promise." These practical rules of conduct were correct for Mill insofar as they tended to promote utility. Any conflicts between these practical rules of morality could be adjudicated only by reference to the ultimate standard of rightness, the greatest happiness principle. Consequently, Mill allowed for reform of rules (such as "the aristocracies of colour, race, and sex") that failed in practice to maximize the quality and quantity of happiness for the whole. He furthermore argued that widely accepted rules of morality (such as "don't break a promise") were the best practical indicators of what people took to be happiness. A utilitarian could thus rely on such moral rules, alongside legal rules such as justly instituted rights, as means toward achieving the greatest happiness. In his *Methods of Ethics* (1874), Henry Sidgwick criticized the aforesaid argument for its conflation of moral preferences (such as "promise-keeping is good") with beliefs about effects on happiness (such as "promise-keeping produces happiness"). Nevertheless, Sidgwick assumed like Mill that the greatest happiness principle could only be applied in practice via a "fairly detailed and specific set of directives or rules." Even if common moral rules were not in themselves expressions of people's preferences concerning happiness, rules in general (both moral and legal) were necessary practical instruments for the successful application of the greatest happiness principle.[43]

The use of subsidiary moral rules to determine right from wrong produces a dilemma for the utilitarian, however. On the one hand, it becomes unclear how rule utilitarianism is practically different from act utilitarianism. If moral rules can be revised in light of the demands of utility, then the former would seem to collapse into the latter, making each and every act subject to evaluation according to the greatest happiness principle. Rule utilitarianism would then seem to be as vulnerable as act utilitarianism to producing Parfit's "repugnant conclusion" in practice. On the other side of the dilemma, strict compliance with rules appears to be inconsistent with the ultimate goal of utilitarianism. If following a rule is taken to be right, despite generating less utility than another action, then it would seem to contradict the overriding utilitarian requirement to pursue the greatest happiness for the greatest number.[44]

As for the first horn of the dilemma, Mill would respond that while the best rules aim to apply to all cases, they must be open to revision on the basis of their consequences in order to be cemented as general and correct standards of right and wrong. Such revision of rules would not be arbitrary but rather be guided by people's experience of pain and pleasure, and gradually regulated by institutions of culture and law. Furthermore, this experiential revision of rules over time would indirectly lead to the greatest happiness in the long run. As Mill argued in different ways across his *Autobiography*, *On Liberty*, and *Utilitarianism*, a "permanent" happiness for each and all can only be achieved through the indirect path of the human pursuit of virtue and, in this pursuit, learning to prefer the higher pleasures over the lower ones. The subsidiary rules that come to govern this complex process of consequentialist moral reasoning might be best envisioned as nested within Mill's ultimate commitment to the greatest happiness principle. Rights are the most "sacred" form of such nested moral rules because their cultural acceptance and legal enforcement are paramount for individual liberty and thus offer the opportunity to make the moral choices necessary for virtuous self-development. Rights and other rules achieve political inertia over time: while subject to revision with respect to consequences, rules gain a kind of stability through the social process of their moral refinement. For Mill, this stability provided enough security for human rights on the whole, while allowing for the necessary revision of unjust yet legal rights (such as a husband's total ownership of his wife's property under the law of coverture) that had been unreflectively accepted for centuries.[45]

To navigate past the second horn of the rule-utilitarian dilemma, Mill would similarly appeal to his theory of the necessarily indirect path to utility. The indirect realization of utility through adherence to rules (such as respect for equal rights) means that one may justifiably sacrifice short-term pleasure for the sake of the permanent interests of humans as progressive beings. For example, if the granting of women's rights to property ownership in marriage would initially decrease the freedom and power of husbands yet potentially increase the liberty of both sexes, the choice of the latter, complex consequence would be better than simply avoiding the former, short-term outcome. For example, Mill chose the more complex path to happiness in establishing the egalitarian terms of his late-life marriage to Taylor, by signing a document that promised her equal rights to the proceeds of the books published under his name. The complex good of recognizing their collaborative intellectual relationship outweighed any short-term benefits he could have derived from merely keeping the proceeds for himself.[46]

Thus read as a subtle rule utilitarian, Mill can be understood as offering a complex consequentialist foundation for universal human rights. It is complex in the sense that it has several mutually reinforcing levels of moral concerns. The beneficial outcome is the far-reaching concern; the application of the principle of individuality and its legal cognate, the harm principle, is the more immediate and practical concern; and the flourishing of individuality remains the underlying concern at each stage of the process. In this multilevel moral framework, rights function as moral and legal tools that facilitate the permanent happiness of human individuals. Mill defined human (or "moral") rights as fundamental rules of morality that derive from self-regarding and other-regarding duties, requiring that obligations be paid and justice be done to the individual. Over time, some conceptions of moral rights become institutionalized as "legal" rights. The realization of utility through the recognition and respect of moral rights and the legal rights justly instituted from them is the only sure path toward a genuine happiness for everyone, not solely a minority or majority of the whole.[47]

Mill's overall moral system was secular and empirical, not theological and metaphysical like Wollstonecraft's. Nonetheless, both Mill and Wollstonecraft presented normatively rich accounts of the human being as the basis of their theories of rights. While Wollstonecraft's moral view of the embodied human being in nature was ensconced within her metaphysics, Mill's conception of individuality began and ended with humans as they were in the natural world but imagined how they might develop in a moral way if allowed the right constellation of social conditions in which to grow in "eccentric" diversity. As Mill poetically expressed it in chapter 3 of *On Liberty*, "Different persons also require different conditions for their spiritual development; and can no more exist healthily in the same moral, than all the variety of plants can in the same physical, atmosphere and climate." People, like plants, required diverse environments and the freedom to thrive in those personally suitable conditions. Mill's principle of individuality indirectly cultivated a diversity of human capabilities through the social construction of a broader "moral climate" in which people learn to abide by each other's equal rights.[48]

In their respectively secular and theological approaches to grounding human rights on abstract and robust normative conceptions of the human being, Mill and Wollstonecraft both represent versions of what Rawls called "comprehensive liberalism." According to Rawls, Mill's theory of individuality may even be read as "metaphysical," in the sense that it makes controversial moral claims about what all human beings are and should become. Such universalistic normative claims about human nature look "metaphysical" from Rawls's strictly "political" perspective, which accepts the "fact of reasonable pluralism" on morality and religion even among peoples who at least respect basic international human rights norms. The problem with this broad use of the term "metaphysical" is that it neither accounts for the differences between *a priori* and *a posteriori* approaches to reasoning nor distinguishes between theological and secular, or even supernatural and empirically grounded, ideas. It assumes rather that any abstract normative idea that may be subject to moral debate is metaphysical. To better capture the similarities and differences across Wollstonecraft's theory of rights and Mill's, I describe Mill's abstract conception of the human being and its free and full self-development as secular, nonmetaphysical, empirically grounded, yet normatively rich. Wollstonecraft's metaphysical/ethical system, on the other hand, affords a multilevel view of the human being: at the most abstract level of analysis, it is a theological and purely metaphysical conception of the person as a moral and rational being made in the image of God; but from an empirically grounded vantage point, it is a richly normative conception of the embodied human being as ensconced within the divinely created natural world. Although Mill also used an abstract and normative conception of the person as the basis of his theory of rights, he made no appeal to metaphysical ideas.[49]

For Mill, the rights held by human beings are either moral or legal. A "moral right" is derived from a duty, or a widely accepted moral rule that entails the fulfillment of a "perfect," or mandatory, "obligation" toward self or others. For example, the duty to keep promises to others generates the corresponding right not to have one's own promises breached. With this correlative theory of the basis of moral rights, Mill coincided with both Wollstonecraft and Kant, without sharing their metaphysical/deontological foundations for the view. Rather, in the concluding chapter of *Utilitarianism*, Mill theorized duty in complex consequentialist terms as grounded upon utility "in the largest sense": "I account the justice which is grounded on utility to be the chief part, and incomparably the most sacred and binding part, of all morality. Justice is a name for certain classes of moral rules, which concern the essentials of human well-being more nearly, and are therefore of more absolute obligation, than any other rules for the guidance of life; and the notion we have found to be of the essence of the idea of justice, that of a right residing in an individual, implies and testifies to this more binding obligation." This passage provides the best evidence of Mill's rule-utilitarian conception of justice, since it conceives the following of "certain classes of moral rules" as producing the "essentials of human well-being" better than "any other rules." The rights "residing in an individual" are one such class of utility-enhancing moral rules. As such, moral rights "testify" to the "binding obligation" we have to abide by the rules of justice, because moral rights are derived from duty. Rights are thus "the essence of the idea of justice" because they are correlates of duties or obligatory moral rules that are justified by way of a conception of utility in the broadest sense.[50]

Mill understood moral rights as rationally justified independent of positive law because they need not have a formal means of enforcement to be justly held and demanded by individuals. Claims of moral rights may hypothesize how the marginalized or powerless (such as women) need access to public goods that would enable their individual self-development, when society has in fact failed to recognize its duty to provide such rights. Wollstonecraft had predominantly made such moral arguments (or what Sen calls "allegations") for women's rights as humans, since women in Britain and beyond had relatively few socially or legally recognized rights as compared to men in the late eighteenth century. By the time Mill embarked on his political career in the 1860s, Britain had institutionalized more legal rights for women (such as divorce in cases of domestic violence as of 1857), but even then most rights claims for women (such as national-level suffrage) were moral and thereby alleged.

On the political level, Mill understood legal rights to be just when they derived from a correlative moral obligation, rather than from a bad law. In his 1869 treatise *The Subjection of Women*, he contrasted the unjust but legal rights of husbands to commit regular "bodily violence" against their wives with the moral rights of individual women to be free from "personal violence." Here, he strongly implied that sexual violence against women in marriage was shamelessly and unjustly treated as an exception to the criminal law against rape. Through practical applications of the harm principle, legislators could gradually replace such bad patriarchal laws with egalitarian laws that prescribed legal penalties for unjustified interference with the rights of individuals, regardless of color, race, or sex. Examples of the establishment of such legal rights in Britain were the 1830s acts of Parliament that expanded working men's suffrage and set slaves free in most regions of its empire. Allegations for moral rights might still be made in reference to these legal rights. If some but not all groups enjoy a legal right, then the excluded groups might make moral claims for social or legal inclusion in the use of such rights. If access to legal rights for some groups is more extensive than others, then the group with less access might make moral claims for legal inclusion in the full use of such rights. In his early 1830s unpublished correspondence with Harriet Taylor on marriage, Mill had alleged women's equal right to divorce, at a time when only men, such as his friend's husband, legally held this right. Dramatizing the gap between moral rights and legal rights on the political stage, Mill alleged women's human right to vote by formally representing in Parliament the 1867 suffrage petition signed by thousands of disenfranchised women. His *Subjection of Women* alleged the "equal moral right of all human beings" to the free choice of occupation, so that women would no longer be subjugated to the opinion that their proper roles belonged only in the family. Such public and private, written and oral, political and personal allegations of women's human rights contributed to the growth of individual, elite, and popular concern with their institutionalization.[51]

Both moral rights and the legal rights that are based on them are human rights for Wollstonecraft and Mill, because both types of rights are grounded upon their respective conceptions of the human being as a moral being. Although Wollstonecraft takes a theological and metaphysical approach and Mill a secular and nonmetaphysical one, they both offer robust normative accounts of the human being's organic and ethical development through freedom and rights. This is the most important commonality in their theories of universal human rights: their joint grounding of rights claims on normatively rich accounts of what it means to be human. Their respective conceptions of humanity gave them strong normative standards by which they could judge the defects of culture and law with regard to the rights of humans, and subsequently advocate for reform that would advance justice for each and all through the equal provision of rights. We now turn to a comparative assessment of the practical value of their two foundationalist schools for advocating the moral rights of women that are not yet recognized or respected by people within a culture or protected by the law.

Theological and Secular Approaches to Alleging Women's Human Rights: The Issue of Religious Polygamy

Rawlsian nonfoundationalist approaches to justifying human rights assume rights as cultural and legal givens that ought to be articulated and developed further in law and policy, particularly in the context of the post-1948 international political landscape of the Universal Declaration and the other institutions and policies of the United Nations. From a feminist perspective, the problem with this assumption is that many human rights of women have not yet achieved the status of cultural or legal givens. Women's human rights have not even been fully realized in the domain of international law, in which the U.N. Convention on the Elimination of All Forms of Discrimination against Women, CEDAW, is taken more seriously than in nation-states such as the United States and Iran, which are still among the mere seven countries in the world that have yet to ratify it. In contrast to Rawlsian nonfoundationalist approaches to justifying human rights, foundationalist approaches to justifying women's human rights allow for extralegal and extracultural claims about women's desert of rights on the basis of their human nature. Such naturalistic claims about women's shared humanity with men have been politically instrumental in the allegation and advancement of women's human rights, especially since the time of de Gouges and Wollstonecraft.[52]

Moving beyond an analysis of the role of naturalistic foundations in Wollstonecraft's and Mill's rational justifications for human rights, I now respond to a practical moral and political question raised by each of their systems of feminist thought. When women's human rights are not yet recognized in law or policy, or are culturally or religiously controversial even to allege, which of these foundationalist approaches works best as a moral basis for advocacy and political

persuasion? Religious polygamy poses a serious test of both the ethical and the rhetorical value of these approaches for human rights
advocacy, as it has been morally controversial in a variety of cultures
since Wollstonecraft's time and often has been seen as incompatible
with women's rights. Furthermore, practices of religious polygamy
continue to raise questions of which women's rights (for example,
the right to divorce) ought to be respected in culture and protected
under the law. By applying Wollstonecraft's and Mill's theories to
assess the human rights of women within religious polygamy, I il-
luminate how their respectively theological and secular foundations
may serve as ethical and effective platforms for alleging the rights of
women in distinctive yet complementary ways that are sensitive to
religious and other cultural differences. When I speak of polygamy,
I mean a kind of plural marriage in which a man has more than one
wife. This is technically called polygyny.

Wollstonecraft advanced moral views on polygamy early in her
writing career. When she wrote for the *Analytical Review* in London
from 1788 to 1792, she acquired a taste for travel memoirs, especially
those concerning North African Muslim peoples. She researched
works by the German explorer Johann Reinhold Forster and the
English theologian James Cookson, who discussed the practice of
polygamy in Africa. Following the French Enlightenment philosopher Montesquieu, Forster even made theoretical claims about why
polygamy seemed to be more prevalent in warm climates. In her
Rights of Woman, Wollstonecraft philosophically challenged Forster's
argument that the natural environment determined polygamy. By rejecting the natural necessity of polygamy, she sought to discredit the
patriarchal view that woman "must be inferior to man, and made for
him" and his sexual pleasure. This critique of polygamy supported
her general moral argument in favor of monogamous marriages in
which women were respected as ends in themselves, not merely used
as means to other ends.[53]

In her *Rights of Woman*, Wollstonecraft set forth an extended
moral justification of marriage as primarily a relationship between
equal moral beings and secondarily a relationship that concerned

natural functions such as sexual reproduction. She defended marital pairs over multiple spouses, for the reason that marriage is ideally a dyadic, perfectionistic (or virtue-oriented) friendship. Polygamy or polyandry might be permissible if marriage was meant to be like a business or corporate contract, in which maximum productivity for the group was the goal. In a perfectionistic friendship, however, the goal was the mirroring and mutual inspiration of the higher virtues in one another.[54]

Like Aristotle, Wollstonecraft upheld the dyadic form to be the best, or virtue-oriented, friendship, but she explicitly and unequivocally extended this idea of higher friendship in an egalitarian way to male-female marital relationships. Beyond the practical consideration that such lofty virtue might prove more difficult to achieve in plural marriages, her defense of the smaller dyadic form belied her normative assumption that the process of sexual reproduction itself produced supplemental reasons for the moral practice of monogamy. The best evidence of this assumption is found in her 1797 *Lessons*, which envisioned and even idealized the active roles of biological parents in joint childcare of their toddler. More broadly, her metaphysical perspective allowed for Cookson's view that divine providence mandated monogamy as a beneficial moral ideal for humanity. Wollstonecraft disagreed, however, with Forster's culturally biased and morally relativistic claim that God ordained monogamy for Europe, while nature dictated polygamy for Africa.[55]

In theory, Wollstonecraft's metaphysics should accommodate a variety of religious and secular conceptions of monogamous marriage, under the condition that all people are treated as ends not means within marriage and the broader laws of their societies. Wollstonecraft's novel *Maria, or the Wrongs of Woman* vividly represented how her deontological theory of human rights would absolutely prohibit any exploitation of women by their husbands, regardless of the cultural or religious context. When her husband attempted to sell her into prostitution, Maria finally sought a way out of the bad relationship. Her escape symbolically alleged for the eighteenth-century audience a married woman's human right to protect her bodily integrity. As illustrated by Maria's response to her predicament, Wollstonecraft's deontological approach to defending women's human rights would be an appropriate basis for strong criticism of any cases of marriage, whether monogamous or polygamous, which are exploitative of women's bodies.

Wollstonecraft's broader theological approach uncovers a deeper level from which polygamy could be strongly judged: the immanent feminist perspective on patriarchal oppression. Such an immanent feminist perspective speaks against a patriarchal practice from within a culture for the benefit of women in that culture and potentially beyond it. For example, when a Muslim woman, such as the Iranian feminist lawyer Shirin Ebadi, challenges polygamy on metaphysical grounds—as in, the Koran states I am equal to man, thus I should be legally treated as a moral equal to man and not as "'half' a human being"—she is enacting a broadly Wollstonecraftian critique of the institution from within. Islamic polygamy as it is practiced in her homeland of Iran requires that polygamous wives be legally subsumed under and subordinate to their husband, thus undercutting the Koran's theological view of the sexes as moral equals. Interestingly, Wollstonecraft had used a mathematical metaphor similar to Ebadi's to critique how Rousseau's theory of education perversely turned woman into a "half-being" who was primarily defined by her marital relationship to her husband rather than her independent ontological status as a moral, rational, and equal human being made in the image of God.[56]

As the Indonesian Muslim feminist activist Lily Munir explains, the Koran supports polygamy only as a "privilege" of widows and children in times of need, not a general "right" of men. Striving to return her Muslim culture and Islamic religion to their moral roots, the 2003 Nobel Peace Prize winner Ebadi continues to criticize Iranian laws as "discriminatory and misogynist" for allowing "a man to marry four wives . . . and divorce his wife at will," while women do not have the same access to divorce. In her Muslim feminist view, these laws are "not Islamic" because they "cannot be found in the Koran." She advises her fellow Muslim feminist critics of religious polygamy: "It is essential for women to master religious discourse because patriarchal culture is usually protected and strengthened in the name of Sharia law, and by political forces who exploit Muslims' ignorance of various interpretations." Such a sacred-text-based approach may not, however, work as well for religious and other cultural outsiders, who run the risk of seeming imperialistic by making such arguments from without.[57]

Mill's secular approach to justifying and subsequently alleging women's human rights poses its own set of challenges for judging the issue of religious polygamy. Mill shared Wollstonecraft's philosophical view of marriage as ideally conceptualized and practiced as a perfectionistic, or virtue-oriented, friendship between moral equals. On a nonideal and personal level, Mill appeared to be tolerant of polyamory, if sexual intercourse is not understood as essential to its practice. Harriet Taylor was married to another man for most of their platonic and perfectionistic friendship. This was a forced choice for Mill, as he would have preferred to have an exclusive relationship with Harriet under ideal circumstances. Harriet and Mill appear to have refrained from intercourse for the duration of their intellectually and emotionally passionate affair and late-life marriage. Harriet ceased to have a sexual relationship with John Taylor once their last child was born, soon after she met and fell in love with Mill. Mill's awkward domestic situation with the Taylors compelled his toleration of a type of sexually restrained, Victorian polyamory even when he personally considered it morally deficient.

In chapter 4 of *On Liberty*, Mill's application of the individuality and harm principles to the issue of Mormon polygamy explained his tolerance of this particular plural form of religious marriage under two conditions. First, the practice may be tolerated at "a remote corner of the earth" where such "barbarism" or cultural backwardness may be practiced without becoming widely institutionalized. His use of the culturally biased, liberal imperial language of "barbarism" was consistent with his *Subjection of Women*, in which he identified patriarchal marriage as a "relic of primitive barbarism" that caused women's oppression worldwide.[58]

Apart from his belittling attitude toward Mormonism, Mill's moral concern with polygamy centered upon the inverse relationship between women's tendency to adapt to their culture and the heterogeneity of that culture. In other words, the more that women conformed to their culture, the less varied that culture would be; conversely, the more uniform a culture, the less diverse women's life choices would be. It followed that if, generally, patriarchal culture teaches women "to think marriage the one thing needful," then, in a polygamous community, women "should prefer being one of several wives, to not being a wife at all." Consideration of this problem of adaptation elicited Mill's second condition for the toleration of polygamy: its practitioners must "allow perfect freedom of departure to those who are dissatisfied with their ways." In these cases, his complex consequentialist justification for human rights provided a strong ground for alleging women's human right to exit polygamy when the religious institution harmed their self-development. Education about exit options, likely provided by outsiders to the polygamous community, would be one way to combat the problem of women's adaptation to conditions of patriarchal domination.[59]

Mill's secular liberal utilitarian approach to advocating for women's human rights might be most useful to reformers from outside the polygamous community. *On Liberty* proposed such reformers could use educational writings to shape Mormon polygamists' critical understanding of the ethical implications of their own religious practice, just as women's rights advocates used education to challenge their own brands of patriarchal "barbarism" in Britain. Wittily playing both sides of the argument, Mill inveighed, "Let them send missionaries, if they please, to preach against it; and let them, by any fair means (of which silencing the teachers is not one), oppose the progress of similar doctrines among their own people." If taken, this secular educational approach would rely not on controversial religious or metaphysical views to make its moral claims but rather on a comparatively thinner, nonmetaphysical and nontheological, set of values such as human individuality and freedom. It would also need to be applied to similar problems in the outsider's own culture, in order to be morally consistent and not hypocritical.[60]

For societies that do not value individuality or freedom in a liberal sense, this secular educational approach to women's human rights advocacy may not work from without or within. In these cases, Mill's secular liberal utilitarianism theoretically generates a long-term reformist approach to human rights advocacy: observation of the issue from afar, so as to ensure that women's human rights are not sacrificed for the utility of the patriarchs of the commune. This remote observational model is implicit in Mill's recommendation of toleration of polygamy on the Utah frontier instead of making it "a scandal to persons some thousands of miles distant." Although his spatial appeal to distance had imperial implications (as in, the unconquered frontier was the nadir of civilization), it also may be read in more abstract psychological terms: maintaining a reasonable sense of cultural and emotional distance from other people's cultural practices.[61]

The latter mode of reasonable psychological distance might animate the work of a Millian reformer who is monitoring a polygamous religious culture from without. Mill did not assume that polygamy was inherently incompatible with women's rights, but he remained concerned with protecting women against potential violations of their rights in this and other historically oppressive marital arrangements. Consequently, he supported reformers' remote observation of polygamy in Utah as a moral means of judging whether the practice was in fact harmful to women. If violations of female self-sovereignty were tracked and verified, then the monitoring Millian reformer faced a predicament: alleging women's human rights on naturalistic grounds that might seem culturally insensitive or imperial to the people she sought to aid. The allegation of women's human rights, in these cases, is a Millian outsider's last-resort act of political instigation. Ideally, this instigation would stir the local community to discussion of the ethics of their practice of polygamy and provoke critical reflection on similar issues in the reformer's home culture.

Mill's secular liberal utilitarianism produces indirect models of women's human rights advocacy, such as toleration, education, observation, and instigation. In contrast, Wollstonecraft's theological and deontological approach to justifying rights generates strong and direct moral judgments on the best content and scope for women's human rights. It also enables the allegation of women's human rights in universalistic terms that may resonate with a variety of religious worldviews. Mill's indirect strategies for reform are better suited for cultural or religious outsiders to a morally controversial issue such as polygamy, whereas Wollstonecraft's direct approach to rights advocacy would fare better with cultural and religious insiders who seek to effectively criticize or defend a morally controversial practice from within.

From 1872 to 1914, a group of female Latter Day Saints (LDS) in Utah modeled the latter mode of immanent defense. Their newspaper, the *Woman's Exponent*, made pro-polygamy arguments based on Mormon theology and contemporary women's rights discourse. Its editor, Emmeline Wells, was a reader of Wollstonecraft, and, in 1874, the paper defended the feminist ethical logic of the *Rights of Woman* against charges of its irreligion and immorality: "Eighty years ago Mary Wollstonecraft published her 'Vindication of the Rights of Woman.' It was a book laid under ban as irreligious and immoral. Yet it consists simply of a forcible and logical plea for the higher education of women, and an exposure of the false sentimentality of Rosseau [*sic*]." Wells blended Wollstonecraft's rational theological and deontological style of women's human rights advocacy with her own Mormon conviction in the sacredness of women's everyday work, starting in the family. In a relief society handbook, Wells argued that Mormon women's duty in life was to help restore humanity's original, God-given equality: "Woman must be instrumental in bringing about the restoration of that equality which existed when the world was created. Perfect equality then and so it must be when all things are restored as they were in the beginning." The slogan of the *Woman's Exponent* also fused Mormonism and women's human rights: "The Rights of the Women of Zion, The Rights of Women of All Nations."[62]

These LDS women's internal support for Mormon polygamy from a gospel and feminist perspective warranted Mill's cautionary approach to judging their community from the outside. Indeed, the women's rights leaders Susan B. Anthony and Elizabeth Cady Stanton—who opposed polygamy on much the same grounds as Wollstonecraft—chose such a Millian pragmatic route in working with LDS women on their common cause of universal suffrage in Utah. An avid reader of *On Liberty*, Stanton criticized those feminists who opposed the involvement of Mormons such as Wells in the national women's suffrage convention of 1878: "I should think Mormon women might sit on our platform without making us responsible for their religious faith."[63]

The *Woman's Exponent* suggested the rhetorical and political power of Wollstonecraft's theological approach to defending women's human rights for cultural insiders who sought to reconcile religious commitments, such as to polygamy, with other normative commitments, such as women's right to suffrage. Plural marriage and universal suffrage had coexisted in Utah from 1870 to 1887. In 1887, the passage of the Edmunds-Tucker Act in the U.S. Congress took away women's right to vote and the right to polygamy in Utah—partly because male legislators from other states were angry that LDS women did not "free themselves" from polygamy through the vote. In response to the government's attempt to strip their rights as women and as religious people, Wells and others argued in the *Woman's Exponent* that polygamy and women's suffrage were both morally consistent and socially beneficial in the context of democratic, feminist, and gospel values.[64]

The historic and contemporary controversies surrounding religious polygamy illustrate the ethical complexities of making arguments for the institutionalization of the moral rights of women, especially in cases where law and culture do not yet provide guides for reformist action. Because of these complexities, allegations of women's human rights must often refer to some kind of moral foundation as a justification for their broader public recognition as a valid claim for reform. A conception of humanity itself is one such foundation.

Foundationalist approaches to justifying human rights run into the problem of the pluralism of values across peoples, cultures, and nations, however. Not all peoples will agree on what it means to be human, or wish to dissociate religion or other cultural traditions from their definitions of humanity. Not all women will agree on policies that affect them, such as laws concerning marriage, suffrage, or health care. For example, a liberal pluralistic society such as the contemporary United States sees significant gaps in public opinion emerge between women who primarily identify as religious and women who primarily identify as feminist. When faced with what Rawls called "the fact of reasonable pluralism," a human rights advocate must attend to reasonable differences among people's worldviews (or comprehensive doctrines) in adopting an ethical approach to judging how to respond to the disputed issue at hand. Understanding one's own basic relationship to a contested issue is a crucial first step toward making rationally justified and culturally respectful claims for human rights.[65]

To allege women's human rights in cases of strong disagreement may be a morally courageous act for a cultural insider such as Ebadi, but it is also a political step toward justice. Since 2009, Ebadi has been forced to live in exile from Tehran due to her successful yet controversial feminist activism; worse, the Iranian government has persecuted her family in order to try to stop her work for women's rights in her Islamic nation. Such brave and persistent activism by cultural insiders puts the issue on the national or global agenda for cultural outsiders. This is Wollstonecraft's gift to human rights activism: modeling the value of people speaking up for women's human rights from the foundations of their own cultural and religious traditions.[66]

With a comparatively thinner set of moral foundations than Wollstonecraft's approach, Mill's liberal utilitarianism lends itself more to the outsider perspective for advocating women's human rights. Pragmatically akin to Rawlsian nonfoundationalist theorists of human rights yet philosophically grounded in his foundational value of individuality, Mill provides another compelling secular model for judging and alleging women's human rights. This liberal utilitarian approach to rights-based reform begins with a basic stance of tolerance toward other people's cultural practices. If necessary, it educates people directly and indirectly affected by a women's human rights issue. It proceeds to monitor violations of those human rights. The last resort is invoking a thin set of secular yet foundationalist human rights values in order to instigate reform. This outsider perspective on contentious women's human rights issues ultimately strives to resist the strong imposition of one's most contestable moral standards on different cultures. In the long run, the dynamic interplay of a variety of insider and outsider perspectives on human rights may lead to reform of laws and policies concerning controversial women's human rights issues, such as those on religious polygamy. This dynamic of insider and outsider reforms might make liberalism more accommodating to practices that at first look incompatible with its principles of justice, while encouraging people to adapt their cultural practices such that they resonate with basic human rights values, both moral and legal.

three

THEORIES OF HUMAN DEVELOPMENT
WOLLSTONECRAFT AND MILL ON SEX, GENDER, AND EDUCATION

Virtue Ethics and the Human Right to Education

Despite their contrasting religious and secular approaches to the justification of universal human rights, Wollstonecraft and Mill saw the purpose of rights in a similar light. To claim any human right, moral or legal, was to simultaneously claim an even more expansive right to live, develop, and flourish as a human being. The enjoyment of some basic human rights—such as sustenance and security—was a minimal yet necessary condition for the sound growth of people, as individuals and in groups. However, many persons lacked the means—individually, socially, or politically—to initiate, let alone actualize, this process of human development. Wollstonecraft and Mill were keenly aware that systematic sexual discrimination posed formidable obstacles to girls' and women's exercise of basic human rights and thus their free and full self-development as human beings.

To solve this gender-inflected political problem, Wollstonecraft and Mill knew that they could not stop at the general justification of the equal moral rights of the sexes. Beyond this first step, they had to make a case for why there was a specific human right by which human beings could best develop their capabilities as individuals, in groups, and as a whole. Each of them identified education as this basic right, especially but not exclusively for children, and without discrimination as to sex. This universal right to education presumed the enjoyment of other basic human rights (such as sustenance and security), but it aimed at loftier moral and political goals than these bare necessities for survival. As Mill powerfully put it in *On Liberty*, it was a "moral crime" that women and children were not guaranteed a "right" to "education" in his supposedly advanced country, because not only "food" but also "instruction and training for [the] mind" were necessary for individual well-being. While adequate provision of food could meaningfully satisfy the right to sustenance in the short term, the satisfaction of the right to education could be determined only in light of its long-term process of character development.[1]

Because of their joint concern with education as the perfection of moral character, Wollstonecraft and Mill drew from some of the ancient wisdom of Aristotelian ethics. For them, the Aristotelian telos, or final goal, of human life is the realization of eudaimonic, or virtuous, happiness. Wollstonecraft's foundational conception of duty led her to define "virtue" in universalistic and metaphysical terms: "to obtain a character as a human being, regardless of the distinction of sex," by ruling oneself and respecting others through rational adherence to God's moral law. Mill's complex consequentialist distinction between aggregate human happiness and the "real, permanent" happiness of self-cultivation led him to think of virtue as asserting one's individuality in a way that was conscientious of the freedom of others. This, in *On Liberty*, he called "a Greek ideal of self-development, which the Platonic and Christian ideal of self-government blends with, but does not supersede." In their liberal variants of virtue ethics, Wollstonecraft and Mill agreed that to experience virtuous happiness—or the ultimate human good—was to cultivate an independent yet caring moral character. Because people must learn how to be virtuous in their relationships to self and others, education is the most important human right in their perfectionistic ethics.[2]

Martha Nussbaum has made the point that Aristotle's theory of *eudaimonia* may be read as allowing the perfection of a range of virtuous characters, from the contemplative philosopher to the courageous warrior. I follow Nussbaum in understanding Mill as continuing this perfectionistic tradition of ethics even as he opens up the possibility of an even richer variety of virtuous outcomes for human character development. Mill's liberal utilitarianism diversifies eudaimonia by setting down the freedom, eccentricity, and higher pleasures of individuals as the expansive parameters for human flourishing.[3]

I further propose that Wollstonecraft should be understood as an important predecessor to Mill in developing this liberty-centered school of virtue ethics. Although virtue ethics is often understood as an alternative to both deontology and consequentialism, Wollstonecraft and Mill demonstrated how a deep philosophical interest in character as the primary marker of virtuous happiness was in fact compatible with their respective duty-based and utilitarian justifications for human rights. Their resultant liberal school of virtue ethics is explicitly egalitarian and democratic in its political implications. Its egalitarianism—meaning, its applicability to each and every human being, regardless of gender, class, race, or other social status—made it universalistic in scope in contrast to Aristotle's ethics, which largely confined its attention to the character formation of elite men. Wollstonecraft and Mill aimed at nothing less than the inclusion of all people in the experience of eudaimonia through the establishment of a universal human right to education. In her *Rights of Men*, Wollstonecraft explicitly contrasted her views on "democracy" with "Aristotle." Specifically, she rejected Edmund Burke's conservative interpretation of book 4 of the *Politics* to mean that democracy inevitably produces tyranny. In the spirit of the early, liberal stage of the French Revolution, she contended that "democracy" leads not to "tyranny" but rather to the empowerment of the people. In her *Rights of Woman*, she argued that representative democracy was the best political framework for instituting the "rights and duties" of humanity and the "human virtues (or perfections)" that "naturally flow" from them.[4]

In recent scholarship on Wollstonecraft and Mill, each of them has been independently assessed as a virtue ethicist. Virginia Sapiro's landmark 1992 book *A Vindication of Political Virtue: The Political Theory of Mary Wollstonecraft* situated Wollstonecraft's political theory in eighteenth-century republican discourse on virtue and laid the groundwork for the more recent turn toward reading Wollstonecraft in terms of her moral theory of virtue. Philosophical readings of Mill's *Autobiography* alongside his *Utilitarianism*, such as by Nussbaum, have underscored the centrality of virtue to his ethics, especially his theory of happiness. While a consensus has formed around conceptualizing each of their ethical systems in perfectionistic terms, the status of rights in their moral and political thought continues to be debated. Scholars have lately emphasized Mill's view of freedom as nondomination over his theory of rights, and Wollstonecraft's conceptions of virtue and duty over her theory of rights. I seek to connect Wollstonecraft's and Mill's well-discussed virtue ethics with their more contested theories of rights, via a comparative analysis of their views on the fundamental human right to education.[5]

Wollstonecraft and Mill ideally conceived education as broader in scope than a mere process of socialization and higher in purpose than a simple system of discipline or social control. To apply a distinction made by Alan Ryan (and Mill before him), they perceived that the "narrower" use of terms such as "education" and "socialization" discouraged the "wider" human quest for freedom and virtue, and even obscured the ways that people may be made unfree and vicious by learning and norms. As do Nussbaum and Amartya Sen, Wollstonecraft and Mill viewed education as a long-term process of realizing the abundant variety of capabilities of human beings, first and foremost as individuals and secondly as a species.[6]

Wollstonecraft and Mill theorized the process of eudaimonic human development as having several, mutually reinforcing levels: (1) the education of children in the habits of body, affect, and mind to become virtuously self-governing adults; (2) the simultaneous, reflexive reform of educational practices to better enable such free and full self-development; (3) the allegation, recognition, and institutionalization of the basic human right to education undifferentiated by sex; and (4) the simultaneous, reflexive reform of policies and laws concerning the right to education, in order to promote virtuous human development. Each accepted that the various levels of human development would not always take place at the same intensity or pace, be linear, consistent, or progressive in results, or ever be final. Yet for both thinkers, the goal of virtue remained the common point of moral orientation.

Although they were perfectionists in the Aristotelian sense that they posited virtue as the end of their ethical worldviews, they were not perfectionists in the contemporary psychological sense of defining one's purpose in life in terms of an unrealizable excellence. The latter view was self-defeating and demoralizing, as Mill poignantly chronicled with his account of his "mental crisis" and subsequent, life-saving discovery of the "indirect" route to personal happiness. According to his *Autobiography*, a "real, permanent" happiness could only be found via an inward turn, to the culture and habits of the self, which would precipitate a virtuous shift in the public habits of individuals. It was education that would spread and solidify this virtuous shift in personal and public habits. The most important outcome of this educational process would be citizens' development of the taste for higher-order utility (above all, the flourishing of individuality) over lower forms of utility (such as short-term personal pleasures).[7]

In a similar spirit, Wollstonecraft prescribed education as a political solution to the deeper moral problem of how to inculcate the virtues necessary for the practice of equal yet "ennobled" citizenship among men and women. As a starting point for this educational process, she consistently advised girls to focus on meaningful practical goals that enhanced their own sense of self-worth. Women should not define themselves in terms of superficial markers of their sex's prescribed social value, such as a passive feminine demeanor. As she surmised in the *Rights of Woman*, "If fear in girls, instead of being cherished, perhaps, created, were treated in the same manner as cowardice in boys, we should quickly see women with more dignified aspects." This shift in girls' self-understandings would encourage boys to do the same, in their views of themselves and their female counterparts. In the long run, the cultivation of personal virtue would contribute to the global human good: a shared sense of human entitlement to reasonable conditions of equal dignity and respect.[8]

As a philosophical proponent of the capabilities approach, Nussbaum has argued that normative theories of human development must begin with an account of the fundamental capabilities of human beings and also establish the minimum threshold at which their actual or potential voluntary realization characterizes a life of human dignity. Whereas Sen has focused on the capability for freedom as a gateway to the growth of other human capabilities such as education or political participation, Nussbaum has provided a detailed list of ten basic human capabilities (life; bodily health; bodily integrity; senses, imagination, and thought; emotions; practical reason; affiliation; relationships with other species; play; and control over one's environment). Despite these differences in their definitions of the capabilities, both have argued that the Aristotelian ethical distinction between the actual and the potential—what humans can do, versus what they could do and should do—is vital for theories of just human development. If we judge human activity solely on an empirical basis, rather than also invoking a normative idea of what humans could and should choose to do, we will never gain a critical perspective on "what is" versus "what ought to be." This application of the Aristotelian distinction between actuality and potentiality permits the derivation of rights from capabilities. For Nussbaum, the right to education may be derived from a number of human capabilities, including practical reason, play, bodily integrity, and the emotions. Because education typically empowers humans with the choice to potentially or actually exercise their other capabilities, it is a basic or fundamental right of the human being. Furthermore, the application of the Aristotelian distinction between actuality and potentiality allows humans to allege rights as extralegal or extracultural moral standards for assessing the limitations of present social and political norms. For Sen, such criticism of the actual may stir reform toward the potential.[9]

Wollstonecraft and Mill applied the actual-potential distinction in their diagnoses of the moral problem of sex inequality, and their joint prescription of the universal human right to education as its political remedy. Males and females were unequal in society and politics not because of nature but rather because of their socialization within the patriarchal norms of the family. Almost eighty years apart, Wollstonecraft and Mill insisted that the potential of females to contribute to human society and progress would be unknown until they were given a chance to develop without the fetters of patriarchy. Wollstonecraft hypothesized that women "will change their character, and correct their vices and follies, when they are allowed to be free in a physical, moral, and civil sense." Concerning women's "capabilities," Mill empirically reasoned that "nobody knows" what they are or could be, "not even [women] themselves, because most of them have never been called out."[10]

The first step toward realizing the capabilities of girls and women would be the reform of education—in families, schools, and culture as a whole—such that it produced more egalitarian norms of character development for the sexes. Wollstonecraft's theory of education was twofold in its innovative treatment of the psychological development of the girl child's gender identity. First, Wollstonecraft diagnosed how bad educational practices led girls to adapt to conditions of patriarchal domination by playing the standard, limited gender roles assigned to them by society. Second, she prescribed a cure for this problem in the deep coeducational reform of public schools such that they would train girls and boys to see themselves and each other as equally entitled to the "birthright" of humankind: "such a degree of liberty, civil and religious, as is compatible with the liberty of every other individual." Less focused on the curricular details of educational reform at the primary or secondary level, Mill offered a pragmatic model for criticizing the negative effects of patriarchal gender roles on human development in general. Both theorists envisioned how the state-level institutionalization of a basic human right to universal primary education (UPE) would establish national venues for systematic, virtuous reform of gender and other social roles.[11]

Because Wollstonecraft and Mill wished to convince governments to provide the fundamental human right to education, they were faced with a political predicament. On the one hand, their primary justification for the human right to UPE was the intrinsic value of equal education for individual girls and boys. On the other hand, elite men in power had to be persuaded to extend this right to females. Responding to these unfavorable political circumstances, Wollstonecraft and Mill made consequentialist arguments that foregrounded the extrinsic benefits of reforming female education for society at large, including the men who ran it. However persuasive, such consequentialist arguments for women's human rights had the

countervailing rhetorical effect of portraying girls and their education as mere means to larger social and political ends. This chapter
concludes by engaging the questions of whether and how women's
human rights advocates and educational reformers may avoid this
moral contradiction between their deeper philosophical principles
and their rhetorical practices.

Diagnosing Bad Education via the Sex-Gender Distinction

Wollstonecraft began her philosophy of education by assessing the
bitter reality of social inequality in her time. Her "observations" on
women's "state of degradation" led her to argue that such degradation was predominantly caused by bad educational practices that systematically disadvantaged girls at the same time that they advantaged
boys. The remedy to such bad, gender-specific educational practices
was the institution of an equal human right to education, especially
formal primary education. Wollstonecraft proceeded to propose the
reform of educational institutions and practices such that they would
guarantee this basic right and generate virtuous characters for individuals across the sexes and the species as a whole.[12]

Wollstonecraft's treatment of gender—or the socially constructed
aspect of human sex identities—was the most groundbreaking dimension of her observational and politically situated approach to
defending the universal human right to education. While she and
other eighteenth-century thinkers did not use the term "gender" in
this way, she came remarkably close to articulating in her philosophy the conceptual distinction between gender as a social construction and sex as a biological trait that has become fundamental to
social science research since the 1940s. The *Rights of Woman* presented her most complete account of the social construction of gender identities, masculine and feminine. Continuing a theme from
the *Rights of Men*, the first chapter reviewed how unnatural social
hierarchies—such as slavery, the aristocratic class system, the Catholic and Anglican Churches, monarchical government, and standing
armies—provided the context in which people assigned limiting and

corrupting identities to one another. She then moved, in chapter 2, to discuss how the same process formed "the prevailing opinion of a sexual character."[13]

What Wollstonecraft meant by "the prevailing opinion of a sexual character" was the way in which society prescribed unduly sexualized identities for both women and men, but especially women. "Prevailing opinion" consisted of culturally shared, comparative, and competitive judgments and beliefs about one another. Such opinions were the mechanism that created stereotypical gender identities. The power of "prevailing opinion" to shape people's beliefs meant that it could impose a set of sexual stereotypes upon people—such as the male rake, the dandy redcoat, the vain girl, and the despotic mistress—which they often unreflectively, even happily, accepted as their own social identities. These gender identities situated men and women in a sexualized hierarchy of roles and relationships; they also reflected and intersected with the other artificial hierarchies that defined society, including those inflected by class and race.[14]

Wollstonecraft identified education as the means by which culture reinforces both economic and legal constructions of patriarchal power. Through education, women come to be seen as "cyphers" in the eyes of themselves and others. Wollstonecraft pinpointed "education" as principally responsible for giving an "appearance of weakness to females." This appearance quickly became reality, as education trained girls to internalize this collective social judgment of their gender's supposed physical or natural inferiority. The frivolous character of female education, with its focus on "novels, music, poetry, and gallantry," tended to "make women creatures of sensation, and their character is thus formed in the mould of folly." Such a poor education had "a more baneful effect on the female than the male character" because women were denied the economic and political opportunities that would at least give them a chance to break out of this culturally imposed mould.[15]

Likewise, Mill was morally troubled by the social construction of gender to support male power and female powerlessness. In comparing husbands to slave owners, he caustically asked: "Was there ever any domination which did not appear natural to those who possessed it?" The first chapter of his *Subjection of Women* thus opened with Mill's engagement of this problem as if he were the lawyer for the defense of women's equality with men. Similar to Wollstonecraft with her observational and politically situated approach, he proceeded from the realistic assumption that the "burthen of proof" lay on his side, because "the subjection of women to men being a universal custom, any departure from it quite naturally appears unnatural." Despite the odds against him, Mill pitched his case for human equality in the hope that the jury of society would change its mind on the basis of his arguments about the arbitrary and artificial character of sex inequality. Because humans made gender, gender could be unmade and remade by them. Mill thus underscored the practical possibility of rethinking and reforming gender norms such that they unleashed both women's and men's full human capabilities.[16]

The beginnings of Mill's relationship with Harriet Taylor, in the early 1830s, inspired some of his first meditations on gender. In private correspondence in the fall of 1833, Mill challenged his friend Carlyle's description of Madame Roland as "almost rather a man than a woman" by way of querying, "*Is* there any distinction between the highest masculine and the highest feminine character?" Over the next three decades, Mill developed a theory of gender as a social construct independent of biological sex—particularly in his private musings on marriage and women's rights, and in his public engagement of the suffrage debate.[17]

In his unpublished essay "On Marriage," exchanged with Taylor sometime around 1832–33, Mill began to theorize the role of "education and custom" in the social formation of constricting gender roles for women. He used the example of a married woman's "artificially desirable" condition in contrast to the lowly, yet comparatively freer, single woman of his time. Although the wife lacked "any superiority of legal rights" due to coverture, her position in life was still preferable to the single woman. To unravel this paradox, Mill argued that "it is not law, but education and custom which make the difference" between the lower status of the single woman and the higher status of the wife. He concluded that women were particularly subject to the ill effects of bad education. From girlhood, they "are educated to *be* married." The perverse effect of this lifelong push toward marriage was to deny girls the chance to experience freedom, even "in the mere physical sense." Instead, girls were "brought up" to depend upon men for their basic subsistence and security. This deep cultural inculcation of women's dependency on men made it unlikely that they would seek "to subsist" independently or "to protect themselves."[18]

An undated essay on women's rights, cowriten with Taylor in the late 1850s, similarly argued that the difference between men's and women's social roles "is principally if not wholly the effect of differences in education and in social circumstances, or of physical characteristics by no means peculiar to one or the other sex." Here, Mill and Taylor perceptively disaggregated physical differences dependent on sex from physical differences independent of sex, suggesting that the latter were actually more relevant to determining choices in occupation. Mill's 1861 treatise *Considerations on Representative Government* cemented this distinction between "physical" and "social" differences between men and women. In his defense of "universal yet graduated suffrage," he paid no attention to "sexual difference" because it was "entirely irrelevant to political rights, as difference in height, or in the colour of the hair." By the early 1860s, Mill drew a bright line between sexual difference determined by biology and gender difference produced by socialization. Sexual differences were nowhere near as significant for society as the gender roles produced by education and custom. Moreover, sexual differences were less relevant to choice of occupation than species-wide physical differences like height, and as "irrelevant" to political issues as hair color.[19]

Mill's 1843 *Logic* had used the term "gender" in the grammatical sense, in the context of his definition of universal propositions. Mill argued that the proposition "man is mortal" is universal, meaning, its subject's referent logically denoted all "human beings," not only "man" or male humans. In propositions in which the universality or particularity of terms such as "man" was not clear, there was no logical reason to "enumerate the *doubtful* gender." The meaning of the term "man"—whether it was intended to denote "humans" or "males"—could be construed from the context of the proposition.[20]

Beyond this point of grammar, Mill never used the term "gender" in the modern sense of the social construction of human sex identities. His involvement in the women's rights cause, however, pushed him to more strongly consider the ethical implications of universalistic propositions about "man" that did not "enumerate" women as part of the general category of humanity. While there was not an abstractly logical reason to specify women or use a sex-neutral term, there were plenty of contextual moral and political reasons to foster a more inclusive discourse on humanity. Mill's *Subjection of Women* and his other political arguments on behalf of women's human rights explored the problematic ethical implications of making universalistic propositions about "man" without considering women's education into conditions of arbitrary subordination.[21]

In May 1867, Mill's speech before the House of Commons, "The Admission of Women to the Electoral Franchise," put this gender-sensitive ethic of universalistic argumentation to political use. Before the assembly of fellow male legislators, he proposed an amendment to the Reform Bill concerning the qualifications of voters in British counties. This amendment stated that the word "person" should be used instead of "man," in order to legally denote women's right to vote. Before applause, he argued against the current state of affairs, in which "neither birth, nor fortune, nor merit, nor exertion, nor intellect, nor even that great disposer of human affairs, accident, can ever enable any woman to have her voice counted in those national affairs which touch her and hers as nearly as any other person in the nation." His gender-sensitive rhetoric specifically denoted woman in his universalistic moral argument for every person's right to vote. Although his motion lost, 196 to 73, Mill's case for legal recognition of women's status as "persons" had already been publicly recognized as an expression of his "logic," in a recent issue of the satirical London magazine *Punch* (figure 1).[22]

From the earliest responses to their theories of the social construction of gender roles, Wollstonecraft and Mill had been accused

MILL'S LOGIC ; OR, FRANCHISE FOR FEMALES.
"PRAY CLEAR THE WAY, THERE, FOR THESE—A—PERSONS."

Figure 1. "Mill's Logic; or, Franchise for Females," in
Punch (London, 30 March 1867), 129. The subcaption is
"Pray clear the way, there, for these-a-persons."

of professing strange views on the expression or repression of sexuality in human life. She was spoofed as a sexual wanton, while Freud mocked Mill's *Autobiography* for its "prudish" ideas on the relationship between men and women. Although they exaggerated some truths about Wollstonecraft's revolutionary-era sexual radicalism and Mill's Victorian reserve, the critics had their moments of insight. Intriguingly, the press caricatured Wollstonecraft and Mill as manly women or as womanly men for their ideas on how women's rights ought to transform gender roles in society. Indeed, seventy years apart, cartoonists presented them as cross-dressing philosophers of women's human rights (figures 2 and 3).[23]

Engraved by J. Chapman from an original Painting.

Mrs GODWIN.

Figure 2. "Mary Wollstonecraft," 1798 stipple engraving by
John Chapman, in the National Portrait Gallery, London.

MISS MILL JOINS THE LADIES.

[See Page 47.

Figure 3. "Miss Mill Joins the Ladies," in *Judy* (London, 25 November 1868), 46–47, and the National Portrait Gallery, London.

Wollstonecraft and Mill both shrugged off such crude satires of their radical views on the difference between bodily sex and gender norms. Wollstonecraft deflated such criticisms by anticipating them: she exploded the notion of "manly virtues" in the opening pages of the *Rights of Woman* by invoking the universal human standard of moral virtue and depicting "masculine" activities such as hunting and shooting as vicious regardless of which sex performed them. Mill persisted in making his logical argument for the human right to be legally recognized as a person. His unsolicited 1867 letter to Kansas state senator Samuel N. Wood, later printed in Topeka and New York papers, praised the legislator for proposing a constitutional amendment for universal suffrage that would abolish "the unjust political privileges of sex at one and at the same stroke with the kindred privilege of color."[24]

Contemporary scholarship has carried on the nineteenth-century tradition of supposing that Mill wished to impose asexual androgyny on others, and presuming that Wollstonecraft wanted women to be like men. These interpretations do not, however, make sense of why Wollstonecraft and Mill made human embodiment the starting point for their practical ethics. Their philosophical distinction between gender and sex relied upon their conceptions of the embodied, sentient, sexed human being.[25]

For Wollstonecraft and Mill, sex mattered because the body mattered—physically and morally—as the vehicle for human life. Wollstonecraft argued that both children and adults should study sexual reproduction as part of natural science, beginning with botany. Sexuality had important public health ramifications, as she and Mill acknowledged in relation to prostitution and venereal disease, and so it needed to be treated as a vital issue in political discourse.[26]

Like most people of their times, Wollstonecraft and Mill sometimes predicated their arguments about sexual politics on moral presumptions about how the sexed body generates social preferences. As discussed in chapter 2, Wollstonecraft assumed that sexual reproduction gave reasons for monogamous marriage and male-female partnership in early childcare. In a highly contested statement in *The*

Subjection of Women, Mill assumed that most married women would (and perhaps even should) choose to focus upon family and motherhood, rather than careers outside the home, even once granted full legal and economic equality with men: "Like a man when he chooses a profession, so, when a woman marries, it may in general be understood that she makes choice of the management of a household, and the bringing up of a family, as the first call upon her exertions, during as many years of her life as may be required for the purpose; and that she renounces, not all other objects and occupations, but all which are not consistent with the requirements of this." The meaning of this passage has been much debated by feminist scholars. Some, like Nadia Urbinati, have interpreted it as a rhetorical strategy to persuade men to enfranchise women at no risk to their current domestic situations. Others, like Susan Okin, have interrogated it to expose Mill's inconsistency or limitations as a feminist, particularly on the sexual division of labor.[27]

In light of his moral concern with human embodiment, it is interesting to note that Mill cited "the physical suffering of bearing children" and the "bodily and mental exertion" of running a household as reasons why married women focused on work within the family during their reproductive years. Lending social scientific evidence to this hypothesis, political economists Torben Iversen and Frances Rosenbluth have recently explained why women are more likely to slow down in their work beyond the home when they are in their childbearing years, whether or not they have children. The embedded causes of this trend are found in politics, economics, and patriarchal family structures. In a patriarchal society that allows women at least some access to the marketplace, women face greater pressure than men to calculate the costs and benefits of reproduction and other caregiving roles to them. The possibility of pregnancy, childbirth, and elder care is a significant determinant of action, including choice of work, from women's perspectives as economic actors. Whether because of actual or anticipated caregiving burdens, women focus less on their careers outside the home during their fertility windows, which feeds back into patriarchal patterns of employment and salary discrimination against women in general. As Mill contended long ago, female embodiment does matter, but so do patriarchal gender norms.[28]

The bulk of Wollstonecraft's and Mill's arguments concerning the sexes clearly fell on the side of addressing the moral problem of the social construction of patriarchal gender norms. In response to this problem, Wollstonecraft called for a "revolution in female manners" by which women could reform themselves as individuals, and in so doing, "reform the world." Mill likewise envisioned the holistic, egalitarian transformation of education so that it cultivated self-sovereign individuals who would reform gender and society along virtuous lines. As Urbinati has shown, Mill embraced the British Romantic ideal of androgyny—or the positive blending of the "highest" feminine and masculine qualities in human psychology—found in the writings of Samuel Taylor Coleridge and Percy Bysshe Shelley. It is clear, however, that Mill understood this androgyne ideal to be a psychological or moral disposition that one could adopt to pursue a life of virtuous happiness, not an innate facet of the human mind or body.[29]

Wollstonecraft's and Mill's theories of gender identity formation are strikingly similar to contemporary social scientific accounts of gender. When psychologists formally introduced the sex-gender distinction in the 1940s, they used it to distinguish between sex (male and female biological traits) and gender (socially constructed norms of masculinity and femininity). Wollstonecraft took note of male homosexual prostitutes, transvestites such as the French diplomat Madame d'Eon (who now might self-describe as transgendered), and other "equivocal beings" who broke down a strict gender binary between masculine and feminine plus the prevailing assumption of the biological basis of femininity. Although contemporary literary theorists such as Claudia Johnson have criticized her hetero-normative perspective, Wollstonecraft acknowledged homosexuality and transvestitism as practices in her time and seems to have tolerated them among adults except in cases of sexual promiscuity, infidelity, and prostitution (which she judged to be morally wrong in general).

By contrast, Mill's general moral preference for the pursuit of the higher, mental pleasures may have led him to focus more on issues of gender than on issues of sexuality. Unlike his utilitarian mentor Jeremy Bentham, Mill did not boldly engage controversial sexual questions such as the morality of homosexual relations (then censoriously labeled as sodomy or pederasty). As we saw in chapter 2, even his consideration of Mormon polygamy in *On Liberty* hinged on the social and political question of whether such plural marital arrangements ought to be tolerated from afar, rather than on close moral evaluation of their sexual practices. Although he and Harriet Taylor chose to practice a platonic, intellectual love together, free from the obsession with sex and reproduction that dominated most couples' relationships, Mill never prescribed asexuality, chastity, or childlessness for people in general; in fact, he devoted a large portion of his life to advocacy for people's access to and education regarding birth control and family planning, especially for the working classes, who sadly lacked the means to support the many children they currently brought into the world.[30]

What distinguishes Wollstonecraft and Mill from many postmodern invocations of gender is their consistent use of a philosophical distinction between sex, understood as biological, and gender, understood as a social construction. In the late twentieth century, the rise of postmodern theories of gender as a kind of social performance had the effect, in academic and even more in popular discourse, of treating gender as a general category under which cognate yet distinct identity traits, such as sex and sexuality, are subsumed. Especially in current popular discourse, gender serves as a nebulous umbrella concept that covers all dimensions of sex and sexual identities, rather than as a specific concept that distinguishes between what is biological and what is socialized in these aspects of human identities. The distinction between biological sex and socially constructed gender, as applied in contemporary social sciences such as anthropology and sociology, better promotes such rigorous analysis of gender, sex, and sexuality. Wollstonecraft's and Mill's philosophies have more in common with this social scientific approach to understanding the differences between gender and sex than with the popular, postmodern usage of the term "gender" to diffusely describe any and all aspects of sex and sexual identities.[31]

Within their critical theories of gender socialization, Wollstonecraft and Mill typically distinguished between the sexed body and the social roles that had become culturally and legally associated with sex. This distinction served as a point of departure for their common judgment of patriarchal gender roles as arbitrary, artificial, and damaging to all humans. Their use of the sex-gender distinction grew out of their perfectionistic ethics. The reference point of biological sex aided the critical analysis of patriarchal gender roles as vicious yet culturally contingent, and therefore transformable. According to the highest standard of moral virtue, gender could be reconceived along egalitarian lines so that it promoted, rather than inhibited, the free and full self-development of embodied, sexed human beings.

Vicious Cycles of Bad Education: Women's Adaptation to Patriarchal Gender Norms

Wollstonecraft and Mill identified education as the vicious means of women's subjection but also, once holistically reformed, as the primary means of their exit from patriarchal domination. Mill eloquently conveyed the distinction between good and bad education, as well as their dialectical relationship, in his 1867 inaugural address at the University of St. Andrews: "Whatever helps to shape the human being; to make the individual what he is, or hinder him from being what he is not—is part of his education. And a very bad education it often is, requiring all that can be done by cultivated intelligence and will to counteract its tendencies." A good education—which promoted the "virtue" and "self-culture" of the human being—was the outcome of the "always slow" process of reforming "bad education."[32]

The most perplexing problem with the patriarchal system of bad education was that women did not want to graduate from it. As a highly observant woman, Wollstonecraft was struck by her sex's complacent enjoyment and even willing, malicious perpetuation of patriarchy: "Women are told from their infancy, and taught by the example of their mothers, that a little knowledge of human weakness, justly termed cunning, softness of temper, outward obedience, and a scrupulous attention to a puerile kind of propriety, will obtain for them the protection of man; and should they be beautiful, every thing else is needless, for, at least, twenty years of their lives." Mill also recognized most women's contented acceptance of their subordination. As an extremely conscientious man, Mill blamed his sex for using "the whole force of education" to make woman "not a forced slave, but a willing one." Despite different emphases in critiquing his or her own gender, he and Wollstonecraft agreed that it was the overarching patriarchal structure of family, society, and the state that occasioned such vicious choices, concessions, and strategies, and worst, ignorant acceptance, among human agents.[33]

Sen and Nussbaum's theories of human development have described such responses to suboptimal circumstances as adaptive preferences. Wollstonecraft and Mill understood the phenomenon of women's adaptation to patriarchy as vicious in three senses. First, it was morally bad, as in contrary to the realization of the individual's potential for happy, virtuous self-governance. Second, it was self-perpetuating, as it spread vice throughout society via the repetitive processes of socialization within marriage and the family. Third, and worst of all, it was a mind-set deeply rooted in the agent's subjective sense of self.[34]

Building on her personal experiences and observations as a girl, a woman, a mother, and a teacher of girls, Wollstonecraft made an important contribution to understanding the subjective psychological experience of women's adaptation. Wollstonecraft used first-person narration in her 1798 novel *Maria, or the Wrongs of Woman*—most vividly with the destitute character of Jemima—to reveal the bleak interior psychology of patriarchal oppression. Jemima recounted to Maria her sad experience as a street prostitute: "Fate dragged me through the very kennels of society; I was still a slave, a bastard, a common property. . . . I picked the very pockets of the drunk-

ards who abused me; and proved by my conduct, I deserved the epi-
thets, with which they loaded me at moments when distrust ought
to cease." Her desperate situation drove Jemima to steal from the
"drunkards" who "abused" her; her shame for this crime, even in
light of the sexual abuse she suffered, poignantly showed how female
victims of patriarchal oppression internalize society's estimation of
their worthlessness.[35]

Mill, as a conscientious man, assessed the problem from the outside; his perspective yielded far-reaching insights into the political
psychology of not only women's adaptation to patriarchy but also
their capability to resist it. While he acknowledged the thesis that
women's subjection "is accepted voluntarily; women make no complaint, and are consenting parties to it," he challenged its power to
explain all women's attitudes toward patriarchy. He pointed out that
"a great number of women do not accept it." Women had long used
the pen, and more recently other forms of activism, to record their
"protests against their present social condition." On the other hand,
Mill conceded, "All causes, social and natural, combine to make it
unlikely that women should be collectively rebellious to the power
of men." Because women had been raised to "make complete abne-
gation of themselves," they were unlikely to do more than independently complain about bad treatment at the hands of their husbands.
But it was a "political law of nature" that people "under power of
ancient origin"—such as slaves or women—would only gradually
move from complaint of the power's "excessive exercise" to complaint of "the power itself."[36]

Wollstonecraft's subjective psychological account of adaptation
explained girls' early adherence to socially prescribed gender roles
alongside adult women's rationalization of their limited options.
For example, Wollstonecraft often criticized aristocratic women's
sour designation of early infant care as beneath them so they could
focus on frivolous pastimes. But she was equally, if not more, concerned with how their frivolous lifestyles set up a dangerous model
for their daughters. Raised to play with dolls and admire themselves
in the mirror, these girls were surrounded with an array of gender

"stereotype threats" in their upbringing. As social scientists discuss today, a "stereotype threat" is the use of powerful stereotype (such as girls play with dolls) to compel a group to behave in a way that conforms to social expectations (such as being conventionally feminine) and thereby reduces their ability to successfully perform in other areas (such as doing well in math). Indeed, it has been shown that if girls are asked to play with pictures of dolls before taking a math test, they will significantly underperform on the test as a result of confronting this gender stereotype threat.[37]

In challenging the Rousseauian assumption that girls by nature enjoy so-called feminine pastimes, Wollstonecraft diagnosed the deeper educational problem of the "stunting" of the girl child's preferences and behavior from the time of her infancy through exposure to various gender stereotype threats. She thus isolated the efficient cause of adaptation as women's lack of knowledge of any other way to live. Since bad education was the origin of women's stunted development, deep reform of education could open their psychological horizons in a way that would at least allow women to choose their lots rather than simply accept them or unreflectively impose them upon the next generation. Her response to the problem of women's adaptation to pernicious gender norms and stereotype threats spurred Wollstonecraft to conceptualize how education ought to be reformed to advance women's human rights despite women's ingrained preferences for oppression. Although she has sometimes been unfairly charged with misogyny, her sharp criticism of women's vicious behavior in her time was not antiwoman but rather antipatriarchy and therefore against women's adaptation to it.[38]

Mill's theory of adaptation was just as subtle, and thus prone to misinterpretation as well. Mill has been mistaken for a conspiracy theorist of why women adapt to subjection. On this reading of *The Subjection of Women*, men supposedly gang together to get women to prefer things the patriarchal way. This view of Mill's theory of adaptation fails to account for his broader social scientific explanation for global patriarchal institutions such as the family. The first chapter of *The Subjection of Women* dispensed with the traditional explanation for "patriarchal" power, the natural dominance of fathers, as a posthoc justification of male authority. Men had power neither because it was natural nor because they schemed together to get it but rather because they arbitrarily acquired it through use of "force."[39]

Mill empirically reasoned that patriarchal institutions grew and persisted because individual men in power perceived them as economically and politically advantageous to them, and protected their self-interest accordingly. According to chapter 1 of *The Subjection of Women*, these patriarchal institutions emerged from the older, feudal social order, so they could not be interpreted in isolation from broader patterns in political and economic development. In addition, Mill argued that women have adapted to the social expectation that "being attractive to men" should be their "polar star," and thus have contributed to their own subjection. With a sympathetic regard for women's predicament, he noted it would have been a "miracle" if they hadn't taken up this "yoke." For Mill as for many social scientists since, patriarchy is not a collective conspiracy among men against women but rather a long, cumulative feedback loop through which all members of society gradually reinforce institutions of male dominance.[40]

Wollstonecraft's and Mill's profound accounts of the moral and political psychology of patriarchal oppression led them to posit a correspondingly deep form of education as its remedy. This model of education is a kind of realistic perfectionism, as it aims to take "women as they are" (oppressed, and largely adapted to such oppression) to what they could and should be (individuals empowered to choose, if they so wish, a life of virtuous self-governance). Using the capabilities approach as a framework, Mozaffar Qizilbash has insightfully argued that Mill's rich conception of human flourishing is meant to be a realistic standard and goal for reforming society and politics. On this reading, Mill's liberal virtue ethics is thus akin to Sen's capabilities approach in upholding a holistic, liberty-centered, individual-empowering moral education as one such realistic policy. In what follows, I argue that this model of eudaimonic education supported both Wollstonecraft's and Mill's visionary defenses of

UPE as a basic human right that, if institutionalized, could success-fully undercut the vicious cycle of patriarchal domination.[41]

Perfectionism Meets Egalitarianism: Wollstonecraft and Mill on the Human Right to Universal Primary Education

In her *Rights of Woman*, Wollstonecraft was the first philosopher to publicly propose and systematically defend a national system of government-supported primary schools, free for boys and girls of any social status to attend during the day in their localities. In a chal-lenge to the "enlightened nation" of France and Charles Maurice de Talleyrand-Périgord's recent report on public education there, she argued that they should try an "experiment" in permitting women "to share the advantages of education and government with man." Anticipating patriarchal criticism in the guise of masculine chivalry, she satirically remarked that women "cannot be injured by the ex-periment; for it is not in the power of man to render them more insignificant than they are at present." She outlined the experiment as follows: "Day schools, for particular ages, should be established by the government, in which boys and girls might be educated together. The school for the younger children, from five to nine years of age, ought to be absolutely free and open to all classes." This overlaps with the twenty-first-century definition of UPE used by the United Nations in its second and third Millennium Development Goals: enabling all children, boys and girls, to complete education from grade 1 through grade 5.[42]

Wollstonecraft systematically argued for a right to UPE when the concept had only recently and partially emerged in Western educational thought and practice. In the context of the eighteenth-century expansion of primary-level parish and charity schools in his native Scotland, Adam Smith had defended government-sponsored primary education for working-class boys in book 5 of *The Wealth of Nations* (1776). This schooling was intended to serve as a psychologi-cal corrective to the narrow, mechanical lines of work that they faced in the capitalistic division of labor. Smith did not apply this argument to girls, despite the fact that they dealt with similarly narrow lines of work in the domestic realm. Given that girls were already being trained to read and to spin in Scottish charity schools in the 1770s, Smith's patriarchal bias is all the more evident.[43]

With a similar slant toward the rights of men, Talleyrand-Périgord's *Rapport sur l'instruction publique* (1791) proposed that orphan girls ought to receive government-sponsored primary education in the new French republic, but it defended full access to public education only for boys. Talleyrand-Périgord's partial inclusion of females had the instrumental goal of saving these orphans from a projected life of prostitution, not the empowerment of women in general. Likewise, the turn-of-the-century Swiss educator Johann Pestalozzi inspired a progressive, "child-centered" movement in primary education, but his reliance on Rousseauian ideals of womanhood oriented his followers more toward educating girls to be better mothers than toward equalizing the options of the sexes.[44]

Across the Atlantic, Boston's tax-supported primary schools had been coeducational since 1789 and flourished alongside several private female academies. Wollstonecraft's *Rights of Woman* resonated deeply with Boston's feminist educators at the turn of the nineteenth century, including Hannah Mather Crocker and Susanna Rowson. In his 1798 political tract *The Key of Liberty*, the rural Massachusetts farmer William Manning argued that mandatory, free, public coeducation was foundational to democracy.[45]

Six years earlier, the *Rights of Woman* had culminated with a comprehensive moral argument for UPE as a public policy solution to the vicious cycle of bad, patriarchal education. UPE would provide a public space in which governments could apply Wollstonecraft's perfectionistic theory of women's capability to realize moral and political equality alongside men: "By allowing them to share the advantages of education and government with man, see whether they will become better, as they grow wiser and become free." UPE ought to be a "grand national concern" because "private education" in the family could not be relied upon alone to bring about the "good effects" of moral and political virtue among all.[46]

In Wollstonecraft's theory of UPE, her perfectionism met her egalitarianism: "My observations on national education are obviously hints; but I principally wish to enforce the necessity of educating the sexes together to perfect both."[47] Wollstonecraft envisioned UPE as operating according to three core moral principles that would together undermine harmful social norms by instilling an egalitarian ethic of mutual respect among children: (1) holistic universalism (general education of body, mind, and character for all); (2) duty-based individualism (teaching children that their first duty is to govern themselves); and (3) psychological optimism (educating children to believe in their human capabilities to develop). Applied in concert in a primary school, these principles would guide children to avoid playing out the damaging gender roles that their culture had foisted on them.

Universalism in primary education, for Wollstonecraft, meant holism and fairness. Holism entailed the education of the whole person, and fairness required equality of opportunity for such a holistic education. Fairness arose from national standards for UPE and local schools' implementation of the government policy of holistic education for all. The national standards of equity that Wollstonecraft imagined were "absolutely free" primary education for "boys and girls, rich and poor"; uniformity in schoolchildren's clothing, discipline, and curriculum; and a local parish school committee system to which teachers could be held accountable by parents.[48]

Holism meant an education that developed, rather than "stunted," the potential of the "body, heart, and understanding." By playing together during hourly recess in the grounds surrounding the school, girls and boys would learn to see and treat each other as embodied human equals. Differences in body or sex did not translate into differences in moral status or rules. The only rule specified for their coeducational outdoor play ought to be "national" in scope: the general prohibition of brutality toward animals. By learning to treat animals benevolently in their games, children would discern the Rousseauian idea that all embodied, sentient creatures (including humans) had natural rights to respect of their bodily integrity. Finally, holism demanded day schools because children needed their families for a complete moral education: it is by "making children sleep at home that they may learn to love home."[49]

Individualism was about inculcating a sense not of social isolation but rather of moral responsibility to oneself and others. Children ought to be treated as moral equals by their teachers. Girls and boys would learn to see themselves as capable of the same self-respect if they governed themselves according to the same rules of morality. Raised to think themselves worthy of equal respect, children could better resist the threat of external gender stereotypes: "Were boys and girls permitted to pursue the same studies together, those graceful decencies might early be inculcated which produce modesty without those sexual distinctions that taint the mind." Integrating boys and girls of different class backgrounds was the key to the deeper psychological transformation of their images of themselves and each other: "They should be sent to school to mix with a number of equals, for only by the jostlings of equality can be formed a just opinion of ourselves." Such "jostlings of equality" on the playground and in the classroom would lead to a general ethic of respect for human potential, regardless of ascribed social roles.[50]

Optimism, or a belief in one's capability for positive development, would be inculcated through a standard yet stimulating curriculum. Girls and boys would be similarly encouraged to believe in their human capabilities to better themselves in body, mind, and character. They would be taught botany, mechanics, astronomy, reading, writing, arithmetic, natural history, and simple experiments in natural science, but such intellectual training would "never encroach on gymnastic plays in the open air." In Socratic conversation with their teachers, they would learn elements of religion, history, anthropology, and politics. In this way, optimistic teaching methods and goals reinforced the holistic dimension of UPE. Religion and morality were not dissociated from other elements of instruction in the government school system Wollstonecraft desired. Britain's long tradition of royal-chartered, Anglican, charitable day schools for poor boys and girls—such as Christ's Hospital, founded in 1552—gave her a cultural framework for thinking these elements compatible.[51]

Mill likewise defended UPE, which had become a mainstream political issue in his time. It was on the legislative agenda in Britain during his service as a member of Parliament from 1865 to 1868. Soon after his single term in office, the Education Act of 1870 established the rudiments of modern UPE in England and Wales but also permitted Anglican religious instruction in the government-sponsored schools. Since the early 1830s, Mill had been in favor of "the compulsory principle in education" for children in the primary school years, but against the use of public funds for the support of religious instruction. Before the National Education League Meeting in London, he gave a speech against the passage of the 1870 Education Act. If he had still been an MP, he would have voted against it on the grounds that it did not separate religious and public instruction. For Mill, the general division of religious and governmental institutions was necessary to prevent the trampling of the individual conscience.[52]

Although Mill consistently valued UPE's power to promote virtuous and happy outcomes in human self-development, he differed from Wollstonecraft in the emphases he placed on the three core moral principles that drove the policy. The guiding roles of the principle of individuality and the harm principle in his practical ethics meant that Mill prioritized duty-based individualism over universalism and optimism. A case in point was his desire to prevent harm to the private conscience by excluding religious instruction from government schools. In contrast, Wollstonecraft's curricular holism imagined a seamless integration of religion with other elements of rational, moral learning. From Mill's secular liberal utilitarian perspective, any government control over religious education of children seriously hampered the freedom and diversity of individual thought and conscience.

Mill also privileged duty-based individualism above universalism in upholding the moral responsibility of parents for the education of their children. While Wollstonecraft made a universalistic case for "absolutely free" UPE for all children, Mill deployed the principle of individualism to defend a scalar fee structure for UPE, based on parental income, with the poorest families receiving "state aid" for their children's educations. Even more crucially, Mill considered "the home, the family" to be the appropriate place for "moral and religious education," which "consist in training the feelings and the daily habits." Because "these are, in the main, beyond the sphere and inaccessible to the control of public education," it was the primary responsibility of parents to inculcate morals and, if they chose, faith in their children.[53]

Although he supported a national mandate for UPE and the separation of religion from government schools, Mill entertained "the strongest objections to any plan which would give a practical monopoly to schools under government control." He instead defined compulsory education as requiring parents "to have their children taught certain things" while being "left free to select the teachers." Despite his own wariness about faith-based education, Mill's broader commitment to duty-based individualism supported diverse schooling options—secular and religious—for parents to choose within the national mandate for UPE. He also argued for local autonomy in school committees' oversight of the government's primary schools, and for a range of women and working-class people to serve on such boards to represent the wider public opinion.[54]

On Liberty's principle of individuality fleshed out how duty-based individualism was to work within Mill's vision of UPE. In chapter 3, Mill dramatically situated the free yet responsible cultivation of human individuality as standing in tension with the potentially crushing influence of cultural uniformity. If facilitated through education, the diverse and spontaneous development of human beings would first enrich the well-being of individuals and subsequently the sentient creation as a whole: "In proportion to the development of his individuality, each person becomes more valuable to himself, and is therefore capable of being more valuable to others." Children's education aimed toward the lofty moral goal of individuality but nevertheless relied upon a certain amount of curricular standardization en route: "Nobody denies that people should be so taught and trained in youth, as to know and benefit by the ascertained results of human experience. But it is the privilege and proper condition of a human being, arrived at the maturity of his faculties, to use and interpret experience in his own way." Standardization of primary education could and should be done in a way that fostered, not stultified, individuality.[55]

In his 1867 inaugural address at St. Andrews, Mill supported a broad-ranging curriculum for primary education in "the islands" of Great Britain, focused on the acquisition of general knowledge, yet adapted to the needs of particular populations. While classical schools for university-bound children ought to continue teaching Greek and Latin, "history and geography" should be taught "in elementary schools for the children of the laboring classes, whose subsequent access to books is limited." Mill offset the class-based biases of such curricular differentiation with his commitment to guaranteeing the right to a quality "general education" for all children, regardless of economic status. This general education inculcated virtue as a consequence of imparting a broad knowledge of a variety of subjects, from math to literature: "Education makes a man a more intelligent shoemaker, if that be his occupation, not by teaching him how to make shoes; it does so by the mental exercise it gives, and the habits it impresses." Mill thus envisioned UPE as a programmatic yet flexible public policy for cultivating a variety of virtuous individuals, confident in their abilities to insightfully interpret and ethically interact with the world around them. Indeed, he saw primary education as part of a holistic and continuous process of personal growth: "Where does elementary instruction end, and the higher studies begin?"[56]

Although Wilhelm von Humboldt (1767–1835) was a major inspiration for *On Liberty*'s theory of individuality, Mill differed from the Prussian philosopher in defining free and full self-development in a virtue-oriented direction. Rather than being an open-ended process, as Humboldt allowed, free and full self-development ought to produce an active, creative, and virtuously self-governing individual. In his *Utilitarianism*, Mill's distinction between the higher and lower pleasures led to his moral demarcation of virtuous versus vicious pursuits. In *On Liberty*, he equated the "the most passionate love of virtue" with "the sternest self-control." He mourned that "the majority of young persons" lose their taste for "keeping that higher capacity" for virtue "in exercise," if their educations and occupations do not encourage them to do so.[57]

Mill's moral egalitarianism generated his pedagogical anxieties about steering all young persons to appreciate virtue and the other higher pleasures in life. He acknowledged that "virtue, according to the utilitarian doctrine, is not naturally and originally part of the end, but it is capable of becoming so; and in those who love it disinterestedly it has become so, and is desired and cherished, not as a means to happiness, but as a part of their happiness." Mill insisted that virtues were "besides being means . . . part of the end" of utility. Young people had to be taught to love virtue in a disinterested way, so that they loved it for its own sake. Once people loved virtue in itself, they could experience virtue as integral to their happiness, not simply an instrument to it. In an 1829 speech, Mill upheld Wordsworth's poem "The Character of the Happy Warrior" as illustrating "the most important features of the happiest and most virtuous character." Wordsworth's warrior was happy not because he was pleased by war but because he had come to cherish above all else the intrinsic value of a life characterized by personal excellence and self-control. It was incomparably happier for the warrior to be virtuous though displeased by his circumstances, like Socrates, than vicious and pleased, like a pig. Despite its apparently elitist distinction between higher (especially intellectual and moral) pleasures and lower (especially physical) pleasures, Mill's conception of happiness sought to promote democratic political ends. In *Considerations on Representative Government*, Mill argued for plural voting as a reward for educational attainment in order to urge the poor to pursue higher schooling as well as experience greater powers of personal and democratic self-governance.[58]

His substantive account of virtuous yet diverse self-development led Mill to support a universalistic national policy that mandated, at minimum, primary education for all children regardless of sex or class. Neither he nor Wollstonecraft specified the inclusion of all races in UPE, but this ethical implication could be logically derived from their strong antislavery politics and general critique of arbitrary, artificial inequalities. In his *Political Economy* (1848), Mill codified the educational policy that he and Harriet Taylor had discussed since the 1830s. He approved "universal education" for the complex consequence of empowering the laboring classes to control their fertility and improve their chances at realizing the higher pleasures in life for themselves and their children.[59]

According to Ryan's study of his educational philosophy, Mill spoke more of the cultivation of the individual in the "wider," or character-forming, sense than in the "narrower," or curricular, sense. As a political economist, not a teacher, Mill did not approach UPE from the grassroots perspective of Wollstonecraft. His very consistent views on UPE largely overlapped with Wollstonecraft's comparatively more detailed proposal, however. Fundamentally, both Mill and Wollstonecraft envisioned children's holistic education of body, mind, and character. As Mill claimed in his *Autobiography*, children of average abilities could handle the broad-ranging education of his childhood. With his university audience at St. Andrews, Mill shared his amazement "at the limited conception which many educational reformers have formed to themselves of a human being's power of acquisition." For this reason, he might have endorsed Wollstonecraft's ambitious liberal arts curriculum for her ideal day school. In a striking parallel to the *Rights of Woman*, *The Subjection of Women* observed that girls benefited from sharing the "healthful physical education and bodily freedom of their brothers." The physical education of girls was another core, practical component of Mill's and Wollstonecraft's theories of UPE.[60]

For both philosophers, a long-range goal of such a holistic primary education was to improve the life chances of girls and other historically disadvantaged groups. While Wollstonecraft's universalism directed her to focus on the value of a national educational system, Mill's liberal utilitarianism—especially the primacy of individuality within it—guided him to support a variety of public and private schools within UPE. Mill's distrust of uniformity also made him wary of centralization, bureaucratic inefficiency, and the loss of parental rights and responsibilities in any national educational system.

Mill shared Wollstonecraft's optimistic belief in the human capability for self-development toward virtue. But as a political economist and a liberal politician, he tended to be optimistic more about the long-term effects of educational policy than about particular teaching methods or learning experiences. Mill's theory of progress was hopeful about the power of free yet responsible choice to eventually produce beneficial social outcomes. On this account of progress, proponents of UPE and other optimistic social policies should generally seek to reinforce individual responsibility for personal choices, and expect a process of slow, not necessarily linear, but effective reform.[61]

Effective yet Ethical Argumentation for Women's Human Right to Education

Despite their differences at the policy level, Wollstonecraft and Mill judged the goodness of UPE in terms of its beneficial consequences: (1) enabling duty-based individualism and (2) encouraging other positive outcomes for human society as a whole. Unlike Mill's liberal utilitarianism, Wollstonecraft's rational theology required her to address the question of goodness separately from the question of rightness. While goodness could be defined as relative to beneficial outcomes, rightness was absolutely based on the rational demands of God's moral law. In contrast, Mill posited utility as the standard by which all normative measures—including goodness and rightness— were made.[62]

Supplementing her foundational duty-based argument for the human right to education, Wollstonecraft argued that UPE would yield better citizens, spouses, and parents. Like any effective rhetorician, she knew her political audience. Men in power, such as Talleyrand-Périgord, had to be persuaded of the benefits of extending equal civil and political rights to women. She thus presented an additional series of consequentialist arguments that focused specifically on the benefits of women's education for men and children: "I entreat them to assist to emancipate their companion, to make her a *help meet* for them! Would men but generously snap our chains, and be content with rational fellowship instead of slavish obedience, they would find us more observant daughters, more affectionate sisters, more faithful wives, more reasonable mothers—in a word, better citizens. We should then love them with true affection, because we should learn to respect ourselves; and the peace of mind of a worthy man would not be interrupted by the idle vanity of his wife, nor the babes sent to nestle in a strange bosom, having never found a home in their mother's." On a moral level, these consequentialist arguments served as supplements to Wollstonecraft's core deontological justification for women's human rights. Human rights derived from human duties, and such duties were expressions of a rational standard of moral "virtue" that had "no sex" but rather applied universally to all people. On a metaphysical level, both forms of moral argumentation for women's human rights—deontological and consequentialist—fitted, rank-ordered, within Wollstonecraft's belief in the benevolence of God's overarching plan for humanity. These consequentialist arguments, however, stressed the extrinsic value of women's human rights for men and children. Wollstonecraft's direct entreaty to the opposite sex, her pleading tone, combined with her suggestion that liberated women would more dutifully care for their fathers, husbands, brothers, and sons, produced a real tension between her philosophical justification of women's human rights and her rhetorical presentation of it.[63]

After her sustained argument for national education in chapter twelve of the *Rights of Woman*, Wollstonecraft repeated that UPE would produce better mothers: "Besides, by the exercise of their bodies and minds women would acquire that mental activity so necessary in the maternal character." A few lines later, however, she reminded her readers that this reasoning actually applied to both sexes. UPE would in fact cultivate good parents and spouses, not just good mothers and wives. She also indicated that these beneficial consequences for family life would arise from the sexes' reciprocal enactment of the duty to show mutual respect to one another: "Make women rational creatures, and free citizens, and they will quickly become good wives, and mothers; that is,—if men do not neglect the duties of husbands and fathers." Like Mill, she did not set education as a legal prerequisite for citizenship but rather considered it a comprehensive basis for the virtuous character development of future citizens, male and female. If educated together as equals, then men and women would practice, rather than neglect, the moral and civic "duties" from which their basic human rights were derived. In her prioritizing of the right before the good, Wollstonecraft was more like Kant in his 1795 essay "Perpetual Peace" than like Mill in *On Liberty*. Kant envisioned the ultimate beneficial political consequence (world peace) as a by-product of all nations doing the right thing (following requirements for establishing a pacific international league of republics). Similarly, Wollstonecraft's supplemental consequentialist arguments predicted that the pursuit of the right path in politics (for example, human rights to education and political participation) would have long-term public benefits (for example, virtuous citizenship and social justice), without establishing utility as the basis of her ethical system.[64]

On Mill's side, consequentialist arguments for the personal and public benefits of rights were basic to his liberal utilitarian enterprise. With regard to UPE's public benefits, he argued that it would decrease the fertility of the working classes, liberate women from the burden of excessive childbearing, reduce poverty, and thus advance the development of society as a whole. In the *Autobiography*, Mill confided that he and Harriet "only hoped that by universal education, leading to voluntary restraint on population, the portion of the poor might be made more tolerable." Most important, UPE would give women literacy, and the corresponding opportunity for a broader range of work inside and outside the home. As individuals and as a sex, women would finally activate their unknown human potential. In the process of virtuous self-development, girls would undercut the vicious cycle of socialization into patriarchal gender norms. Finally, they would gain a better basis of knowledge for voting and other forms of political participation.[65]

Mill's liberal approach to utilitarianism generated many powerful arguments for women's rights, including the human right to education, because it emphasized both the public and the personal utility of such rights. Yet the idea of public utility yielded instrumental arguments for women's rights that could rhetorically portray women's social, economic, and political opportunities as tools for other development goals, rather than as good outcomes for individual women. Chapter 4 of *The Subjection of Women* contained several examples of instrumental arguments for women's rights: equality of rights will make men less selfish and more intellectually stimulated by marriage, plus double "the mass of mental faculties available for the higher service of humanity." While such instrumental arguments might be, prima facie, persuasive, they also give the appearance that the standard utilitarian justification for rights is not sufficient in the case of women.[66]

In isolation, Wollstonecraft's and Mill's arguments for the extrinsic benefits of women's right to education have the rhetorical effect of portraying female education as a tool for other, superior development outcomes, such as happier families, universal suffrage, democracy, and population control. This rhetorical practice threatened to derail the orientation of their moral theories away from the end goal of human life, the virtuous happiness of the individual. By underscoring how the education of girls would make men and society happier and better developed, Wollstonecraft and Mill ran the risk of perpetuating the dangerous gender stereotype of women as instruments for male pleasure and power. An undesired (yet likely foreseen) by-product of pitching their arguments to men in power was to rhetorically reinforce the gender biases that they originally sought to uproot with their egalitarian theories of education.

Their predicament can be captured in a question: How can one defend universal human rights to the very people whose power depends on the current system of inequality? The reformer appears to face a trade-off between maintaining her principles (by arguing that women deserve rights simply by virtue of their humanity) and being effective in practice (by persuading male leaders of the personal and public benefits of granting rights to women). Because philosophical argumentation often sounds like futile rationalization when used in actual politics, the trade-off between holding principles and having practical effectiveness has been one contemplated by every modern political theorist seriously concerned with reform, from Wollstonecraft and Mill, to Marx and Rawls, to Nussbaum and Sen. This dilemma is also still a real one for women's human rights advocates working on a variety of issues, such as domestic violence, sexual discrimination, and family law. Yet the dilemma is perhaps most widely faced with regard to the issue of state provision of the universal human right to education, because UPE is a right that literally applies to all children, and therefore to all humanity, at the most vulnerable stage in their lives.

In our time, the Millennium Development Goals (MDG) have drawn attention to the problem of gender inequality in primary education by arguing that the education of girls is essential for the reduction of extreme poverty worldwide. Since the adoption of the MDG by the United Nations in 2000, there has been significant progress in achieving some overlapping aims of goals 2 and 3: universal primary education and gender equity in education. In 2013, the United Nations documented that the gender gap in literacy is narrowing in developing countries, especially in Southeast Asia and northern Africa, where general literacy rates have grown to 80 to 90 percent of the population. From 2000 to 2011, there was a remarkable drop in the number of children out of school worldwide—from 102 million to 57 million. U.N. Women, the agency devoted to gender equity in global justice, has nuanced this data by tracking the enduring gender disparities in primary education and literacy rates. It is a sobering fact that twelve years after the espousal of the MDG, "ten million more girls than boys" remained out of primary school and "nearly two-thirds of the world's 780 million people who cannot read are women." Given these dramatic gender inequalities, women's human rights advocates face a dilemma similar to that facing Wollstonecraft and Mill. While it is morally necessary and philosophically consistent to defend the equal right of girls and boys to UPE, it may be ineffective or even counterproductive for correcting the actual gap in their access to education.[67]

Wollstonecraft and Mill modeled some ways to navigate past this dilemma. As we have seen, Wollstonecraft reminded her readers that women deserved rights because of their human capability for virtue, not because men would benefit from their more virtuous behavior. Following her example, reformers might balance any economic or political arguments for the extrinsic value of UPE with repeated and clear public appeals to its intrinsic value for children. Near the end of his career, Mill modeled a morally stronger yet politically riskier rhetorical tactic: stressing the intrinsic value of education for all people over and against its extrinsic advantages for society. In his rector's address to the students of St. Andrews in 1867, he explained that the ultimate reward of education "is not a consequence, but is inherent in the very fact of deserving it." Intrinsic to education was "the deeper and more varied interest you will feel in life: which will give it tenfold its value, and a value which will last to the end." Education was inherently meaningful in the sense that it inculcated the virtues necessary for a human being to see, and deeply feel, just how interesting life was to live for its own sake. Given its strong moral and spiritual appeal, Mill's argument for the intrinsic good of education—and a happy life—was both ethical and effective in its rhetorical formulation. Although such arguments might not independently persuade men in power to promote gender parity in schools, they might at least counteract the cruder patriarchal connotations of arguments for the extrinsic value of female education for men. Learning from the examples of Wollstonecraft and Mill, feminist theorists and reformers should strive to avoid rhetorical constructions of women's human rights that overstress their benefits to families, males, societies, governments, religions, or (often implicitly Western) models of development. Chapter 4 turns fully to the latter issue: particularly, the problematic place of Western European cultural biases in Wollstonecraft's and Mill's theories of women's progress.[68]

THE PROBLEM OF CULTURAL BIAS
WOLLSTONECRAFT, MILL, AND WESTERN
NARRATIVES OF WOMEN'S PROGRESS

Confronting Cultural Bias

Although Mary Wollstonecraft and John Stuart Mill aspired to transcend time, place, and personal bias in the development of universalistic arguments for women's human rights, they fell short of this noble moral goal. As Michel Foucault, Carol Gilligan, and Charles Taylor have diversely argued, it is improbable that any human mind could move wholly beyond the epistemological frames set by epoch, gender, culture, religion, nation, and politics. But does the psychological fact of mental rootedness absolutely prevent a person from thinking more globally than locally?[1]

This is a particularly important question of practical philosophy for human rights advocates. Human rights advocacy in the wake of the 1948 Universal Declaration relies on the universalistic status of human rights in international law and policy. Human rights are meant to apply across nations and cultures to each and every human being—for the grave reason that we wish to prevent atrocities like those of the two world wars. For philosophers from Jürgen Habermas to John Rawls, the terrifying fact of the mass genocide of minorities as in the case of the Holocaust has spurred a return to political conceptions of human rights as a defense against such deadly treatment of humans as objects and instruments for the cruel ends of others. Human rights advocates, especially those who cautiously seek to reform aspects of other people's cultures, are thus faced with a moral quandary. May one advocate a global standard of human rights without an imperial mind-set that imposes one's own cultural values and biases upon others?[2]

Given their legacies for the idea of universal human rights, Wollstonecraft, Mill, and their philosophical followers are crucial historical cases to study with regard to this fundamental ethical problem within global politics. Despite the nearly ethereal perspective of her metaphysics, Wollstonecraft failed to extend her rational theological arguments for women's human rights in a perfectly universal way in rhetorical practice. Although she boldly strove to overcome the patriarchal biases of Enlightenment political philosophy in defending women's human rights, she did not rise above this intellectual tradition's cultural prejudices concerning non–Western European peoples and religions, especially Turkish Muslims. Similarly, Mill moved well beyond the cruder cultural biases of his father, James Mill, and other employees of the East India Company, particularly in rejecting the imperial supposition of India's incapacity for self-rule. He nonetheless incorporated negative stereotypes of non–Western European peoples and religions, especially Muslims and Hindus, into his liberal utilitarian arguments for human development, liberty, and rights.[3]

One explanation for these persistent cultural and religious biases is found in Wollstonecraft's and Mill's joint intellectual debt to eighteenth-century philosophies of history. Enlightenment-era theories of the history of human progress, exemplified by Scottish economist Adam Smith's *Wealth of Nations* (1776), were typically conjectural and stadial, imagining the growth of human society from its origins in terms of economic stages of hunting, shepherding, agriculture, and commercial trade. These philosophical narratives usually (at least implicitly) assumed a Western European model of commercial civilization at the pinnacle of the development process. Worse, they coded modern Western Europe as the antithesis of the "barbarian" or "savage" peoples beyond it. According to Charles W. Mills, this opposition contributed to the racist idea that white settlers and colonizers had a right to dominate nonwhites under their supposedly more "civilized" systems of republican government.[4]

Even Jean-Jacques Rousseau—whose 1749 *Discourse on the Sciences and the Arts* sought to overturn the prevailing consensus that more civilization, education, and commercial growth was better than less—still employed prejudicial assumptions about non–Western European cultures in his construction of an alternative conception

of human development. With irony that exploited and perpetuated Orientalist stereotypes, he cited the "stupid Muslim" (with his
barbaric tendency toward violent conquest, and accidental push of
classical philosophy into medieval Spain) and the ancient Egyptians
(with their superstitious and primitive science) as the progenitors of
the indolent and slavish modern civilization he hated. More obviously Eurocentric in his relative lack of irony, he specified the island
of Corsica or the mountain villages of the Swiss Valais as the ideal
locations for a truly free society.[5]

Continuing in this Enlightenment-era tradition of thinking in Eurocentric terms about human development, Wollstonecraft and Mill
upheld Western European women's social status as a cross-cultural
standard for economic, political, and cultural progress. Wollstonecraft was deeply read in the tradition of the Scottish Enlightenment
that put modern European women on such a pedestal. For example,
she defined her monistic view of the human species as a single group
with diverse potentialities against Scottish philosopher Lord Kames's
essentialist view that the species originated with plural racial groups.
Rejecting Kames's scientific racism, Wollstonecraft nonetheless took
up his Occidental slant on sex and gender. Kames contrasted "matri-
mony among savages, having no object but propagation and slavery,"
with "European education," which enabled women to be raised as
the "virtuous and refined" wives of monogamous men. As we saw in
chapter 2, Wollstonecraft eerily mirrored this Kamesian language in
her ethical objection to polygamy. While such arguments in the abstract were morally universalistic (for example, polygamy is bad for
women), they were rhetorically rooted in symbolic binaries between
the West and the rest of the world.[6]

Mill, too, was heavily influenced by the Scottish Enlightenment,
for his father's philosophy of history—found in *The History of British
India* (1817)—was part of the utilitarian tradition of applying principles of classical liberal political economy to determine the happiest
direction for humanity. John Stuart Mill's theory of human development, with its optimistic orientation toward the realization of individuality and diversity, was more speculative and forward-looking

than his father's rigid, linear, historically grounded model of stadial progress.

The cultural bias and epistemological blinders of James Mill's approach were apparent in the preface to *The History of British India*. Defending his historical method, James Mill brazenly claimed that "use of his eyes and his ears in India" was unnecessary to justify his philosophical prescription of imperial domination for it. He could learn more about India during a year of study in "his closet in England" than by traveling there or acquiring the languages. From this standpoint of cultural isolation, he could cherry-pick historical examples of Indian incompetence at self-government to legitimate British rule via his employer, the East India Company.[7]

Given James's intensive private education of John Stuart, perhaps it is to be expected, though not excused, that there was some spillover of his disturbing biases in his son's mature political philosophy. As with other historians of nineteenth-century liberalism, such as Jennifer Pitts and Karuna Mantena, I am interested in the problematic intersection of liberal and imperial ideas in John Stuart Mill's political thought, particularly in relation to India. Mill had worked for thirty-five years at the London office of the East India Company before publishing his major political works. He troublingly deployed many imperial ideas in arguing for a fundamental human right to self-development in works such as *On Liberty* and *The Subjection of Women*. These liberal imperial ideas included: (1) the conception of the relative cultural superiority of Western Europe to developing and colonized nations, (2) the use of Orientalist imagery, or symbolic caricatures of the East in opposition to the West, to support liberal reforms, (3) a tendency to contrast civilized peoples with so-called barbaric ones, (4) the assumption of the need for temporary and nontyrannical despotic government of such barbaric nations in order for them to ultimately realize republican self-government, and (5) condescension toward supposedly primitive religions beyond modern "Christian Europe."[8]

Scholars have explored how this constellation of ideas aided complex defenses of colonialism and empire in Mill's writings. Oddly, his

Subjection of Women has been left relatively untouched by such criticism. On the other hand, literary and historical scholarship has long situated Wollstonecraft's feminism in the context of eighteenth- and nineteenth-century European imperialism. Further merging the literatures on feminism, liberalism, and imperialism, this chapter provides the first extended comparative analysis of the ethics of Wollstonecraft's and Mill's Eurocentric rhetoric for women's human rights.[9]

Although they criticized the bad educations, oppressive marital arrangements, poor economic opportunities, and political disenfranchisement of women in general, Wollstonecraft and Mill typically contrasted the higher status of women in Western Europe and the United States with the lower status of women in non–Western European cultures, such as India and Turkey. Although they both deployed images of Eastern women's oppression to undermine the perceived legitimacy of patriarchy at home and abroad, such rhetorical moves were predicated on, and thus perpetuated, a slanted cultural perspective from which the Occident condescendingly looked down upon the Orient. The most pressing problem with these Eurocentric and liberal imperial ideas was their cumulative effect: the creation of a Western-biased rhetorical model for women's human rights argumentation. Wollstonecraft's Eurocentric arguments for women's progress through the advancement of their human rights, coupled with her growing iconic status as the founding philosopher of this school of thought, enhanced the salience of Orientalist prejudices within the emergent feminist cause. Published in twenty-six non-English editions, seventeen countries, twelve European languages, and three non-European languages between 1869 and 1928, Mill's *Subjection of Women* was stunningly popular on a global scale. Its international reach made it more influential than the *Rights of Woman* among both non-Western and Western first-wave feminists.[10]

Building on the work of Edward Said, Chandra Mohanty, Joyce Zonana, Inderpal Grewal, and other postcolonial theorists, I expose the power of Wollstonecraft's and Mill's Eurocentric idiom to insidiously shape prejudicial political rhetoric toward non-Western, colonized, and developing peoples. To this end, I trace the origins of an Orientalist rhetoric for women's human rights in Wollstonecraft's *Rights of Woman* and the writings of several of its most prominent early American readers: Abigail Adams (1795), Hannah Mather Crocker (1818), and Sarah Grimké (1838). I assess *The Subjection of Women* alongside the forewords to four of its earliest non–Western European editions—by Grigory Blagosvetlov and Maria Tsebrikova in Russia (1869–70), Martina Barros Borgoño in Chile (1872), and Govind Vasudev Kanitkar in colonial India (1902)—to reveal its synergies and tensions with other cultures on the woman question. Two of Wollstonecraft's non–Western European interlocutors, Olive Schreiner of South Africa (1889) and Elvira López of Argentina (1901), respectively show the struggle with cultural bias in feminist thought and the successful crafting of an international and intercultural feminist narrative.[11]

This exercise in comparative political thought makes clear how Wollstonecraft and Mill established problematic rhetorical models for women's human rights arguments that would incline toward representing non–Western European women and cultures in belittling and instrumental terms. The internalization and replication of some of these biases by Blagosvetlov, Schreiner, and Kanitkar show the insidious power of this rhetoric in colonized and developing countries. By comparing Wollstonecraft and Mill and their historic non–Western European interlocutors, I enable a cross-cultural dialogue on women's rights that underscores the importance of thinking critically about Western-biased and instrumental arguments for ending women's subjection around the globe.

This comparative reception history additionally reveals that the *Rights of Woman* and *The Subjection of Women* were used and presented as resources for thinking through problems of Westernization and women's human rights by non–Western European intellectuals. Although their particular views of Westernization varied from time, place, and ideological perspective, these non–Western European respondents to Wollstonecraft and Mill help to show how a general conception of Westernization emerged in the late nineteenth and early twentieth centuries. Whether they interpreted it as good, bad, or mixed in effects for their societies, they saw Westernization as a process of exporting or importing Western models of development (grounded in the liberal, utilitarian, and capitalist ideas of the European Enlightenment) beyond the developed nations of the North Atlantic. Non-Westerners adapt and innovate in the face of Westernization, but the process is nonetheless predicated on their dependence on the Occident.[12]

Although they sometimes perpetuated prejudice, often unreflectively, these international dialogues on the *Rights of Woman* and *The Subjection of Women* also spurred some profound critical reflection on the problem of cultural bias for feminism. Organized feminism became a global trend, with national and transnational social movements, from the early 1870s through the 1910s. Several of the earliest non–Western European interpreters of Wollstonecraft and Mill—Tsebrikova of Russia, Borgoño of Chile, and López of Argentina—show us why and how we should avoid the moral traps set by Wollstonecraft's and Mill's discriminatory language. This chapter concludes with a hopeful assessment of these non–Western European feminist thinkers' achievement of a partial yet sufficiently ethical transcendence of cultural bias, through the self-reflective adoption of "rooted," or culturally attuned, cosmopolitan perspectives in crafting universalistic, or globally applicable, arguments for women's human rights. By looking back to their examples, we may look forward to a contemporary reformulation of feminist liberalism in light of its historic concern with making culturally sensitive claims for the rights of women worldwide.[13]

The Problem of Western Prejudice in
Wollstonecraft's Rights of Woman

Wollstonecraft opened the *Rights of Woman* with a trenchant critique of the irrational prejudices of European civilization. "Men, in general," she dryly noted, "seem to employ their reason to justify prejudices." This attempt at reasoned justification was more apparent than real. As she scoffed, "They can scarcely trace" how they "imbibed" these biases, let alone use reason to "root them out." She later defined prejudice as any belief held without a reason to support it: "A prejudice is a fond obstinate persuasion for which we can give no reason; for the moment a reason can be given for an opinion, it ceases to be a prejudice, though it may be an error in judgment." Prejudices, or unjustified opinions, were prevalent and persistent because of a human tendency to think emotionally and circularly about their beliefs. People typically assumed the truth of their beliefs "because they love[d], or believe[d] them."[14]

Like Gilligan's recent rejection of the patriarchal biases behind the idea of girls' inferior moral reasoning skills, Wollstonecraft insightfully critiqued how this "mode of arguing" was "vulgarly termed a woman's reason." From Wollstonecraft's metaphysical standpoint, even the epistemological process by which prejudice was widely mistaken for true and justified belief was in itself an example of the formation of patriarchal bias. Given her universalistic view of the human mind's capabilities, there was nothing essentially female about an emotivist claim such as "it is true because I believe it, and I believe it because I love it." Rather, women were particularly susceptible to holding such prejudicial beliefs because of early gender socialization. Girls were not educated to use reason to see through the irrationality of the opinions inculcated in them by their patriarchal culture.[15]

Wollstonecraft's analysis of prejudice grew out of her reinterpretation of John Locke's and David Hume's empirical epistemologies. She entitled chapter 6 of the *Rights of Woman* "The Effect which an Early Association of Ideas Has upon the Character." Here she built on Locke and Hume to argue that the mind's "first impressions" were sense-based reflections of the empirical world. These impressions bombard our minds and together forge an "association of ideas."[16]

Whereas Hume's "laws of the association of ideas" were simply his surmise as to the laws of his science of the mind, Wollstonecraft thought humans could and should use reason to challenge the prejudicial associations of ideas that form in their minds. Hume's "laws" explained the mental formation of prejudice and nonprejudice alike.

In contrast, Wollstonecraft thought of the "association of ideas" as a process we must analytically challenge in the case of prejudice. In her hands, the epistemological concept of the "association of ideas" became a tool for critical social theory.[17]

While Hume had a more benevolent view of the ethical implications of the association of ideas, Wollstonecraft saw its insidious potential for women. Sensory impressions quickly developed into a chain of "associations that do violence to reason" if children were not given a good education. A good education would teach them how to use reason to think through the difference between rational and irrational beliefs, rather than simply imbibe the prejudices pushed upon them.[18]

Because of their bad educations, girls were more victims of this problem than boys were. Setting forth a feminist theory of subject formation, Wollstonecraft argued that girls were shaped from the crib by a "cruel association of ideas": "Every thing that they see or hear serves to fix impressions, call forth emotions, and associate ideas, that give a sexual character to the mind." Anticipating feminist readings of Foucault, Wollstonecraft interpreted the embodied psyche as a prison for girls and women under patriarchy. Patriarchal power structures set the bounds of women's meager senses of self, agency, rationality, and knowledge: "Taught from their infancy that beauty is woman's sceptre, the mind shapes itself to the body, and, roaming round its gilt cage, only seeks to adorn its prison." Because women were educated only to be attractive mates for men, their mental contents were conflated with the rudimentary sensory experiences of their bodies. Exacerbating the problem, society valued women's bodies primarily in terms of their sexual functions. Exercising their reason within the constraints set by patriarchy, women perceived their only route to power as manipulation of men through their sexuality and fertility.[19]

Although Wollstonecraft posited a rational education as the solution to the problem of prejudice, her own education did not prevent her from slipping into cultural bias—over and over again. Perhaps it was the haphazard quality of her early education, similar to that of other girls of her time, that made her less than systematic in how she identified and eradicated prejudice in her own worldview. On the other hand, her education did not prevent her from analyzing the problem of patriarchal prejudice toward and for women in general. Proceeding as though she were the exception to the rule, she at least recognized that it would be difficult for other women to overcome the tendency to think in prejudicial terms: "Still I know that it will require a considerable length of time to eradicate the firmly rooted prejudices which sensualists have planted; it will also require some time to convince women that they act contrary to their real interest on an enlarged scale." Yet her enlightened awareness of the problem of prejudice, especially for women, did not fully extend to her own case. As she strove to take what Thomas Nagel has called the "view from nowhere," she was able to see through the problem of prejudice in others, but was largely blinded to it in herself.[20]

One likely culprit was the abstraction of her metaphysical framework. The attempt to adopt a universalistic perspective on morality may mask the fact that the perspective is ineluctably rooted in a particular historical, cultural, and personal context. As Taylor has noted in his analysis of Foucault, this tendency to generalize from one's own perspective colors even the deepest critiques of our psychological bounds. For example, feminists have widely criticized Foucault for assuming a male perspective in his *History of Sexuality* (1976), even as they praise him for including the male homosexual point of view. Theorizing general patterns in human consciousness and behavior often leads us to overlook some prejudices in favor of overturning others.[21]

Immanuel Kant, like Wollstonecraft, had employed an abstract approach to defending rights for humans in the wake of the French Revolution. Despite his moral universalism on an abstract level, he denied political rights to women in modern republics because he prejudicially judged them incapable of rational self-governance. Wollstonecraft fell prey to the obverse problem: exposing the prejudices that harmed women in general but failing to critically assess a range of cultural biases that compromised the universalism of her feminist argumentation.

Another culprit for Wollstonecraft's cultural biases was her religious standpoint. Given the dissenting Christian theological foundation for her ethics, Wollstonecraft had "imbibed" many Protestant biases toward non–Western European religions, especially Islam and Russian Orthodoxy. Wollstonecraft also followed French and Scottish Enlightenment philosophers such as Montesquieu, Voltaire, and Smith in casting the Roman Catholic countries of southern Europe as nests of indolence and other forms of cultural backwardness. She followed her theological mentor Richard Price in designating the "blind" slavery of "a Spaniard, a Russian, or a Turk" as the antithesis of free and responsible Western Protestants—particularly those noble Christians in the abolition movement. What these three non-Protestant religions—Roman Catholicism, Russian Orthodoxy, and Islam—had in common were origins and institutional centers beyond Western Europe.[22]

Although Wollstonecraft found the "civilization of the bulk of the people of Europe" to be "very partial" toward men in power, she was certain it was worse elsewhere for her sex—particularly in the Muslim cultural outpost of Turkey. She was well traveled within Europe, trekking to Portugal, Ireland, France, Sweden, Norway, Denmark, and northern Germany. Yet her journeys seemed only to reinforce her haughty cultural preferences for Paris and London. Despite what she judged as her culture's condescending view of women's capabilities, Wollstonecraft consistently judged Western Europe and its North American colonies as superior to virtually every other culture in the world. "Scarcely human" and "sluggish" peasants of rural Scandinavia, wife-abusing Russians, Chinese foot binders, lazy southern Europeans, Roman Catholic "vermin," tyrannical Egyptians, oversexed Tahitians, and voluptuous Turkish Muslims were all symbolic targets of her culturally biased arguments in favor of women's human rights. Ironically, all this disdain came from an endlessly indebted, middle-class, Anglo-Irish woman from a broken home.[23]

Wollstonecraft drew her negative caricatures of non-Western cultures, especially the Muslim peoples of Turkey and North Africa, from books by European explorers. Like the elder Mill, she followed the Enlightenment-era approach of studying Eastern cultures in her "closet." Wollstonecraft's frequent resort to anti–Turkish Muslim rhetoric probably arose from the politics of the time. Turkey was at war with both Russia and Austria from 1787 until 1791, the year she wrote the *Rights of Woman*. Earlier in the eighteenth century, Lady Mary Wortley Montagu had written home to Britain with relatively kind words about her experiences within Turkish culture, including the secret female world of the seraglios. By the late eighteenth century, however, the Ottomans were generally misrepresented to the Western European public as "barbarians" who viewed women as soulless creatures, unworthy of the same afterlife as men. In fact, it was a Western-made myth that Muslims believed women had no souls and thus no access to paradise.[24]

The rhetorical power of such Orientalist prejudices was not lost on Wollstonecraft. She literally began and ended the *Rights of Woman* with images of women's servitude in Eastern cultures. In the opening lines of the introduction, she inveighed against "men of genius" who "in the true style of Mahometanism" conceptualized women as "subordinate beings," not as "part of the human species." A few paragraphs later, she bewailed that women were raised to be "weak beings . . . only fit for a seraglio!" In the final sentence of the book, she rebuked European men for being "Egyptian task-masters" to underscore the injustice of their enslavement of women even in the age of "reason" and "rights."[25]

As Marilyn Butler and Janet Todd argued in their annotations to the *Rights of Woman*, each of these symbolic references to the Orient was likely rooted in contemporary British prejudices toward Turkey. As early as 1717, Lady Montagu had challenged the British misconception that the Turkish Muslims were barbaric because they did not believe women had souls. The Turkish seraglio, or the private living quarters of the wives and concubines in a Muslim household in the Ottoman Empire, likewise fascinated the European public. Such polygamous Muslim households often served as symbols of Oriental sexual perversity, which buffed the veneer of Occidental sexual restraint. Since the Ottoman Empire occupied Egypt for most of the eighteenth century, Wollstonecraft's "Egyptian task-master" metaphor obliquely jabbed the Turkish even as it rallied Protestants around a familiar biblical and abolitionist trope.[26]

There is a likely unintended irony in Wollstonecraft's use of anti-Turkish rhetoric to shore up her feminist critique of the master-slave dynamic. Wollstonecraft denounced the vicious cycle of patriarchal oppression—with its arbitrary husbands, manipulative wives, despotic mothers, and tyrannized children—in morally universal terms. She nonetheless exploited the view of Turkish Muslims as particularly prone to the moral vices that civilized Europeans ought to avoid. Revealing her superficial understanding of Ottoman culture, she compared European wives to "Turkish bashaws" (sic). Technically, these pashaws were high-ranking Turkish military officers, but Wollstonecraft reduced them to an instrumental stereotype. She deployed the "bashaws" as symbols of the master-slave dynamic that she sought to expose in male-female relations. Women, she wrote, like the Turkish officers, "cunningly obtain power by playing on the weakness" of their male superiors but sacrifice "virtue" and "respectability" to the "temporary gratifications" of such "illicit sway."[27]

Moving beyond metaphor into a kind of Montesquieuian sociology, Wollstonecraft claimed that this type of "despotism that kills virtue and genius in the bud" may "hover over Europe," but it "desolates Turkey." The sexual subtext of her argument surfaced alongside her Orientalist prejudices: Turkish despotism, especially in the seraglios, had caused the spread of venereal disease, making "men, as well as the soil, unfruitful." Her account of Turkey as desolated by male infertility functioned as a veiled threat to European men (perhaps especially those who frequented the Turkish baths in London) and especially their wives. After all, the women faced the dire consequences of their husbands' extramarital sexual traffic: venereal disease was a major contributor to eighteenth-century mothers' and children's ill health and early deaths.[28]

Wollstonecraft proposed a solution, which was predicated on a culturally biased binary: either Western women could ignore the cyclical problem of despotism and be "shut up" in their homes like "eastern princes," or they could be "educated in such a manner as to be able to think and act for themselves." Both routes negated the worth of the Muslim wife by transforming the Western wife into either an "eastern prince" or a bearer of equal rights. This binary, in turn, presumed that Eastern governments were despotic and therefore inferior to emergent Western conceptions of rights-based republicanism as nondomination.[29]

By framing and interweaving the first major philosophical treatise on women's human rights with such Orientalist metaphors, Wollstonecraft was the author of a double-edged tradition: a feminist liberalism with both humanist and imperialist sides. Contra the patriarchal apologists, such as Edmund Burke and Rousseau, she upheld the feminist humanist idea of women as part of the human species and therefore entitled to the same rights as men. Yet she relied on demeaning images of Eastern, especially Turkish Muslim, peoples to signal the moral importance of the liberation of women in general. She thus implied that Eastern women and men must be Westernized in order to be free. The obverse implication was that Western women and men must resist a "return" to the passions of Eastern "barbarism" in order to fully realize the rational freedom of their superior culture. These two sides—humanist and imperial—of the feminist liberalism born of Wollstonecraft are not necessarily tied together, for we shall see in the remainder of this chapter how later feminist liberals have achieved partial yet sufficiently ethical transcendence of such Western imperial biases. Rather, the prejudices of Wollstonecraft and some of her followers ought to be understood as historically situated products of a Western European culture that was, according to Pitts, in the midst of a "turn to empire."[30]

Wollstonecraft's reproduction of the symbolic binary between Eastern seraglios and Western morality may be read as an early iteration of a trend in British imperial feminism. According to Grewal's study of late nineteenth-century British feminist activism concerning India, "the discourse of the woman 'caged' in the harem, in purdah, becomes the necessary Other for the construction of the Englishwoman presumably free and happy in the home." Wollstonecraft offered an Enlightenment variation on this theme: the women in the seraglios of Turkey served as the "necessary Other" to construct the greater possibility of women's freedom in Europe, and the rest of the world's hopeful emulation of it. As Zonana cogently observed, the "feminist orientalist" rhetorical strategy of the *Rights of Woman* was to demand that "the West rid itself of its oriental ways, becoming as a consequence more Western—that is, more rational, enlightened, reasonable." While Wollstonecraft's primary goal was to make Western Europe "more Western," she also reinforced the notion of the subordinate position of the East in relation to Western advancement.[31]

In the *Rights of Woman*, Wollstonecraft exposed the hypocrisy of Rousseau's unduly sexualized prescriptions for female education by insinuating their affinities with the luxury and decadence of Turkish Muslim polygamy: "In a seraglio, I grant, that all these arts are necessary; the epicure must have his palate tickled, or he will sink into apathy; but have women so little ambition as to be satisfied with such a condition?" When Wollstonecraft summoned "women" in this highly rhetorical question, she connoted that European wives ought to have more "ambition" than their counterparts in the seraglio. The rhetorical dimension of this question, however, does not rebuff its prejudice. Although she took an ironic, or unexpected, position by granting the "necessity" of women's sexual "arts" in the seraglio, she clearly demarcated such Eastern homes as ruled by "necessity" and thus inhospitable to Western ideas of freedom.[32]

Wollstonecraft's Orientalist women's human rights discourse represented a kind of global feminist imperialism. From her late eighteenth-century standpoint, she presumed women's current oppression not only in the East but worldwide. Yet she situated patriarchal oppression on a slope—with non–Western European cultures at the bottom, and Western Europe and its North Atlantic colonies at the top. As Samara Cahill has shown, there was nothing absolute or "essential" about this slope: Wollstonecraft thought that Eastern peoples could, and should, close the gap between themselves and the West. Like Mill after her, she did not assume that non–Western

European peoples were absolutely incapable of progress, because of some essential flaw in their natures or cultures. Her rhetoric, however, publicly bolstered the idea of Western supremacy in a way that stood in conflict with her universalistic ethics.[33]

For Wollstonecraft, Western culture was almost as culpable for women's oppression as the non-Western cultures it had partly surpassed. Western European culture, through reverence for its "men of genius," continued to profess unenlightened ideas about women. Even John Milton, the author of the greatest English Protestant epic poem, wrote in the "true Mahometan strain" with regard to Eve being "made to please" Adam. Burke likewise had not "steered clear of the mussulman's creed" when he endorsed women's seclusion in home and family. Wollstonecraft accused Rousseau of the sensuality of a Turkish sultan for professing that "a girl should be educated for her husband with the same care as for an eastern haram [sic]." By mocking these Western "men of genius" with her caricatures of Islam, Wollstonecraft suggested that Western culture had advanced to a point where it could and should cast off patriarchal hierarchies and other "vestiges of barbarism."[34]

Given the international success of the *Rights of Woman*, Wollstonecraft established a morally problematic yet politically influential rhetorical model for making women's human rights arguments. Historians of feminism and imperialism have traced the lingering impact of this Orientalist idiom on nineteenth-century feminist authors and activists from Britain—such as Mary Robinson, Emily Brontë, Harriet Martineau, and Millicent Fawcett. Grewal has inventively shown the ideological drift of this discourse among late nineteenth-century colonized Indian women, who reversed many Western stereotypes of their "harems" to expose the moral problems with British imperial ideas of womanhood and family. According to Grewal, such symbolic reversals challenged imperial domination yet reproduced the binaries between East and West on a different bias.[35]

Both the humanist and the imperialist sides of Wollstonecraft's feminist liberalism found a welcoming home in the United States. It was a conflicted young liberal democracy, which had recently rewritten its constitution. Between 1787 and 1791, the Americans had reinforced the legitimacy of chattel slavery at the same time as they pushed forward a bill of individual rights for white male citizens. In postrevolutionary America, we find further evidence for Zonana's provocative thesis that "the feminist orientalist strategy introduced by Wollstonecraft came to pervade nineteenth-century feminist discourse," whether "through direct influence or simply because the ideas on which she drew were circulating freely within the culture."[36]

From its publication in Boston and Philadelphia in 1792, the *Rights of Woman* attracted an enthusiastic audience among American Protestant women who advocated education reform, abolition, public benevolence, temperance, and suffrage. In this book they found a rhetorical style that resonated with their own modes of argument for women's human rights. In 1795, soon after reading the *Rights of Woman* with Vice President John Adams, First Lady Abigail Adams complained to her husband about the "more than Egyptian Bondage, to which the Female Sex, have been subjugated, from the earliest ages." The *Rights of Woman* had argued that women were "educated in worse than Egyptian bondage."[37]

The "Egyptian bondage" metaphor had multiple meanings in Wollstonecraft and the Adamses' shared Anglo dissenting Christian context. When John Adams was an ambassador in London in the 1780s, he and his wife had frequented Price's church at Newington Green at the same time as Wollstonecraft. Although it is not known if they met, they certainly heard similar sermons, fraught with allusions to the "darkness and superstition" of the "Mahometans and Papists." On both sides of the Atlantic, the allegory of the liberation of Moses and the Jews from Egypt was a common framework for late eighteenth-century Christian abolitionist narratives of progress—such as by the freed African slave and poet Phillis Wheatley of Boston.[38]

Like Wollstonecraft, Abigail Adams exploited the salience of these symbols and their multiple meanings for different audiences. Perhaps to assuage her conservative husband, she made her critique of patriarchy less universal by claiming that the "attention paid to the Education of Females in America" had raised their nation above the rest of the world just "within these last 15 years." Framed within this rising imperial feminist idiom of the North Atlantic, Eastern despotisms appeared more prone to subjecting women to "Egyptian bondage" than Western rights-based republics such as the United States and France. This was certainly an ironic contrast given the constitutional legitimacy of the evil of slavery and the formal exclusion of women from citizenship in the United States, and the systematic retrenchment of women's rights in France during the radical stage of the French Revolution and the Napoleonic era.[39]

In the early nineteenth century, the two most significant American philosophers of women's human rights were Crocker and Grimké. Crocker's *Observations on the Real Rights of Women* (1818) and Grimké's *Letters on the Equality of the Sexes* (1838) were both published in Boston. These book-length treatises reflected the city's long-standing openness toward issues of abolition, female education reform, and women's public activism. Crocker and Grimké's books also contributed to the feminist imperial discourse that the reception of Wollstonecraft's *Rights of Woman* had helped to transport around the Atlantic world.

Crocker favorably cited Wollstonecraft several times in the *Observations* and continued her philosophical forerunner's assault on "the idea of the inferiority of female nature." A liberal Congregationalist theologian, Crocker followed Wollstonecraft in her concern with refuting the religious notion that women have inferior souls to men, or no souls at all, leaving them incapable of the same (or perhaps any) salvation. Building on a widespread Western misconception of Islam at the turn of the nineteenth century, they both associated this "general view" of a metaphysical sex inequality with the "mahometans both of Asia and Europe." Crocker cited Lady Montagu's rejection of the Western presumption that Turkish Muslims did not believe women have souls. But Crocker held on to the view that "mahometans" believed in the natural inferiority of the female soul. She represented this patriarchal idea as backward and Islamic, and pointedly contrasted it with the egalitarian views of "our God," found in the "religion of the gospel."[40]

This (often implicit) contrast between our God and your Islamic barbarism also animated Grimké's attempt to craft a transnational feminist abolitionism in her *Letters*. In an extended section of the book in which she examined the lowly status of women across the world's cultures, Grimké reported that "pigs, dogs, women, and other impure animals" are treated as equivalents under the "Mohammedan law." A Quaker preacher who began life on a Southern plantation, Grimké presented her comparative reflections—drawn from books and personal witness—as sociological fact. Capitalizing on the stereotype of Muslim women's severe oppression, she noted the "resemblance between the situation of women in heathen and Mohammedan countries, and our brethren and sisters of color in this Christian land." Her use of impersonal language imparted an emotional distance to her description of the condition of Muslim women, while her invocation of the "our" sought to foster a sense of deep sympathy in her American abolitionist audience for their "sisters of color" in the South. Such rhetorical moves illustrated what Grewal has identified as the (often latent) imperial and cultural biases of transnational feminist narratives. Next, we shall see how Mill's *Subjection of Women* also fell into this pattern of presenting a North Atlantic standard for women's (and civilizational) progress, in a time when British imperialism had reached peak power.[41]

The Ethics of Instrumental and Eurocentric Rhetoric in Mill's Subjection of Women

Mill's liberal utilitarianism was his philosophical attempt to correct classical utilitarianism's neglect of individual rights in favor of promoting the greatest good for the greatest number. His answer to his father and Jeremy Bentham was to define individual self-development, in all its rich eccentricity, as the indirect path to the greatest good, or utility, of the human species. His liberal utilitarian emphasis on both the public and the personal utility of human rights made his school of thought a rich philosophical and political resource for feminism. Yet the utilitarian dimension of his liberalism lent itself to a rhetorical pathology: defending women's human rights in terms of public utility may make it look as though (or worse, feel as though) women's freedom was primarily a tool for development outcomes beyond their individual well-being.

In the context of debates on Westernization, such instrumental arguments might conceive of women's human rights as a means for advancing Western models of economic growth or education. Perhaps most problematically for feminism, instrumental arguments can imply that the issue of women's human rights is secondary to some other purpose. Conditions of cultural or political imperialism, including colonialism, can exacerbate the ethical problems associated with this form of reasoning. If an argument for women's human rights assumes the superiority of Western culture over another culture, then it contributes to the legitimation of the idea of Western domination over other cultures. Women's human rights, ironically, can become a means for supporting cultural imperialism, even though the concept's aim is to liberate all women from conditions of domination.[42]

The inequalities of power that colonized or developing peoples face in national and international politics make the rhetorical and ethical implications of such instrumental feminist arguments even worse. As Mohanty has argued, feminism can be represented as a tool handed down to colonized or developing peoples for their advancement according to a higher Western standard. The construction of women's human rights as an instrument of Western reform only contributes to the misperception that the indigenous culture is inferior and lacking its own resources for enabling women's empowerment.[43]

Through an analysis of the Western biases and instrumental feminist argumentation of *The Subjection of Women*, we see how its rhetoric sets up a liberal imperial model for women's human rights arguments. The book opens with Mill's attack on the customs that keep women subjected to men in nineteenth-century society, even in "all the countries of Christian Europe." Mill critiqued the endurance of the antiquated practice of the "social subordination of women" in an otherwise civilized Western Europe by confronting his readers with an extended counterfactual: imagine that St. Paul's Cathedral in London—the epicenter of the Church of England—did not exist, but instead a "gigantic" megalithic "dolmen" or a "vast" Roman pagan temple of "Jupiter Olympius" was still used by British Protestants for their daily worship. This complex metaphor suggested that the subjection of women was a "relic" of primitive culture and religion, which Western Europeans ought to entirely transcend.[44]

These locutions had the effect of locating Mill's conception of modern civilization in Western Europe, particularly a "civilized and Christian England." Granted, this bias is unsurprising for a man of Mill's culture and status, but it is nonetheless one that contributes to a series of rhetorical oppositions between Western Europe and the rest of the world. In chapter 2, he stated that Christianity "has been the religion of the progressive portion of mankind, and Islamism, Brahminism, &c., have been those of the stationary portions; or rather . . . the declining portions." Although Mill scholars have shown that he did not designate Muslim and Hindu cultures as permanently stagnant or absolutely incapable of development, the quoted statement implied their relative—yet likely long-term—cultural inferiority to "Christian Europe." Trading on the religious biases of his Western European, and especially English Protestant, audience, Mill employed a series of mutually reinforcing rhetorical binaries in *The Subjection of Women:* women's rights/women's subjection; Western Europe/Eastern cultures; European Christianity/Hinduism and Islam.[45]

In chapter 2, Mill identified the institution of patriarchal marriage as the effective cause of the enduring subjection of women across modern societies from East to West. Although he identified it as a global source of women's contemporary subjection to men, he conceptualized patriarchal marriage not in universal and culturally nonspecific but in primitivist and Orientalist terms. Patriarchal marriage was a "relic of primitive barbarism" and thus existed "under a varnish of civilization and cultivation" in developed countries. In a series of prejudicial rhetorical moves, he associated the barbarism of patriarchal marriage with Eastern cultures and religions.[46]

Mill used familiar Orientalist symbols such as the "odalisque" to develop his critical account of female domestic servitude in patriarchal marriages. In contending "it was wrong to bring up women with any acquirements but those of an odalisque, or a domestic servant," he likened European wives to female slaves sequestered in the Turkish seraglio. Capitalizing on his nineteenth-century Occidental male audience's intrigue with the dark, sensual Middle Eastern "other," he cast a female Muslim servant as a negative yet sexually charged trope in his argument for women's right to higher education. The odalisque, in this discursive context, represented the basest yet most exotic form of female subordination: enslavement to female slaves and their polygamous sultan. She was a metaphorical object of conflicted, Christian European male desire and judgment, not a human subject in a different religious tradition who was as entitled to education as the European wife.[47]

Mill furthermore adopted the alluring yet taboo setting of the seraglio as a mirror for exposing to European eyes the perverse effects of patriarchy on both spouses. He compared a European wife to a "Sultan's favorite slave," in order to show that "the desirable thing would be that she should neither have slaves nor be a slave." He complained of the "sublime and sultan-like" self-image of men in the patriarchal family. Breaking down the distinction between the symbolic and the real, he went so far as to speak for "the women in the harem of an Oriental" by claiming that they "do not complain of not being allowed the freedom of European women. They think our women insufferably bold and unfeminine." Like Wollstonecraft with her Orientalist strategies, Mill took advantage of the European salience of anti-Muslim stereotypes to make arguments for women's human rights that treat Muslim culture as contrary to the progressive feminist values of Western Europe.[48]

Mill's rhetorical strategies on behalf of women's rights also targeted Indian culture. Mill cited the "violent abuse" of women in "Hindoo writings" as evidence of the "Oriental" view that "women are by nature peculiarly voluptuous." By contrasting this sexual and violent "Oriental" view of women with milder and merely "ridiculous" European chauvinistic attitudes, he reinforced the idea of European preeminence over Asian cultures on the question of women's status. He also belied his "latent," or unreflective, Orientalism in sketching Asian women as what Said has called "creatures of a male power-fantasy."[49]

Invoking the authority of his work for the East India Company, Mill explained how his "long official knowledge of Hindu governments" gave him insight into the "natural capacity of women for government." In a backhanded compliment, he noted that Indian women have been competent and prolonged legal regents of principalities during the minorities of male heirs, despite the fact that "these princesses have never been seen in public, have never conversed with any man not of their own family except from behind a curtain, that they don't read, and if they did, there is no book in their languages which can give them the smallest instruction in political affairs." Despite his other writings on the value of indigenous Indian cultures and languages, Mill here marshaled British presumptions about the colonized Indians—including illiteracy, cultural bankruptcy, and political ineptitude—for the sake of an argument for women's "natural" capacity for governmental leadership.[50]

In chapter 4, Mill laid out his major instrumental argument for the institutionalization of equal rights between the sexes. The effect of "giving to women the free use of their faculties," "leaving them the free choice of their employments," and "opening to them the same field of occupation and the same prizes and encouragements as to other human beings" would be "that of doubling the mass of mental faculties available for the higher service of humanity." By arguing that women's full development as human beings would double economic and civilizational progress, Mill opened the door for women's rights to be seen and used as a tool for development, rather than for the well-being of individual women. He concluded the book with a telling reminder that his own end goal in defending women's rights was to enhance "all that makes life valuable to the individual human being." In light of this, he cannot in all fairness be understood as a straightforward imperialist on the issue of women's human rights or any other political issue. While his feminist arguments were sometimes imperial in implication and (as we shall see) in subsequent application by other thinkers, his rights-based individualistic liberalism also endowed his political theory with cosmopolitan potential for the woman question.[51]

The rhetorical advantage of privileging the Western-biased point of view over the cosmopolitan, or culturally attuned yet universalistic, perspective on justice was not lost on Mill, however. He freely admitted that he had to persuade British and European men in positions of political power to adopt the cause of women's human rights in order for the movement to succeed. In chapter 4, he likened discrimination against women to the discrimination that men in "unenlightened societies" face: "What, in unenlightened societies, colour, race, religion, or in the case of a conquered country, nationality, are to some men, sex is to all women; a preemptory exclusion from almost all honorable occupations." Even as he was issuing a universal critique of unjust discrimination on the basis of race, religion, and sex, he wielded the prejudiced binary between "unenlightened" societies and Western societies to motivate European men to protect their wives and daughters from such discrimination. Ironically, both the Western biases and the instrumental feminist arguments of *The Subjection of Women* have led it to be engaged on the issues of women's human rights and development, as illustrated by the comparative analysis of two of its early non–Western European forewords from Russia and colonial India.[52]

Reflecting Cultural Bias: The Subjection of Women in "Westernizing" Russia and British India

James Scanlan and Douglas Howland have provided the most extensive studies of Mill's translation and reception beyond Western Europe, in late nineteenth-century Russia, Japan, and China. *The Subjection of Women* has been credited as an inspiration for feminists in nineteenth-century North and South America, Russia, Japan, and Continental Europe, as well as Britain and its empire, including India and New Zealand. By comparing the forewords to *The Subjection of Women* by Blagosvetlov (1869) and Kanitkar (1902), we see how local intellectuals from Russia and colonial India situated the book's ideas in the context of their own debates on development and Westernization. Demonstrating the power of Mill's Orientalist rhetoric to insidiously shape public discourse, these two non–Western European intellectuals reproduced some of his cultural biases in crafting their own arguments for women's human rights.[53]

The Russian feminist movement had gained steam in the late 1850s with a debate over medical careers for women, as some had served as nurses in the Crimean War. Vera Pavlovna—the heroine of Chernyshevsky's influential novel *What Is to Be Done?* (1863)—expressed the radical idea that economic independence, not merely sexual or personal freedom, enabled a woman's realization of her full humanity. Women's clubs, devoted to charity, education, and business ventures such as publishing Russian translations of English works, emerged in St. Petersburg in the early 1860s. The "drive to higher education" for and by women in Russia commenced in 1868. Six printings of *The Subjection of Women* in St. Petersburg in 1869–70 was another milestone for the growing Russian feminist movement.[54]

Prior to 1869, Mill was already influential in Russian intellectual and political life. Around the time that he sponsored the women's suffrage petition in the British Parliament in 1867, he corresponded with a friend in Russia about the movement to establish a women's university there. Evident in the letter was the Western bias of Mill's theory of women's rights, as shown in his supposition that Russia would "prove that a nation relatively recently civilized grasps the great ideas of amelioration sooner than the older ones." Blagosvetlov and the other radical journalists who penned forewords to Russian editions of Mill's *Subjection of Women* duly noted the Western bias of Mill's philosophy of women's rights that led him to situate their nation as "recently civilized" on the scale of European civilization. To varying degrees, they accepted or disputed this view in using Mill's ideas to outline their distinctive accounts of how to advance the rights of women in the context of political debates on Westernization, economic development, and populist reform in Russia.[55]

Blagosvetlov (1824–80) was born in Stavropol. He trekked to England in 1857 to live and study with the radical expatriate Russian journalist Alexander Herzen (1812–70). Returning to St. Petersburg via Paris in 1860, he founded the journal *Delo* (the *Cause*) there in 1866. For his commitment to the 1861 emancipation of the serfs, the rights of women, and individual liberty, Blagosvetlov was described in one nineteenth-century Russian biography as an "extreme radical Westernizer." The Westernizers challenged the philosophy of the Slavophiles, pitting the idea of "free, autonomous personality" against the demand to a return "to the old Slavic principles of 'community life.'" According to Andrzej Walicki, Russian Westernism was not "a homogenous school of thought" but rather a "common denominator" for intellectuals who "believed Russia might and should follow the general pattern of European progress." Blagosvetlov's foreword to his 1869 edition of *The Subjection of Women* set forth his vision of Westernization in Russia by building on the Orientalist and instrumental feminist arguments, as much as the liberal individualism, of Mill.[56]

Blagosvetlov began his foreword by upholding the "social status of women" as one of the "main issues of contemporary European philosophy." Yet he situated Russia outside this debate, since it was "two centuries behind from where, in the sphere of intellectual culture, the English find themselves in the present time." He called for the immediate practical implementation of Mill's philosophy of women's rights in Russia: "The question is not whether it is timely to hold here a discussion of emancipation of women as it is understood by people of higher intellectual culture" but rather "to what extent a Russian society is able to reduce and eliminate those obstacles that stand in the way of carrying out this great life goal of the contemporary generation."[57]

Deploying the Orientalist imagery found in Mill's work to rhetorically distance himself from the Slavophiles, Blagosvetlov stated that

"Russia can no longer go back to its old Asiatic stillness." Against these nationalists' romanticization of Russia's supposedly republican past, he upheld "European civilization" as the "role model for her future prosperity," not "the aged Eastern heritage that our pseudo patriots are ready to perceive as uniqueness or majestic serenity." Employing one of Mill's images from the Turkish seraglio, he proposed that Russia should face the question of whether it would "benefit by allowing a woman to obtain an independent status, i.e. if we make a real mother out of a simple wet nurse, if we make a free member of the family out of a household maid, a real loving wife out of a harem odalisque, a lively and active force out of a dead social material?" While Mill had contrasted his subversive and "disturbing" ideal of the educated woman with the "odalisque" or "domestic servant," Blagosvetlov revealed the limits of his feminism with his rather conservative opposition of the "harem odalisque" to the "real loving wife" to be produced by Russian women's liberation. Following Mill's rhetoric more closely, he demarcated progress and feminism as Western European values by using Asiatic and Muslim caricatures to mock the backwardness of the Slavophiles on these issues. Although these tropes had an ironic sense in the context of Russia's place between East and West, they still had the rhetorical effect of casting women's human rights as a Western imperative.[58]

Building on Mill's liberal utilitarianism, Blagosvetlov applied the main instrumental feminist argument from chapter 4 of *The Subjection of Women* to Russia. He predicted that equal rights in Russia would mean double the economic productivity: "Two hundred years of people's activity under the same social conditions would be reduced to one hundred years, and for underdeveloped people that saves an enormous amount of labor and time." Advancing women's human rights was not primarily about promoting women's freedom and personal development but rather a step in the process of giving Russia "a right to declare itself to be an educated people rather than a useless one."[59]

Westernization, development, and women's human rights were also at the forefront of the minds of turn-of-the-century Indian intellectuals, who often addressed these issues from the standpoint of their colonization by Britain. Kanitkar of Maharashtra translated and introduced the Marathi edition of *The Subjection of Women* in 1902. Building on the postcolonial theory of Frantz Fanon, Jayanti Patel, and Said, I argue that Kanitkar's philosophical response to *The Subjection of Women* represents the "assimilation" stage of the colonial intellectual. Kanitkar appropriated a colonial British model of using Mill's liberal feminism to endorse Westernization for the development of India. His treatment of the woman question within his colonial predicament in many ways mirrored the ironies of Blagosvetlov's liminal position as a Russian Westernizer who challenged his traditional patriarchal culture.[60]

An indigenous, prenationalistic feminist movement had grown in India by the 1870s, especially in the region of Maharashtra. According to Rosalind O'Hanlan, a public debate emerged in this decade in western India on "the ways in which Indian and Hindu women might develop and transform themselves, whilst preserving what was best in 'traditional' culture." It was in this context that the Marathi translator Kanitkar (1854–1918) came to address the women's issue. Kanitkar was a poet, reformer, and subjudge in the colonial legal system. In the late 1860s, he joined a group of his male, Brahmin friends in implementing their liberal ideas "by educating their own child-wives." These women, led by Kanitkar's wife, Kashibai (1861–1948), organized their own feminist society, Striyancha Sabha, in 1880s Maharashtra. The all-female group read Austen, Eliot, and *The Subjection of Women*, and promoted the cause of women's education in the region. The couple came to embody the model of companionate marriage among intellectual equals that was popular in late nineteenth-century Brahmin society.[61]

Kanitkar recalled his own exposure to *The Subjection of Women* around 1870, when he married Kashibai and entered university. In 1872, he published *Sushikshit Stricharitra*, which explored the traditional ideal of "pativrata," or the chaste and devoted wife, and its compatibility with education. Contrary to traditionalists who thought education would make Indian women unfaithful and rebellious, Kanitkar argued that education would make mothers and daughters more chaste and respectable.[62]

Kanitkar's foreword recalled how he finally fulfilled his "sacred duty" to translate the treatise into Marathi after years of contemplating the project. With a kind of stoicism that belied a deeper sense of loss in the wake of British cultural imperialism, he supplied his motivation for translating the book: "The language of Maharashtra may or may not flourish in the future." His translation also had a reformist agenda: undermine the "ridicule" of the "topic of the 'subjection of women'" in local Indian culture. To show that ancient Hinduism shared Mill's deep respect for women, he cited the Sanskrit epic Mahabharata: "The wife is a man's half. The wife is the first of friends."[63]

Recounting how he first translated selections of *The Subjection of Women* for the "popular magazines 'Manoranjan' and 'Nibandhchandrika' in Pune" around 1890, Kanitkar metaphorically addressed Mill's book as though it was an Englishwoman he had been courting: "O lady! It has been several years—almost 20 years—since I chanced upon your liberal and charming character. At the time, I had just been admitted to university; since the day, I had a deep wish to acquire you! But you were a foreigner! You were born in the bountiful land of the independent and triumphant English! So, how could you be acquired by a poor Brahmin like me! My mind would return to you again and again. Finally, I made the determination to forcefully clothe you in a Maharashtrian costume and bring you to my people!" This strikingly sexual and latently violent representation of Mill's book as a "liberal" English "lady" whom Kanitkar "forcefully" clothed in the "costume" of his native language illustrated his predicament as a colonial intellectual. In attempting to assimilate the Western liberal feminist values of Mill while adapting them to some of the traditional values of his own culture, Kanitkar reproduced in his writing the imbalances of power caused by the intersection of patriarchy and colonialism in India. In imagining the translation of Mill's book as "forcefully" fitting it into the clothing of his language, he indulged in a troubling symbolic reversal of British cultural imperialism. He declared his ambivalence to the "lady" with an emotional reference to the *Mahabharata:* "I both want you and do not want you! Or, like the cursed Dushyant . . . wanted to both accept Shakuntala and reject her, I am in a similarly strange state of mind." Torn by reverence of the English lady and desire to conquer her, Kanitkar modestly chose to clothe her—dramatizing what Fanon has called the colonized male's feeling of emasculation in the face of the political rape of imperialism.[64]

Kanitkar asserted "that the importance of women's rights should be pointed out and discussed with quiet and serious consideration." Demonstrating such "quiet" consideration, he did not use his own words but rather quoted the British colonial Theosophist Annie Besant. Kanitkar implied that he agreed with Besant's views on teaching indigenous Indian women some English alongside their native tongue: "The main motivation for this is so that she develops communion with her English-knowing husband and children." Again borrowing words from Besant, he stated: "The Indian woman will never lose her devotion, but her devotion must be coupled with knowledge." Kanitkar aimed this colonial instrumental argument for female education toward the preservation of indigenous women's "devotion" to, and "communion" with, their more educated, Westernized husbands and male children.[65]

Kanitkar's feminist proposals were muted by design, in order to rhetorically appease his conservative audience's fears that "all women will revolt against men" if liberated. He soothed their concerns: "It is extremely unlikely that conventions and thinking which have been rooted very deeply for thousands of years in this soil called society, will be uprooted or eroded through discussions." Kanitkar's gradualist approach to feminist reform oriented itself toward the advancement of Westernization in British India. Situating the progressive liberal values of the West against the traditionalist indigenous culture, Kanitkar began his discussion of women's rights by stating, "'A woman does not deserve freedom' . . . is a principle or a theory well-known in our country. Taking the opposing viewpoint, Mr. Mill wrote a small excellent treatise with the support of his wife in 1861 and named it *Subjection of Women.*" Although he acknowledged that cultural differences between India and England meant that "Indian ladies" could not be "given the same type of education as in England," he thought that training in English would mean that indigenous women would "get directly acquainted with one of the strongest influences on the recent progress in India." Kanitkar assumed a British standard of excellence for reform of female education, and progress in general, in India. In so doing, he slyly pushed his stubbornly traditionalist society toward a Westernized conception of "equality of rights."[66]

Situated between the 1885 establishment of the Indian National Congress and the post-1917 nationalist independence movement, the Marathi preface to *The Subjection of Women* provides a fascinating example of the internal conflicts that arise when a colonial society faces the prospect of radical political change. Caught up in the colonial assimilationist spirit, Kanitkar attempted to initiate changes within Indian culture—such as the Westernized education of women—to bring it into alignment with British culture, while avoiding suspicion from Indian traditionalists. Separated by decades, languages, and national politics, Blagosvetlov's and Kanitkar's responses to *The Subjection of Women* nonetheless operated within a shared political context: the unequal international power relations set by Westernization. Like Mill's, Blagosvetlov's and Kanitkar's intellectual and rhetorical relationships to Western notions of progress limited the scope of their otherwise visionary commitments to women's human rights.

Struggling with Cultural Bias: The Rights of Woman *in Colonial South Africa*

Olive Schreiner, the white South African writer famous for her 1883 feminist novel *The Story of an African Farm*, grappled with the problem of cultural bias in her reflections on the relevance of the *Rights of Woman* for relations between black and white women in her colonial nation. As Carolyn Burdett has recounted, Schreiner traveled to London in 1881 with the manuscript for her novel. There she was active in Karl Pearson's "Men's and Women's Club" (which originally was to be named after Wollstonecraft) from 1885 to 1886.

In Pearson's circle, she was introduced to the publisher Walter Scott. Learning of her interest in theorizing the late Victorian "sex question," Scott encouraged the young feminist to introduce a new centennial edition of the *Rights of Woman*.[67]

Schreiner worked on her Wollstonecraft project for three years but abandoned it around the time she returned to South Africa in 1889. In the late 1890s, she took the pro-Boer stance in the Second Boer War between British and Dutch settlers over control of the South African territories of the Transvaal Republic and the Orange Free State. According to Burdett, Schreiner's aporetic introduction to the *Rights of Woman* exemplified her lifelong struggle with the difficult questions of colonial and patriarchal power relations without adequately resolving them. Continuing in this vein, I argue that Schreiner's introduction and her feminist treatise *Woman and Labor* (1911) strove for a global female solidarity yet reproduced negative stereotypes of non-Western women in a way similar to Wollstonecraft.[68]

Although Schreiner's introduction began with rehashing the standard British Victorian reading of Wollstonecraft as an inconsequential thinker and bad writer, it quickly turned toward a positive reclamation of the book's prescient grasp of the "necessity" of the "woman's movement." Schreiner underscored how the book's demand for women's rights was rooted in the author's own experiences as a woman: "Being a woman, perhaps there was no necessity for her to see it; she knew it." She concluded the essay with her own observations of black women in South Africa, whom she believed demonstrated the natural, evolutionary roots of a universal female sense of their sex's oppression. Her colonial upbringing gave her a condescending view of these indigenous women as "uncivilised." Schreiner simultaneously felt a strong moral obligation to fight racist prejudice against them. She later resigned from a women's suffrage organization that sought to exclude black women from the vote in the buildup to the formation of the Union of South Africa in 1910.[69]

Despite her colonial prejudices, Schreiner presented her interaction with the local black women as a kind of feminist ethnography. She tried to preserve the cultural distinctions between herself and the indigenous women, in distinguishing between her and her interviewees' first-person voices. She recalled, "I have bent over a woman half flogged to death by her husband, and seen her rise, cut and bleeding, lay her child against her wounded breast, and go and kneel down silently before the grind-stone and begin to grind." Yet Schreiner undercut her poignant sense of solidarity with this abused African woman by attempting to explain such "savage" women's resignation to patriarchal domination in terms of a Eurocentric model of historical progress.[70]

Seeking to understand such "deep" resignation, she interviewed a black woman and translated her explanation at length. Schreiner recorded her interviewee's insight into black women's double burden of sex-based and race-based oppression: "We are dogs, we are dogs. There may perhaps be a good for the white women; I do not know; there is no good for the black." Her register of this African woman's voice echoed Wollstonecraft's lament that girls are born into domination: "We might as well never have been born, unless it were necessary that we should be created to enable man to acquire the noble privilege of reason." Pushing the Eurocentric rhetoric of the *Rights of Woman* in a robustly imperial political direction, Schreiner interpreted the black woman's despair as a sign of the "necessity" of "savage" women's resignation to sexual domination in undeveloped, non-Westernized societies. Ending the essay with a disturbing projection of the "necessity" of an African man's murder of his insubordinate wife, Schreiner coded feminism for the West and the inevitability of submission for the "savage" rest.[71]

Like her feminist counterparts in nineteenth-century Britain and America, Schreiner also reproduced one of the central Orientalist stereotypes of the *Rights of Woman*. In her unpublished introduction to the centennial edition of Wollstonecraft's treatise, Schreiner used the "female in a Turkish harem" to explain her theory of the biological and social evolution of sex difference. Just as she had reduced the abused African woman to the savagery of her social conditions, Schreiner equated the polygamous wives of the Turkish seraglio to "jelly bag" female wood bugs, with none of the "brain power" to escape their domination by the "active, complex" males of their group. The racist implications of this evolutionary narrative were grave. Schreiner wished to claim that women in sex-segregated societies (such as Islamic cultures) became inferior in mind and body to men. She implied that these women lacked mental and physical resources for their own critical engagement with their Muslim culture or its Western critics. Her "jelly bag" bugs of the harem were cast as dispossessed subalterns who could not even talk, let alone speak for themselves so as to be heard by those in power.[72]

In her feminist treatise *Woman and Labor* (1911), Schreiner continued to appeal to this imaginary of the "Turkish harem of to-day" as if it were sociological fact. Presenting European monogamy as a benchmark of women's and human progress, she claimed that "the study of all races in all ages proves that the greater the freedom of woman, the higher the sexual value put upon her by the males of that society." For evidence to support this imperial feminist variation on Enlightenment philosophies of history, she resorted to the Western stereotype of the "pashaws," also found in the *Rights of Woman:* "The hundred wives and concubines purchased by a Turkish pashaw probably have not even an approximate value in his eyes, when compared to the value thousands of European males set upon the one comparatively free woman, whom they have won, often only after a long and tedious courtship." Just as she calculated the worth of the insubordinate African wife at zero, Schreiner presumed the negligible value of polygamous Turkish wives in comparison to their monogamous Western counterparts. Such attempts to understand women's oppression and liberation in terms of a stadial Western conception of development made her wrestle with the issue of cultural difference without fully challenging her imperial prejudices.[73]

Challenging Cultural Bias: The Feminist Liberalisms of Tsebrikova, Borgoño, and López

Not all early feminist readers of the *Rights of Woman* and *The Subjection of Women* imitated their imperial biases against non–Western

European peoples and religions. Some focused on the flip side of feminist liberalism: humanism and cosmopolitanism. Maria Tsebrikova, a radical Russian journalist from St. Petersburg like Blagosvetlov, penned a cosmopolitan—meaning, culturally attuned yet universalistic—prologue to *The Subjection of Women* in 1870. In her feminist liberal approach to reading Mill, Tsebrikova paralleled her contemporary, Martina Barros Borgoño of Chile. Borgoño translated and introduced the first Spanish-language edition of *The Subjection of Women* for the *Revista de Santiago* in 1872. Borgoño subtly adopted a cosmopolitan standpoint that was rooted, yet not entrenched, in postcolonial Chile's mounting debates on women's education and suffrage.[74]

These women from strikingly different political contexts—a developing Russia and a postcolonial Chile, independent from Spain since 1818—illustrate how Mill's book can inspire feminist liberals to conceptualize women's human rights in culturally sensitive and inclusive terms. Likewise, the Argentinian Elvira López's 1901 doctoral dissertation, "El movimiento feminista," traced the international feminist cause to "Inglaterra" and its *Rights of Woman* yet charted the adaptation and flourishing of the movement across the global South in the nineteenth century. Taken together, these non–Western European intellectuals demonstrated the possibility of challenging cultural bias in the feminist liberalisms inspired by Wollstonecraft and Mill.

Borgoño (1850–1941) was born in Santiago to an upper-class, politically influential Chilean family. Her early education was at a school in Santiago run by a British Protestant woman. Her uncle—the historian and liberal political figure Diego Barros Arana—educated her after the age of eleven. Her fiancé, Augusto Orrego, edited the liberal journal *Revista de Santiago*. With his encouragement and translation assistance, the twenty-two-year-old boldly published her serialized edition of Mill's *Subjection of Women*. Her feminist prologue to the edition made her a radical figure among the typically conservative Chilean women of her social class. It was one of the first public feminist writings in Chilean culture, following the 1865 newspaper articles in *El eco de las señoras de Santiago* by elite Catholic women who sought the right to vote in order to defend their religion. Active in the Chilean women's rights movement through the early twentieth century, Borgoño eventually joined the Catholic Conservative Party, which, unlike the anticlerical Liberals, made women's suffrage a legislative priority. Borgoño lived to see the passage of women's municipal suffrage in her nation's Congress in 1934, just seven years before her death.[75]

Tsebrikova (1835–1917) was born in Cronstadt to an Orthodox Russian family with military ties. Her uncle, Nicolai Romanovich Tsebrikov, educated her. He was a Decembrist whose "revolutionary liberalism" of the 1820s had resulted in years of Siberian banishment. Tsebrikova became an editor of the leading leftist Russian journal of letters, *Notes of the Fatherland*, in late 1860s St. Petersburg. In 1870, she published her foreword to *The Subjection of Women* and organized evening classes for women on the topic of women's rights. After a prolific writing career, which produced an internationally known essay on Russian women for Theodore Stanton's *The Woman Question in Europe* (1884), she was banished to Smolensk in 1890 by Alexander III for sending him a letter criticizing his government's "persecution of free-thought."[76]

Beyond the intriguing parallels in their upbringings and careers, Borgoño and Tsebrikova shared an interpretive approach to *The Subjection of Women*, treating it as a philosophical text that invited their own critical reflections on how best to advance women's human rights. Tsebrikova only mentioned Mill to accentuate the political differences between the commentator and the author. She criticized Mill for not thoroughly investigating the solutions to the problem of women's subjection: "Having proven the legitimacy of the woman's right for equality, Mill proves the necessity to set her free. Here, however, he stops halfway." She offered her own solution to women's subjection: the enabling of women's employment outside the home, regardless of marital status. After pointing out that "Mill has a different solution for the problem," she showed that he primarily defended unmarried or widowed women's work outside the home. Departing from Mill, she contended that women were needed to "spread ideas in remote and stagnated corners of Russia, to fight against prejudice by means of words and example, to create societies to enlighten common people, to reduce prostitution, to invent new sources of employment for women, create workshops for people." With an optimistic sense of the breadth of professional opportunity for women in the future, she concluded: "There will be plenty of work; we only need women who will do it. By contributing her time and talent to a useful activity in the sphere of her choice, a woman will prove by action that, as far as she is concerned, the time when she used to be an odalisque or a slave is in the past." Although she sometimes used the Orientalist imagery and Eurocentric ideas of progress that animated both Mill's work and Russian debates on Westernization, Tsebrikova took a feminist liberal stand in upholding the value of women's human rights for the enhancement of Russian women's freedom and self-worth, not economic utility or other development outcomes.[77]

Similarly, Borgoño critically described Mill as "a serene and elevated thinker who, like all those who search for the truth, may sometimes lose his way," then cited him only to support her own distinctive views. She praised the empirical method of *The Subjection of Women* but indicated how its theory of civilizational progress contributed to misrepresentations of women's condition and history. She noted that Mill's binary between the "barbarity" of women's subjection and their civilized liberation obscured the fact that some women had an elevated social status in feudal society. It furthermore downplayed the fact that feminist argumentation had a history: "Ever since books have appeared in the world, women have made their complaints be heard." Borgoño also questioned the feminist import of Mill's utilitarian arguments for civilizational progress: "Stuart Mill, when describing the advantages society would reap from the equal education of men and women, pauses to point out . . . the stimulus which men would receive upon seeing the need to justify their supposed superiority over women; and the more beneficial influence the educated women would exercise over boys and men as their mothers and wives." These consequences were suspect to Borgoño, as they focused on the utility of women's human rights for males. She supplied an alternative list of advantages that derived from women's education, including the development of women's capacity for deductive reason, the scientific progress of humanity, and the egalitarian transformation of marriage and the family such that "respect and mutual confidence will be the patrimony of all homes." Turning Mill's liberal utilitarian ideas toward more robust feminist ends, Borgoño emphasized the value of women's human rights for women first, and subsequently for humanity at large.[78]

Neither feminist liberal sought to mimic Mill's views, or the politics of the West, in developing her arguments for women's human rights. While Tsebrikova to some degree assessed the need for women's rights in Russia in terms of the gap between it and the West, she generally compared the two cultures in sociological not normative terms. For example, she adapted her ideas for reform to the fact that Russia did not have a "society in the sense that Western Europe understands the meaning of the word, i.e. in the sense of an independent force with recognized influence." She also rooted her advocacy for women's rights in the particular social situations of a variety of Russian women. In arguing that "pregnancy and giving birth . . . can be an obstacle only to women who are sick and physically weak," she cited the Russian "peasant women" who "work during the last days of their pregnancy term," whose "health can't be compared to the one of idle society ladies." Tsebrikova differentiated women's experiences within her nation as part of her argument for generally improving women's health, education, and employment options.[79]

Borgoño's prologue was silent on Westernization and Spanish colonialism and their impact on the woman question in Chile. She claimed, "If one thing has encumbered the resolution of this problem it has been the tenacious insistence of considering it through the inflamed prism of politics." She thus treated *The Subjection of Women* as a philosophical point of departure, distinct from the prejudices of any particular culture or political system. She grounded her argument for women's rights on a universalistic theory of human nature. Following Mill, she argued that each human had the same right "to develop oneself; to freely cultivate one's soul." Biological sex differences, however, meant that men and women would naturally excel at different things. Borgoño echoed *The Subjection of Women*'s call to make the human species more "rich" through the activation of women's capabilities, with the twist that sexual difference would be enhanced in this process.[80]

In partly transcending the limits of her political situation in the name of advancing women's human rights, Borgoño avoided direct engagement of the postcolonial political context of the woman question in Chile. Her recently independent nation was embroiled in debates about the scope and purpose of representative government, including the issues of men's and women's suffrage, in the 1860s and 1870s. Her rebuttals of arguments against women's rights mirrored the contemporary Chilean debates without directly mentioning them. Cognizant of the "seditious" import of Mill's book for her conservative culture, Borgoño made a strategic distinction between advocating for women's "social rights" to education, employment, and self-development and women's formal political rights such as voting and office holding. Although she later became an outspoken women's suffragist, Borgoño argued in her 1872 prologue that "women do not call for these political rights; what she wants, what she needs, are her social rights." This gradualist approach to reform made her theory of women's rights fit the values of the Catholic Conservative Party, which introduced the first women's suffrage bill in the Chilean Congress in 1917.[81]

Tsebrikova's universalistic rights arguments, coupled with her attention to the sociological context of Russian women's subjugation, offered an alternative feminist liberal model of how to advocate for women's human rights. Tsebrikova's feminist essays, which used rich descriptions of the life of Russian women to support her arguments for the rights of women in general, were published in nineteenth-century Europe, Britain, and America. Tsebrikova's brand of feminist liberalism bridged Russia and the nascent international feminist movement, which drew insights about women from a variety of countries to marshal global support for the cause.[82]

The prioritization of women's human rights can direct feminist liberals to take a more cosmopolitan, or universalistic yet culturally attuned, perspective on the problem of women's subjection, seeing it as a matter of global—not just local—justice. As Tsebrikova put it, "The so-called women's issue is the issue of enjoying rights and of the liberation of half of humankind, and, thus, it is the issue of a reasonable organization of life for humankind." The comparison of Borgoño's foreword and Tsebrikova's foreword to *The Subjection of Women* demonstrates how the former developed a philosophically cosmopolitan yet nationally salient feminist liberalism, while the latter developed a sociologically rich yet internationally salient feminist liberalism. In theorizing women's rights as a vital part of a just scheme of human development, Borgoño and Tsebrikova gravitated toward the feminist humanist side rather than the liberal imperial side of *The Subjection of Women*.[83]

At the turn of the twentieth century around the globe, the term "feminism" came to be used to describe the social movements devoted to specific women's rights issues, such as suffrage, or to the general liberation of women from patriarchal oppression. López of Argentina was one of the first authors from the Americas to use the term "feminist" to describe the women's movements of her homeland and other nations. She was also one of the first historians to focus on the international character of feminism. Submitted to the faculty of "filosophía y letras" at the University of Buenos Aires, her 1901 doctoral dissertation, "El movimiento feminista," assessed contemporary debates on women's issues across Europe, British India, Australia, Africa, and Latin America, with a chapter devoted to Argentina. López traced the historical roots of international fin de siècle feminism, describing "Inglaterra" as the origin of "la idea feminista." She cited St. Thomas More, Mary Astell, and, with greatest emphasis, Wollstonecraft as the crucial philosophical moments in the English origins of the now global idea of feminism.[84]

Though only discussed twice, Wollstonecraft functioned as the linchpin in the dissertation's development of the English and American idea of feminism. Representing her work as breaking from the typically abstract debates about the equality of the sexes that transpired during the querelle des femmes of early modern Europe and its Latin American colonies, López praised Wollstonecraft's "famous *Vindication*" for directly "calling for freedom of sex instruction and political rights." She described Wollstonecraft as pitting her philosophical views on women's rights to a "complete and solid education" and "work and political freedom" against the retrograde views of Rousseau. López upheld Wollstonecraft as defending women's entitlement to the rights that "the [French] Revolution acknowledged as the heritage of all humanity." She indicated the radical and farseeing quality of Wollstonecraft's theory of women's rights, highlighting her call "for free access to a career in medicine and the right to vote, all of which makes this work truly remarkable and advanced for the time it was written."[85]

López compared Wollstonecraft's conception of the sexes' equal rights to civil and political liberties to the current "English expression of feminism," which throughout her dissertation she associated with Mill. Both Wollstonecraft and the current school of English feminism—with all their "bold aspirations"—were "not exempt from good sense." López concluded with an argument about Wollstonecraft's substantial philosophical and political legacies in the United States. Her practical egalitarianism made her views appealing to the "religious community of Quakers" in early nineteenth-century America. They appropriated this dissenting Christian strand of English radicalism for the arguments of the U.S. abolition and women's rights movements.[86]

Despite this favorable account of Wollstonecraft's legacies, López's dissertation spent more time assessing the influence of Mill—whose women's suffrage advocacy in the British Parliament and in *The Subjection of Women* were widely discussed and emulated in late nineteenth-century Latin America. The popularity of Mill's *Subjection of Women* had helped to reinvigorate international attention to Wollstonecraft's *Rights of Woman* in the 1890s. "El movimiento feminista" demonstrated that López was certainly familiar with the arguments of the *Rights of Woman*, like her fellow Argentinian and women's rights advocate Ernesto Quesada.[87]

López's overview of Wollstonecraft's philosophy was short but symbolically central to the story she told about the international and intercultural character of feminism and the place of the Argentinian women's movement within it. She succinctly yet precisely "translated" Wollstonecraft's philosophy into fin de siècle Argentinian culture. López crafted a careful account of Wollstonecraft's ideas and their early influence in the Americas to ground the various national-level feminist movements, North and South, in a common ancestral source. Moreover, her symbolic use of Wollstonecraft connected the contemporary "movimiento feminista" with the intellectual traditions of Britain and Europe, in a global narrative woven with diverse cultural threads.

Rooted Cosmopolitan Responses to Global Patriarchal Problems

When we think of roots, we tend to think of our families, our communities, and our prejudices shaped by our upbringings. A case in point is my own roots in a small town in northern Maine. Prejudices abound in this village not more than seven hundred strong. The well-bred Congregationalists—and a few Baptists who snuck into their neighborhood—look down on the rest of the town from the Victorian turrets of "Christian Hill." Farther afield is "French Flats," the residential area of the despised Acadian Catholics who could afford to move to the edge of town. For those too poor to escape, there is "Tin Can Alley." Frenchmen are said to squander their time kicking empty beer cans on the streets near the small Catholic mission church, instead of working their way into heaven with the respectable (and profitable) New England work ethic. A town as white as homogenized milk, it attracted the Ku Klux Klan to its parades in the 1920s—presumably to intimidate anyone who thought the culture was too plain. It was sometimes called a "one Indian town," shoring up the community's sense of togetherness by generously acknowledging the presence of a single outsider within its limits. The local Native American tribe, based thirty miles away, was pegged as incapable of self-government. Locals still made boastful claims of exotic Native American ancestry, which they safely positioned in the distant past.

Reading this origin story, you might guess that I identify with none of the groups I mention but do share some of their faults. Descended from a long line of church-hopping Yankees on one side and recent Irish Catholic immigrants on the other, I was raised to think of myself as serving the poor and huddled masses, while wistfully admiring the turrets on Christian Hill. My roots have certainly shaped my prejudices, but they have also endowed me with a strong (though often misguided) sense of social justice.

Such awareness of the rootedness of prejudice, in our psyches and our histories, is not an excuse for complacent acceptance of it, or worse, imposing it upon other people. Wollstonecraft and Mill were aware of the moral problem of prejudice, especially in its patriarchal form, yet they persisted in using stereotypes of non–Western European cultures to fortify their rhetoric for women's human rights. Their lack of critical ethical concern for the negative effects of their use of such prejudicial rhetoric on other people and cultures is far more troubling than the fact of prejudice inhabiting their (or other human) minds.

Wollstonecraft's and Mill's abstract arguments for women's human rights are global in scope—they apply to all women, regardless of social distinctions. Their concrete rhetoric for women's human rights, however, sometimes excluded or caricatured women from Eastern cultures, or treated women and their rights as tools for development and Western civilizational progress. Given the ethical problems with this argumentative framework, the ultimate value of the *Rights of Woman* and *The Subjection of Women* may be their ability to generate a variety of feminist philosophical responses that push us beyond their liberal imperialism toward their feminist humanism.

Through a genealogy of their early international receptions, we have seen how Wollstonecraft and Mill contributed to both the imperial and the humanist sides of feminist liberalism. The insidious power of their Western-biased model of women's human rights argumentation surfaced in its adaptation and reproduction across temporal, cultural, religious, and political contexts. In the postcolonial United States, we saw Christian women such as Adams, Crocker, and Grimké advocating women's human rights with anti-Muslim stereotypes. In a developing Russia of the 1860s, we witnessed the radical journalist Blagosvetlov buy into the Orientalist binaries of the Westernization debate. In India and South Africa at the turn of the twentieth century, we found colonial intellectuals—both the indigenous Kanitkar and the second-generation settler Schreiner—wrestling with prejudiced rhetoric against their local cultures as they struggled with the woman question within the constraints set by imperialism.

By bringing these thinkers into conversation with each other as well as Wollstonecraft and Mill, I have sketched a model for how the history of political thought can foster a cross-cultural dialogue on women's human rights. Contemporary political theorists have contended that such cross-cultural dialogues inspire critical yet sensitive reflection on cultural differences and how they shape the ethical implementation of universalistic feminist arguments. By looking back to the Western and non-Western respondents to the *Rights of Woman* and *The Subjection of Women*, we have discovered not only the flaws in Wollstonecraft's and Mill's forms of feminist liberalism but also the potential of such critical analysis to strip them of pernicious prejudices and thereby give their arguments a truly global reach.[88]

Speaking from non–Western European standpoints, the feminist liberal voices of Tsebrikova, Borgoño, and López show the power of "rooted," or culturally attuned, cosmopolitan approaches to the global problems of patriarchy and other kinds of social prejudice. Tsebrikova and Borgoño produced two varieties of feminist liberal readings of *The Subjection of Women:* the former's sociologically rich yet internationally salient descriptions of Russian women's experiences of inequality, and the latter's cosmopolitan attempt to universalize arguments for women's human rights without losing touch with the realities of her postcolonial Chilean political context. Likewise,

López's history of "el movimiento feminista" situated her Argentinian branch of the movement within a global cause that partly sprung
from, but quickly adapted and diversified, the ideas of Wollstonecraft and Mill. The comparative study of the three writers' responses
to Wollstonecraft and Mill shows the philosophical fecundity of the
Rights of Woman and *The Subjection of Women*, as much for, as despite,
their Western biases. Most important of all, it illustrates the rich
diversity of feminist perspectives that emerge from non–Western
European political contexts.

In "going global," contemporary feminists have converged on the
idea that encouraging women's empowerment in the Two-Thirds
World begins with listening to their stories, their struggles, and their
hopes for justice. Like the nineteenth-century abolitionist feminist
tradition of which Mill was a part, twenty-first-century feminists
have highlighted the cross-cultural moral importance of conceptualizing women as subjects with capabilities for self-direction, self-
narration, and other forms of agency. Similarly, Mill wrote in *The
Subjection of Women* that justice for women and humanity at large
would not commence "until women themselves have told all they
have to tell." Studying the personal narratives of women and other
historically disadvantaged groups is not enough to ground contemporary feminist attempts to theorize global justice, however. The
philosophical voices of women, colonized peoples, non-Western
Europeans, and peoples of the global South also have a place in the
resurgence of interest in putting gender front and center in debates
on global justice.[89]

A like-minded convergence of ideas has occurred within the contemporary philosophical debate on cosmopolitanism. Martha Nussbaum's early turn toward a Stoic conception of cosmopolitanism —
with its almost crystalline rational abstraction — has given way to a
cosmopolitan ethic rooted in those human emotions and local ties
that motivate humans to promote social justice. Kwame Anthony
Appiah pinpointed the origins of his own conception of rooted cosmopolitanism in his family's deep personal connections to Ghana
and Britain, the respective homelands of his father and mother.

These roots gave him a global sense of citizenship, in which "local partialities and universal morality" do not necessarily conflict. As the multicultural theorists Will Kymlicka and Kathryn Walker have put it, "Although cosmopolitanism is usually understood as requiring us to put aside our more local attachments, a new school of thought argues that the outward-bound cosmopolitan perspective requires and involves the very roots it claims to transcend." The emerging consensus is that thinking globally about justice requires and involves critical recognition of roots while resisting the prejudicial tendency to reduce people to them.[90]

Wollstonecraft wrote eloquently about the role of the natural affections that arise from family life and local schooling to inspire a sense of benevolence toward other creatures, both human and other animals. Mill disclosed to the world that it was his love and respect for his wife, Harriet, that inspired him to write his great treatises on individual liberty and women's human rights. In their abstract philosophies and their personal lives, we find materials for building— from the ground up—a rooted cosmopolitan approach to global justice.

Some scholars have attempted to explain away the cultural prejudices of past philosophers such as Montesquieu and Mill, by reference to the trends of their times or through allegorical readings of their symbolic deployments of the Orient. Such backward-looking attempts to explain and justify their biases ignore the forward-looking ethical problems concerning how such biases gain traction in the real world. I hold Wollstonecraft and Mill accountable for their prejudicial rhetoric toward non–Western European peoples not only because of its moral conflicts with their universalistic theories of human rights but also because of the publicity and influence of this contradictory rhetorical model. On the other hand, I resist the righteous urge to reduce them to their prejudices or dismiss the value of their philosophies on the basis of such a reductive reading of their work.[91]

Contextual explanations of prejudicial rhetoric (such as the Orientalist imagery found in the feminist texts of Wollstonecraft and Mill) do not justify the idiom's use in that context or any other context. Furthermore, to focus on the contextual explanation without exploring the ethical implications of the rhetoric is to treat historical context as though it is static or isolatable in a moment in time. This interpretative approach proceeds as if contexts do not beget other contexts or overlap with other contexts. It proceeds as if human agents are simply reducible to a moment in time, rather than empirically understanding their agency as shaped and constrained by a variety of overlapping contexts (historic and current).

Understanding the ethical implications of human rights rhetoric is not primarily about determining intention and blame in a case where the bad consequences are known, such as in a mass murder trial. Theorizing the ethics of human rights rhetoric is rather about articulating the practical need for more thoughtful use of rhetoric in light of the moral commitments of the human rights tradition. Yet special attention must be paid to the negative (and sometimes unforeseen or unintended) consequences of previous rhetorical models, such as the feminist Orientalism of Wollstonecraft and Mill.

Abstractly seen, Wollstonecraft's and Mill's moral contradiction is found in their manipulation of the salience of negative images of women in particular cultures even though they had theorized the damaging consequences of such stereotypes in the case of women in general. Wollstonecraft and Mill both prioritized the intrinsic value of persons as part of their abstract justifications for human rights; and, consistent with this guiding ethical principle, they also made consequentialist arguments in favor of the good effects of promoting human rights for each and all. I take a similarly consistent, two-tier approach in critiquing the ethical implications of their culturally biased rhetoric for human rights. If one cares for the human person, one ought to create respectful rhetorical models concerning the human person. One's language ought to reflect one's human rights values. The beneficial effects of that rhetoric (politically strategic benefits, for example) are always morally secondary to the primary obligation to uphold the intrinsic value of the person. The first concern trumps the second in cases where the second in any way compromises the first.

All this goes to show that there is no perfect separation of intention and consequence in practical ethics, as both Wollstonecraft's capacious metaphysics and Mill's complex consequentialism freely allow. The intention to create rhetoric that reflects human rights values is a consequence of having such values in the first place. The problem of cultural bias means that humans will have their moral blind spots, even the greatest philosophical minds. Given their human rights commitments and their actions as public advocates, Wollstonecraft and Mill opened the door to their readers' critical engagement of their use of rhetoric that compromised the moral integrity of those commitments and actions. Over time, this dialogical process of reader responses to the original texts moves forward the creation of new rhetorical models, including those that challenge cultural bias—if not fully, at least in a partial yet sufficiently ethical way.

The rooted perspectives of Wollstonecraft's and Mill's feminist liberal readers—from St. Petersburg to Santiago to Buenos Aires— gave the *Rights of Woman* and *The Subjection of Women* new, intercultural meanings. Tsebrikova, Borgoño, and López were not perfectly impartial in their cosmopolitan approaches to feminist global justice, nor did they strive to be. The goal of their feminist liberalisms was to approach issues of global justice from their rooted standpoints in order to achieve a partial yet sufficiently ethical transcendence of deeply felt and hurtful prejudices toward women and other oppressed groups. Their status as non–Western European women made them attuned to how gender could not be treated in isolation from other forms of socialization, including nationality, race, ethnicity, class, and religion.

Since it is neither possible nor desirable to fully transcend these intersecting prejudices, we need to find ways of working with them that respect the integrity of other people and cultures. Wollstonecraft, Mill, and their international interlocutors identified patriarchy as a global moral and political problem for humanity. It was not just a problem for women but rather a human problem. It was not solely a culturally specific issue but rather a universal moral problem that took on different cultural forms.

To best respond to this global yet varied problem of patriarchy, we need to avoid reducing other people to the cultural differences that we are raised to see between "us" and "them." A culturally sensitive rhetoric of women's human rights is one such cosmopolitan step toward a feminist and intercultural theory of global justice. In the fifth and concluding chapter, we shall see how the personal, human stories of Wollstonecraft and Mill—especially their autobiographical writings about love and loss—helped to inspire such a rooted cosmopolitan ethic in feminist thinkers from around the world during the nineteenth, twentieth, and now twenty-first centuries.

five

HUMAN STORIES
WOLLSTONECRAFT, MILL, AND THE LITERATURE OF HUMAN RIGHTS

(Auto)biography as Human Rights Advocacy

Not solely philosophers of women's human rights, Mary Wollstonecraft and John Stuart Mill were also literary innovators. They creatively appealed to personal narratives as forms of evidence that made their allegations of women's human rights more legitimate and persuasive in the court of public opinion. Long before the fact-gathering and testimonial approach of the human rights literature—which is based on witness, transcripts, reports, and empirical studies of crimes against humanity since the Second World War—Wollstonecraft and Mill used personal witness to shape a new genre, the literature of human rights.[1]

Wollstonecraft thinly fictionalized her (and her friend Fanny's and her sister Bess's) experiences of patriarchal oppression in crafting her novels *Mary, a Fiction* (1788) and *Maria, or the Wrongs of Woman* (1798). In her *Letters Written during a Short Residence in Sweden, Norway, and Denmark* (1796), she turned the drama of her recent breakup with Gilbert Imlay into a psychological subtext for her philosophical meditations on the possibility of achieving a "single life with dignity." She also developed a distinctive first-person feminist voice across her oeuvre. Speaking with the "I" and the "We," she began to make claims for women's human rights in a solidaristic fashion, seeking to unite herself with all women ("O my sisters") in the cause of "JUSTICE" for their sex.[2]

In his 1873 *Autobiography* and other memoirs, Mill's Romantic representation of his unconventional relationship with Harriet Taylor established another literary model for making women's human rights arguments. By poignantly recalling Taylor's life and impact on others, including the composition of his own great works of political philosophy, Mill legitimated his human rights claims on behalf of women. In Western and non-Western cultures, his male and female readers sympathized with his remembrance of his remarkable wife, and they upheld the relationship as a standard for egalitarian reform of women's status inside and outside the institution of marriage. Especially among male intellectuals and legislators, Mill reinforced his moral authority as a women's rights advocate by virtue of his partial adherence to the customs of marriage while seeking to reform the institution from within.

Mill's disturbing personal experiences of patriarchal conventions, such as Taylor's enduring sense of obligation to her first husband despite moving out of his home, made his feminism more convincing, perhaps especially for other men. He confided in his *Autobiography* the reasons why he tolerated his extramarital predicament with Taylor for almost two decades: "Ardently as I should have aspired to this complete union of our lives at any time in the course of my existence at which it had been practicable, I, as much as my wife, would far rather have foregone that privilege for ever, than have owed it to the premature death of one for whom I had the sincerest respect, and she the strongest affection." Mill's stoic denial of any wishful thinking for the early death of the man who stood between him and his love seems to belie the pain that no doubt characterized the lives of all three adults involved in this unusual domestic arrangement. Mill, alongside John Taylor and other men, had been indirectly though profoundly hurt by the patriarchal system that directly harmed women. Yet by bravely recognizing men's share of this emotional burden—not so much through abstract philosophical arguments as through messy and complex personal disclosures—Mill could make patriarchal marriage an even more urgent problem for the human species to confront and solve.[3]

Wollstonecraft's and Mill's literary writings were as much autobiographical as biographical. Because Wollstonecraft and Mill wove their subjective experiences of their selves and their relationships with beloved others into intersubjective stories of love and loss, these texts are best understood as (auto)biographies. Their life writings blurred the lines between self and other, author and subject, autobiography and biography, hagiography and history, and sometimes even fiction and fact in order to better convey the social context, interpersonal ethics, and emotional basis of their human rights claims. By grappling with the complexity of these literary works, readers of their (auto)biographies were more likely to become engaged with, if not sympathetic to, their moral goals. The stories of Wollstonecraft and Mill had the narrative sophistication and emotional power to become universal human stories, capable of moving people to care about the neglected cause of women's human rights. Indeed, contemporary psychology has confirmed the value of some of their literary instincts. In 2013, the journal *Science* published a study showing that people who read sophisticated literary fiction, rather than nonfiction or popular fiction, are more capable of expressing sympathy toward others and understanding complex social relationships.[4]

Wollstonecraft's and Mill's contributions to the genre of (auto) biography indicate the power of literacy and literature for human rights activism. The spread of literacy enables people to read, write, and speak about self, other, and their relationships with one another, on a broader scale than cultures with only oral traditions or an elite literary class. As Lynn Hunt has argued in her book *Inventing Human Rights* (2008), the proliferation of novel writing and reading in late eighteenth-century Western culture gave traction to the emergent idea of human rights: "Learning to empathize opened the path to human rights." Sensitive and compelling novels, such as Samuel Richardson's *Clarissa* (1748), Laurence Sterne's series *Tristram Shandy* (1759–67) and *Sentimental Journey* (1768), and Jean-Jacques Rousseau's *Julie* (1761), stirred the sympathy of people with their tales of strong yet ill-fated women, and unlucky but stalwart men. Reading, or just hearing others discuss, these and other novels taught men and women to feel more empathy for each other as human equals. Sterne even referred to the "rights of humanity" to which Tristram Shandy was entitled as a "homunculus" in his mother's womb—albeit with irony if not sarcasm.[5]

Eighteenth-century epistolary novels, like the later (auto)biographical writings of Wollstonecraft and Mill, broke down the divide between literature and history in a way that allowed readers to strongly identify with their heroes and heroines as though they were real people. A common trope of Richardson and Rousseau was to use an editorial frame story, by which the author represented the novel as an (actual) collection of letters by the (supposedly real) protagonists. Although Wollstonecraft remained skeptical of some of the gender messages that these eighteenth-century novels directed at women, she was sufficiently moved by the stories of Julie, Clarissa, Tristram, and Yorick to allude to them in her private and published letters. Her epistolary memoir *Letters Written during a Short Residence in Sweden, Norway, and Denmark* referred to Sterne's *Sentimental Journey* and shared its lightly fictionalized (or heavily edited) approach to autobiography. Moving beyond the merely "pleasing" female characters of Rousseau and Richardson, Wollstonecraft was inspired to write two novels with new "models" of "thinking" women who "wish to speak for themselves" and "not to be an echo." But it was hard to completely break ties with her literary mentors. The heroine of *Maria* is deluded into believing she is in love as a result of reading Rousseau's *Julie*, before she comes to her senses.[6]

Mill, too, was indebted to late eighteenth-century literature, especially Rousseau's 1782 *Confessions* as received by William Wordsworth and Johann Wolfgang von Goethe. Alongside these authors he had an interest in autobiography as the genre best suited for relaying the tough yet vital journey of self-discovery. He even quoted Rousseau's *Julie* in an 1831 letter to the *Examiner* that defended the Royal Society of Literature's provision of publically funded stipends for literary writers such as Samuel Taylor Coleridge. For the state to renounce this duty would be to establish a dangerous "maxim" that would in turn produce "ten thousand" bad actions: not just the economic deprivation of the nation's best authors but, worst of all, the cultural deprivation of society. The political import of literature was clear to the young Mill.[7]

By modeling (auto)biographical approaches to women's human rights advocacy, Wollstonecraft's and Mill's literary works raise a series of epistemological and moral questions for their readers. Is it legitimate to use the human stories—of our families, our friends, and ourselves—as evidence to support human rights claims? Do appeals to subjective, or even fictionalized, stories undermine the truth and universal reach of human rights arguments? Finally, can the use of human stories be consistent with the practical ethics of human rights activism—especially the obligation to respect the intrinsic value of the individual human being? It would appear that using personal stories to defend human rights could exploit either the emotions of the audience or, worse, the very lives on which the stories are based.

On the question of whether to use human stories in human rights advocacy, contemporary feminist theorists have generally affirmed the legitimacy of this literary and legal strategy. Personal testimony is a necessary form of evidence for documenting violations of women's human rights. For decades, the radical feminist legal theorist Catharine MacKinnon has chronicled the wide range of women's personal experiences of sexual violence as a way of raising awareness of the depth and breadth of women's subjection around the globe. By recording women's personal testimony of sexual violence, she has also contributed to the prosecution of rape as a weapon of war, especially in the Bosnian War. In another documentary approach, Martha Nussbaum interwove *Women and Human Development* with biographical portraits of two lower-caste Indian women whom she met, interviewed, and befriended as part of her field research for the book. These two personal stories gave weight to her arguments for the necessity of listening to local women's self-interpretations of what is needed for improving human development in a particular region or nation. There is a growing consensus among feminists that only by building into theories of justice a plurality of women's perspectives can we even begin to enhance women's sense of "agency and well-being" in general. The universality of human rights claims is partly established by the personal testimonials of women and other historically oppressed groups who need rights in order to flourish.[8]

On the question of whether human stories can compromise the truth of human rights claims, there is some justified suspicion of the attempts of advocates to closely identify with the people whom they are striving to help. Deep empathy—whether purported, attempted, or actual—can be politically dangerous because of its personal biases. Unduly sympathetic reformers may fail to demarcate a clear space for objective reporting of human rights violations. Given the widespread disregard of the scale of massive crimes against humanity such as the genocidal rape of women during the Bosnian War, human rights advocates have a special obligation to improve knowledge of the facts of these atrocities. Fact-finding may at times require the adoption of a cooler professional demeanor, or even the sacrifice of an emotional sense of involvement in the case at hand. Any storytelling, including (auto)biography and fiction, that blurs the line between author and subject will not achieve this kind of empirically verifiable objectivity, but it can foster a kind of intersubjective perspective that inspires sympathy for the plight of others. Both elements of human rights advocacy—fact-finding work and sympathy-inspiring literature— can productively work in tandem. If they are sufficiently grounded in the culture of the local community, activists might achieve the kind of "multisited" perspective necessary for choosing the right times, places, and people for gathering hard facts or composing quality literary reflections on the issues at hand.[9]

Finally, there is a potential internal conflict between the moral purpose of the literature of human rights and its reliance on biographical narratives. By building human rights arguments on another person's story, the author risks treating the subject of her biography as a means to an end, rather than as an end in herself. A biography would not appear to promote human rights if it does not respect its human subject as such—a person with the capability to tell her own story.

The most influential exponents of the latter line of argument are postcolonial feminist critics of Western liberalism, such as Gayatri Spivak, Chandra Mohanty, and Inderpal Grewal. In their visionary work from the 1980s and 1990s, they identified the moral problems with Western liberal attempts to "speak for," rather than listen to, the subaltern and oppressed in the developing, democratizing, and non-Western world. They theorized why the voices of women in the

Two-Thirds World had to be heard and incorporated into international dialogue on human rights and social justice, in order for such dialogue to be inclusive and egalitarian in process and outcomes. With their grassroots and democratic approach to theorizing the empowerment of women worldwide, they paved the way for feminists in general to frame their human rights approaches to global justice around the voices, stories, and self-interpretations of women beyond the West.[10]

In response to this postcolonial critique, some feminists have advocated a qualitative social scientific approach to surveying and interviewing women of the global South. Brooke Ackerly and Jacqui True, for example, accept ethnographic research (such as formal or informal personal interviews) within a single case study (such as an event, city, or country) as a valid moral platform for alleging and defending women's human rights. The key to good single-case feminist ethnography is sufficient attention to local detail, cultural sensitivity, and transparency about the researcher's outsider standpoint within the group she is observing. Other feminists, such as Nancy Hirschmann, have simply been transparent about the inescapable interpretive dimension of using the stories of other people as a resource for theorizing issues of justice. Hirschmann insightfully explained the rationale behind this hermeneutical approach in her book *The Subject of Liberty* (2003): "These stories are not the result of systematic interviews in the tradition of qualitative empirical political science. But neither are they fiction, in the hallowed philosopher's tradition of creating hypothetical examples to illustrate philosophical points . . . I do not offer any of them as systematic 'proof' of women's experiences, or of their oppression or freedom; but at the same time, I think it is important to acknowledge that the stories I relate are 'real,' that they are not the fantasies of angry feminists, out to blame men for all the evils of the world, but rather represent the experiences of real, live women." In sharing the stories of a diverse range of female humans—whether in ethnographic or anecdotal form— feminists have responded to the postcolonial demand for recognition of girls' and women's powers of self-representation and self-direction in the Two-Thirds World. By incorporating these voices, feminists have expanded the reach of human rights arguments, making them worthy of the descriptors "universal" and "international."[11]

By attending to the epistemological and ethical issues surrounding the use of human stories for human rights advocacy, contemporary feminist theorists have sketched a philosophical justification for a genre with a global history. As we shall see, Wollstonecraft's and Mill's (auto)biographical writings have inspired people since the nineteenth century to feel sympathy for the cause of women's human rights and rethink the principles of justice that govern their societies in light of this feminist commitment. From the United States to Japan, and from Prague to Maharashtra, people retold and sometimes even relived Wollstonecraft's stories of heroic womanhood and Mill's stories of spiritual marriage, in new iterations of the old narratives. Wollstonecraft, Mill, and their international followers together forged a literary approach to women's human rights argumentation that still resonates in twenty-first-century feminist struggles from South Korea to Pakistan.

Wollstonecraft's Stories of Heroic Womanhood

Wollstonecraft's novel *Mary, a Fiction* (1788) initiated the (auto) biographical and literary trends in her writing career. She partly based the plot of the novel on her journey to Portugal in 1785. The twenty-six-year-old Wollstonecraft sailed for Lisbon to care for her recently married, pregnant best friend Fanny Blood, who tragically died as a result of childbirth soon after Wollstonecraft's arrival. The "Heroine of this Fiction," the eponymous Mary, is a composite of the author Wollstonecraft, her sister Bess, who was recently separated from her husband, and Fanny. Wollstonecraft was unmarried at the time she wrote the novel, yet she imagined her namesake Mary struggling to realize independence within the conventions of patriarchal marriage as she strove to aid her dying friend, Ann. Just prior to her trip to Lisbon, Wollstonecraft had assisted her sister Bess in leaving a loveless and possibly sexually exploitative marriage. The struggle of her "Heroine" Mary to avoid a similar marriage trap, in which she would be forced to give her body to a man she loathed, was the dominant narrative thread of the novel.[12]

Although the protagonist Mary was married when she arrived in Lisbon, she "never had any particular attachment" to her husband. Tellingly, she had contracted with him to live apart for a year prior to their living together as husband and wife. The unstated implication was that the marriage was unconsummated. Mary's feelings of "disgust" for her husband suggested that she would have liked to avoid this inevitability as long as possible. Mary's father had arranged this loveless marriage for the sake of preserving the family estate. As the third-person narrator dryly observed, "While this important matter was settling, Mary was otherwise employed." The "heroine" was caring for her ailing friend, Ann, and her impoverished family when her father chose to broker this marital deal that cost her her youthful freedom.[13]

While in Lisbon, Mary chastely fell in love with a wan, pious "man of learning," Henry, with whom she shared passionate conversations about theology, philosophy, and the meaning of life. When Ann's health took a turn for the worse, guilt overcame Mary as if she had committed a "crime" in letting her relationship with Henry divert even one of her thoughts from Ann's needs. When Ann died while Mary helped her cross the room, the bereaved friend found herself overwhelmed with anguish. Her grief "disturbed her reasoning faculties; she seemed stunned by it; unable to reflect, or even to feel her misery." After she recovered her reason and senses after the initial shock of loss, Mary reflected counterfactually: "Had Ann lived, it is probable she would never have loved Henry so fondly; but if she had, she could not have talked of her passion to any human creature." Emotionally torn between her love for Ann and her love for Henry, Mary understood passion and mutual confidence as the bonds she shared with both. By confiding her passions to each friend, especially her grief for the loss of Ann to her new love, Henry, Mary learned to talk her way through an evolving story of her ongoing self-interpretation as an independent, even rebellious, married woman.[14]

Despite the heroine's deft navigation of her personal tragedies and charting of "strange conduct" in friendship and love, the novel ultimately forces us, the readers, to confront the grim realities of eighteenth-century patriarchal marriage. Three months after Henry's death, social pressure compelled Mary to reunite with her husband. Her "disgust" at seeing him again was so strong that she fainted. She negotiated another year's hiatus from cohabitation, but the time abroad flew by, and soon they were living together: "She gave him her hand—the struggle was almost more than she could endure." Mary sacrificed her sense of bodily integrity to enter into a marriage that disgusted her. Without the motive of love of a living human being, Mary lost her wily determination to evade the marriage she hated. While the laws of entail and coverture set into motion this tragic, forced choice, the devastation of her double loss of Ann and Henry propelled it. Mary could only waste away her last years on earth imagining she was "hastening to that world *where there is neither marrying,* nor giving in marriage."[15]

The radical theological message of *Mary, a Fiction* was the same as its feminist message: marriage, as practiced in the eighteenth century, was a profoundly bad deal for women. Even the most heroic and resourceful of them could not escape its insidious spillover effects into personal health, well-being, and, most important, freedom. Looking forward to a heaven without sex or marriage thus emerged as the only complete exit option available to women of her time.

Wollstonecraft's autobiographical *Letters Written during a Short Residence in Sweden, Norway, and Denmark*—initially published in London, Delaware, Hamburg, and Altona in 1796—had as its implicit topic her tragic romance with Gilbert Imlay. Wollstonecraft had met this American trader in Paris in the spring of 1793, during the radical stage of the Revolution. They quickly fell in love and entered into a "republican" (or unofficial) marriage later that summer. Around this time Wollstonecraft became pregnant with her first child, whom she named after her best friend, Fanny. Imlay's infidelities and other deficiencies as a provider for his family eventually led Wollstonecraft to leave the relationship in the fall of 1795.

Around the time that she ended her first (unofficial) marriage, Wollstonecraft wrote her *Letters*. Based on her journey to Scandinavia to assist Imlay in a business matter in the summer of 1795, her *Letters* reworked her correspondence with her husband into a masterpiece of autobiographical literature. The *Letters* did not mention Imlay by name, but readers in Wollstonecraft's tight-knit intellectual circles in France and Britain would have grasped the domestic premise for this ostensible travel memoir. The resultant text is what the smitten William Godwin called "a book calculated to make a man in love with its author."[16] More important than its inspiration of her second, last, and only official husband to fall in love with her was the book's role in securing Wollstonecraft's fresh sense of self in the process of her unofficial yet brutally painful divorce. Wollstonecraft's authorship of the letters that became her *Letters* was bound between the two bleakest moments in her life: her suicide attempts in May and October 1795. These attempts took place immediately before and following her journey to Scandinavia. Both were occasioned by discoveries of Imlay's ongoing infidelities.

Wollstonecraft's reworking of the letters into the *Letters* in the aftermath of her second suicide attempt meant that the autobiographical composition served as a midwife to the rebirthing of her selfhood. Within the literature of human rights, we might describe the *Letters* as a literary exercise in personal agency and its necessary assertion of a basic human right to life itself. Wollstonecraft's Shakespearean rendering of a meditative experience in a Norwegian church, as she took in the startling view of mummified corpses, provided a case in point: "Life, what art thou? Where goes this breath? this *I*, so much alive? In what element will it mix, giving or receiving fresh energy?—What will break the enchantment of animation?—For worlds, I would not see a form I loved—enbalmed in my heart—thus sacrilegiously handled!—Pugh! my stomach turns.—Is this all the distinction of the rich in the grave?—They had better quietly allow the scythe of equality to mow them down with the common mass, than struggle to become a monument of the instability of human progress." Like her literary alter ego Hamlet speaking to the skull of the jester Yorick, Wollstonecraft reflected on human life and mortality, first reveling in the wonder of the "*I*, so much alive," then recoiling from the mummies before her. The corpses bothered her not so much because of their exotic appearance but because of what they symbolized politically: the childish attempts of the rich and privileged to steal a kind of immortality for themselves at the expense of other, poorer humans.[17]

Just a few lines later, Wollstonecraft assured her correspondent (the implied Imlay) that "with more than usual tenderness, I therefore assure you that I am yours." Ironically, she reworked this letter for publication *after* she had left her first love. She embedded this meditation on the fragility of the good of human love within a larger and more pressing moral and psychological narrative: her retrospective forging of a new identity out of the crucible of her near self-destruction. She presented her past affirmation of her devotion to Imlay alongside a melancholic refrain on the passing shadows of earthly human experience. Akin to Mill in his *Autobiography*, she countered this dark observation on impermanence with the assertion of the permanent happiness of discovering the intrinsic value of one's own self: "God bless you! I feel a conviction that we have some perfectible principle in our present vestment, which will not be destroyed just as we begin to be sensible of improvement; and I care not what habit it next puts on, sure that it will be wisely formed to suit a higher state of existence." On a metaphysical/ethical level, the author of the *Letters* thought of the development of her self (and other human selves) as a perfectionistic process, guided by the (perhaps inscrutable) providence of the divine Creator.[18]

On a psychological and empirically grounded level, Wollstonecraft thought of the process of self-development in Humean terms. As David Hume argued in his 1739 *Treatise of Human Nature*, personal identity was not static but dynamic. It was best understood as a process by which our minds took a set of snapshots of our historically contingent selves, each shaped in a different way by time and place. One looked back on the set of snapshots and endowed them with an overarching sense of selfhood. In this Humean spirit, Wollstonecraft cared not "what habit" her self "next puts on." Identity formation was a process of trying on new clothes that were suited for the time and place, but also for the ongoing, retrospective struggle of self-understanding and self-development.[19]

The *Letters* saw a surge of reprinting and translations after Godwin's 1798 *Memoirs of the Author of A Vindication of the Rights of Woman*, probably because of the rise of public interest in Wollstonecraft's unconventional life story. Swedish, Dutch, and Portuguese translations of the *Letters*, a new German translation in Leipzig, and another printing in London were produced between 1798 and 1806. No new editions of Wollstonecraft's *Rights of Woman* appeared between the Danish translation of 1801 and a New York printing in 1833; yet Wollstonecraft remained well known among literary elites in Britain, Europe, and the Americas through the reception of the *Memoirs, Letters*, and *Maria* during this period.[20]

Making her even more famous as an (auto)biographical author and subject at the turn of the nineteenth century, her incomplete novel *Maria, or the Wrongs of Woman*—initially published by Godwin in London in 1798—was soon translated into French, Swedish, and German and published again in English in Philadelphia. The novel was widely read as a semiautobiographical defense of women's right to sexual freedom and divorce. The public salience of her scandalous life story in the first decades after her death shifted the wider public's focus from her ideas on women's rights to her biography.[21]

Wollstonecraft partly based *Maria* on her sister Bess's dramatic exit from what was likely an abusive marriage in 1784. Wollstonecraft and her sister Everina orchestrated the escape of Bess, because their recently married sibling had fallen into a terrible depression. The price of flight was leaving behind Bess's baby, over whom she had no parental rights under the rules of coverture. The child died of illness soon thereafter, making the sisters' decision to liberate Bess even more morally complex in unanticipated consequences.[22]

Yet *Maria* was as much political as it was personal. Through the narration of the life stories of Jemima (a lower-class woman) and

Maria (a middle-class woman), the novel illustrated how class differentiates and stratifies women's experiences of patriarchal, gender-based inequality and oppression. Wollstonecraft drew the fictional characters of Jemima and Maria from the bleak lives of women she observed in London (even at the Bedlam insane asylum) as part of the process of writing this work of Gothic realism. Her anthropological and ethnographic approach, drawing from the real world of English women's experiences of oppression, let the novel express contemporary political criticism.[23]

In one of the narrative frames of this many-layered tale, Jemima worked as a lowly servant at the Bedlam-like insane asylum in which Maria's husband had unjustly imprisoned her. Trapped in the asylum—a Gothic symbol for the corrupt, arbitrary, hierarchical social and political order—Jemima and Maria shared their life stories with one another. Through the comparison and contrast of their stories, the reader discerns that Jemima's struggles as a woman have been even more severe than Maria's.

The double burden of being poor and female made Jemima subject to a devastating array of social prejudices, economic obstacles, and physical violations. While Maria had a basic but not formal education, Jemima had no opportunity to better herself through education of any kind. While the middle-class Maria first experienced economic insecurity as a result of the law of coverture, Jemima faced extreme poverty from birth. While Maria never worked outside the home, Jemima spent her entire life working in demeaning, physically demanding, slave-like jobs, mainly as a servant. While Maria endured a marriage to a repulsive, alcoholic, verbally abusive husband, Jemima was subject to regular physical and sexual abuse, including rape, from adolescence onward. While Maria suffered marriage as a form of legal prostitution when she was married with a dowry of five thousand pounds to a man she did not love, the young Jemima was forced into literal prostitution as her only means of economic survival. While Maria struggled to regain custody of her infant daughter from her husband, Jemima had to abort a baby because she could not support it.

One of the moral objectives of the novel was to show how such intersectional comparisons of women's experiences across classes might inspire a kind of sensitive solidarity among them for their distinct but related struggles. Through the process of telling their life stories to one another, Jemima and Maria developed a potent sympathy for each other's plights as women precisely because they recognized the salient differences between their experiences of oppression. Encountering Jemima's "unmerited sufferings" prompted Maria to promise her jailor "a better fate . . . and I will procure it for you." While moved by Maria's personal narrative to assist her in escaping the asylum, Jemima still understood her own oppression as more severe. She felt displaced from humanity altogether, since others had treated her, from childhood, "like a creature of another species."[24]

As the more privileged woman, Maria returned the favor of liberation by accepting Jemima's poignant plea to "reconcile me with the human race." These two women—despite their radically different backgrounds—became friends, escaped the asylum together, and, in the only optimistic ending drafted for the unfinished novel, created what some scholars have called an all-female family. Jemima reunited Maria with her infant daughter, who was, unlike Bess's baby, rescued despite the lack of maternal child custody rights. Although Wollstonecraft had argued that poor women were among the worst victims of the patriarchal social and political order, she used the unexpected friendship of Jemima and Maria to show that women's mutual recognition of how class stratified their experiences of gender-based oppression can spark a common quest for the realization of women's human rights, such as to care for their own children. As Maria joyously cried before Jemima when reunited with her infant daughter, "I will live for my child!"[25]

Well before writing her last novel, Wollstonecraft had developed a distinctive first-person feminist voice across several genres. As Janet Todd has argued, the frequency of Wollstonecraft's use of "I" can seem egocentric even to a twenty-first century reader familiar with the conceits of postmodernism. But set in its literary context, her pounding, insistent return to the first-person standpoint is reminiscent of the repetition found in Biblical poetry. In both cases, repetitive word choice drives home the moral teaching of the text. The assertion, and reassertion, of the value of her or any woman's voice—"this *I*, so much alive"—is a necessary step toward the development of a general human morality that recognizes the intrinsic worth of each person.[26]

Wollstonecraft also regularly used the first-person plural to locate herself as part of the broader group of women who face patriarchal injustice. "We might as well never have been born, unless it were necessary that we should be created to enable man to acquire the noble privilege of reason," she pointed out with dark humor in her *Rights of Woman*. This first-person plural formulation anticipated what has been called the "radical feminist" turn of Wollstonecraft's final novel, in which the middle-class Maria learned to identify with the suffering of the working-class Jemima by listening to her personal story of lifelong patriarchal oppression: "Thinking of Jemima's peculiar fate and her own, she was led to consider the oppressed state of women, and to lament that she had given birth to a daughter." This sense of solidarity—specifically, the identification of the individual with group oppression—is a psychological precondition for the formation of any social movement to alleviate collective injustice. For this reason, we may read *Maria* as a founding text for modern organized feminism.[27]

Wollstonecraft's innovative use of first-person voices, singular and plural, allowed her to develop a rich personal basis for the literature of human rights. While her *Rights of Woman* provided a universalistic metaphysical foundation for human rights claims on behalf of women, her (auto)biographical works such as *Mary*, *Letters*, and *Maria* erected another, more practical grounding for human rights advocacy: testimony and witness of women's heroic struggles to navigate the tragic choices set by patriarchy. This literary approach to human rights advocacy built on the personal stories of women, drawn from Wollstonecraft's life, including her own loves and losses.

The literature of human rights confronts us with these difficult histories in order to move us, emotionally and physically, to speak up for a better way for each and all.

Voices in the Wilderness: The "Spiritual Daughters" of Wollstonecraft

In 1891, the U.S. historian Annie Meyer wrote in her book *Women's Work in America* that the pioneering women in the field of medicine, such as Elizabeth Blackwell, were the "spiritual daughters of Mary Wollstonecraft." Meyer hailed Wollstonecraft as a "voice crying in the wilderness," who had the courage to speak up for women's rights to professions, including law, politics, and medicine, long before governments had even made equal provision for primary education. In the generous humanistic spirit of Wollstonecraft, Blackwell and her nineteenth-century American peers "did not seek wider opportunities in order to study medicine, but they studied medicine in order to secure wider opportunities for all women." Blackwell followed Wollstonecraft in leaving "the Record of a Heroic Life," which "has since carried hundreds of women over impossibilities."[28]

Meyer was neither the first nor the last women's rights advocate to hail Wollstonecraft as a new kind of political prophet. Many people read Wollstonecraft as a female Isaiah or a feminist John the Baptist—a lone voice crying out for humanity to clear a new way for its liberation. A "legion of Wollstonecrafts" followed her path-breaking example, especially among the Quakers and other dissenting Christians in North America during the nineteenth century. Lucretia Mott, a Quaker preacher who helped to organize the first women's rights convention at Seneca Falls, New York, in 1848, was not only an avid reader of the *Rights of Woman* but also shared the book among her friends—including the controversial feminist theologian Elizabeth Cady Stanton and the Quaker abolitionist Sarah Grimké.[29]

As part of the Anglo-American Quaker tradition of female preaching that dated to the seventeenth century, Mott saw herself as channeling the "indwelling Spirit of God" in feeling moved to speak on matters of religion and public morality. A 1906 speech at a Quaker conference in Maryland equated Mott's legendary talents for public speaking, on issues ranging from abolition to women's rights, with "the voice of the prophet, 'crying in the wilderness, Make ye ready the way of the Lord, make his paths straight.'" Within her religion, Mott was represented as an authentic prophet, who relied only "upon the Word of God, found not in manuscript or book, but written large in souls that are in touch with the spirit of Jesus Christ."[30]

Mott's own preaching recalled Wollstonecraft as a Christ-like figure who modeled the life of selfless sacrifice necessary for clearing the way for women's rights. Her 1866 speech at the National Woman's Rights Convention borrowed the conventions of a sermon in its religious representation of Wollstonecraft: "Young women of America, I want you to make yourselves acquainted with the history of the Woman's Rights movement from the days of Mary Wollstonecraft. All honor to Mary Wollstonecraft. Her name was cast out as evil, even as that of Jesus was cast out as evil, and those of the apostles were cast out as evil; but her name shall yet go forth and stand as the pioneer of this movement." In a kind of feminist eschatology, Mott resurrected Wollstonecraft, turning her from an Eve-like fallen woman who was "cast out as evil" into a female Jesus who had come to lead the American women's rights cause.[31]

It was a close friend and political colleague of Mott, Stanton, who made Wollstonecraft's philosophy of women's human rights into the basis for an American feminist civil religion. In 1840, she had met Mott at the World's Anti-Slavery Convention in London. There they discussed how Wollstonecraft and other dissenting Christian political thinkers had been "tabooed by orthodox teachers." In the *History of Woman Suffrage*, Stanton recalled how she encountered Quaker families in England who "warned against [Mott's] influence" because "in a recent speech in London she quoted sentiments from Mary Wollstonecroft [*sic*]."[32]

Stanton responded pragmatically to the taboo status of Wollstonecraft even within the dissenting Christian tradition. In her own writings and speeches, she invoked Wollstonecraft and her ideas not so much in terms of any particular religious faith as in terms of a new civil religion. This American civil religion was based on rational principles of morality (such as, each person's desert of equal respect due to each person's dignity as a human being). Around the same time, during the American Civil War, Abraham Lincoln similarly resorted to familiar biblical images and phrases to shore up his secular principles and politics. In defining the secular use of religious language in Lincoln's antislavery statesmanship, Steven B. Smith has argued that a "civil religion" is any "non-denominational profession of faith based upon certain symbols, rituals, and public practices that bind citizens of a polity by virtue of their common membership."[33]

Stanton used Wollstonecraft to articulate the feminist principles latent within postrevolutionary America's civil religion, particularly its doctrines of popular sovereignty and equal rights. She and Mott rewrote Jefferson's 1776 *Declaration of Independence* to include women in their 1848 *Declaration of Sentiments*, to show that American civil and political rights ought to apply to all adult persons, regardless of sex. Stanton distinguished her reading of Wollstonecraft from Mott's by making Wollstonecraft a wholly secular icon of women's right to civic equality and nondiscrimination. In an 1871 letter to Mott, Stanton turned Wollstonecraft into a feminist martyr: "We have had women enough sacrificed to this sentimental, hypocritical, prating about purity. This is one of man's most effective engines, for our division, & subjugation. He creates the public sentiment, builds the gallows, & then makes us hangman for our sex. Women have crucified the Mary Wolsencrafts, the Fanny Wrights, the George Sand's, the Fanny Kemble's, the Lucretia Mott's of all ages, & now men mock us with the fact, & say, we are ever cruel to each other. Let us end this ignoble record, & henceforth stand by womanhood." Stanton's mastery of rhetorical amplification transformed Wollstonecraft from a "sacrificed" Christ into a martyr for a wholly secular cause—the cause of "womanhood" itself. While Wollstonecraft was a righteous prophet for Mott, for Stanton she was a noble and willing political victim who embodied a new kind of female heroism. In Stanton's biting analysis, the tragic history of women persecuting other women and thereby perpetuating patriarchy would be the "ignoble record" of the female sex, if they do not finally band together "& henceforth stand by womanhood." This personal letter to Mott was thereby a political demand for women to "stand" against patriarchal domination, yet for civil not revealed religious reasons.[34]

Another leading Quaker feminist, Susan B. Anthony, was Stanton's political partner in establishing the first freestanding national women's rights organization in the United States in 1869. Stanton and Anthony's formation of the National Woman's Suffrage Association (NWSA) effectively split their more radical branch of the women's rights movement from both the civil rights movement for African American men and the mainstream women's suffrage movement. With the founding of NWSA, Stanton and Anthony drew a firm line between their ultimate commitment to women's rights such as suffrage, divorce, and voluntary motherhood, and the limited victory of the Fifteenth Amendment to the U.S. Constitution that activists such as Frederick Douglass and Lucy Stone had embraced for its extension of suffrage to black men and former male slaves. The political cleavages of 1869 over the ratification of the Fifteenth Amendment became the crucible for the consolidation of the American women's rights cause into a freestanding social movement explicitly focused on feminist issues—sometimes, disappointingly, in opposition to the rights of blacks and other minority groups. As it faced forward, toward the realization of Wollstonecraft's abstract vision of social justice, American feminism ironically distanced itself from its iconic philosopher's commitment to universal human rights in the quest to realize the civil and political rights of women.[35]

Anthony, like Stanton, revered Wollstonecraft as a philosophical source for the women's rights cause. It was widely reported that they prominently displayed portraits of Wollstonecraft and Mott in the offices of their feminist newspaper, the *Revolution*, around the time of the founding of NWSA. No longer heard as religious prophets for women's rights, Wollstonecraft and Mott were instead the secular and pioneering voices for the "great cause" of full and formal female citizenship. In 1904, Anthony donated her copy of the *Rights of Woman* to the Library of Congress with the symbolic inscription:

"To the Library of Congress from a great admirer of this earliest work for woman's right to Equality of rights ever penned by a woman. As Ralph Waldo Emerson said, 'A wholesome dissenter is the first step towards progress.' And here we have the first step." In the iconography of the late nineteenth-century American women's rights movement, Wollstonecraft had transmogrified from a female Jesus, to a feminist martyr, to a "wholesome dissenter," even among the dissenting Christians who had popularized her views across the United States. What remained the same across these mimetic iterations of Wollstonecraft was the focus on the clarity, originality, and urgency of her voice as an advocate of women's rights.[36]

As organized feminism grew in popularity at the turn of the twentieth century, there was an international shift toward representing Wollstonecraft as a secular voice of reason and advocate of human rights. In her 1884 biography of Wollstonecraft, the American expatriate and European intellectual Elizabeth Robins Pennell wrote of Wollstonecraft as "the voice of one crying in the wilderness, to prepare the way. What she had to do was awaken mankind to the knowledge that women are human beings, and then be given the opportunity to assert themselves as such." In 1899, the Jewish German feminist Bertha Pappenheim contended in her introduction to the second German edition of the *Rights of Woman* that Wollstonecraft was "the first woman who with overwhelming clarity awoke the consciousness in women—and also had the courage to voice—that women have rights, not assumed through raw force or custom, but rather human rights whose basis lies in irrefutable duties."[37]

Anna Holmová was the Czech translator of Wollstonecraft's *Rights of Woman* in 1904. Her introduction to this edition, published in Prague, captured another trend in the reception of Wollstonecraft at the turn of the twentieth century. As biographies of Wollstonecraft's life and editions of her letters became popular across Europe, Britain, and the United States, the author of the *Rights of Woman* became more important than the contents of her groundbreaking treatise. Wollstonecraft's arguments were now philosophically quaint and politically irrelevant because they fully reflected the "rationalistic religion and rationalistic philosophy of her time." Holmová concluded that the lasting power of Wollstonecraft's *Rights of Woman* lay not in its "philosophical system" but rather in its emotional sway over the "sensibility" of its contemporary feminist readers: "With almost an elementary force stands out the sense that a change, a renewal, is necessary,—and in this immediacy, in this desire, lies the significance of this book, which makes up for its logical and stylistic imperfections. It isolates the author from her [female] contemporaries, but connects her with the striving and longing woman of today, who disagrees with the old ways and who demands freedom to try and to look for new ways." Like an electric charge, the fin de siècle Wollstonecraft jolted the "woman of today" to leave behind the "old ways" in order to seek "new ways" in the wilderness.[38]

In 1907, the British conservative Mrs. Humphrey Ward felt compelled to satirize this tendency of modern feminists to see Wollstonecraft and themselves as secular prophets. In her widely read novel *The Testing of Diana Mallory*, an idealistic young feminist advised the heroine to split up with her fiancé in order to commit herself to the selfless mission of women's rights. Belying her sense of self-importance, the feminist confided: "I fear I may seem to you a voice crying in the wilderness." With this confession aside, she proceeded to matter-of-factly invite her friend to join the "Mary Wollstonecraft Club," devoted to suffrage and pacifism, once she overcame her mere "personal grief" over losing her beloved. Showing Mrs. Ward's fearful satire to be prophetic itself, the British militant suffragette newspaper *Votes for Women* ran an article in 1912 entitled "The Voice in the Wilderness." Citing Pennell, the article praised Wollstonecraft as a "remarkable pioneer" whose views pointed "so unmistakably in that direction" of the "Woman's Movement of the present day."[39]

In his influential 1922 book on the international history of female emancipation, the Dutch historian Jacob Bouten located Wollstonecraft as the ideological source of the globally successful women's rights cause. Using words that have been repeated to the present day in scholarship on Wollstonecraft and feminism, Bouten referred to her as a "lonely voice in the wilderness of British conventionality" who "heralded the great and successful movement of a later century." In 1929, Virginia Woolf canonized within literature this first-wave feminist trend of hearing Wollstonecraft as a secular, rational, yet emotionally captivating voice. For her *Second Common Reader*, Woolf wrote of Wollstonecraft: "One form of immortality is hers undoubtedly: she is alive and active, she argues and experiments, we hear her voice and trace her influence even now among the living."[40]

After modeling a new style of first-person voice and narration in her contributions to the literature of human rights, Wollstonecraft herself came to symbolically represent women's power to speak prophetically, and thus critically, about women's social status. In the rhetorical and oratorical works of her early followers within organized feminism, Wollstonecraft was heard as a "voice in the wilderness," whether she was seen as a religious prophet, a political sacrifice, or a secular suffragist. Even as the mainstream feminist movement lost touch with its explicitly religious foundations, it retained its spiritual motivations in secularized form. Driven by a quixotic desire to help the whole of humanity, the "spiritual daughters of Wollstonecraft" developed a narrative framework by which they could understand their work as answering a political prophet's call to action. Like other forms of politics, nonreligious forms of feminism are still a kind of secularized theology, with Wollstonecraft and her fellow rational Christian dissenters situated at their philosophical and literary base. James Darsey has argued that "Considered as biography, the prophetic *ethos* is a kind of legend." The early American and European feminists built such a prophetic ethos on the legend of Wollstonecraft's visionary life and ideas.[41]

The Wollstonecraft legend and its prophetic ethos were generated by, and continue to generate, a variety of Wollstonecraft memes. Memes—or widely recognizable yet variously replicated symbols of ideas—have become a staple of modern popular culture. Recent feminist theory and scholarship have begun to grapple with the powerful concept of the meme, with satirical yet intellectual web sites such as "Feminist Ryan Gosling" spurring a global Internet discourse on "feminist memes." Richard Dawkins is credited with inventing the term "meme" to describe the nonteleological, evolutionary cultural process by which social symbols are formed, cross-fertilized, and reproduced in new and diverse iterations of an original (or "genetic") idea. Richard Rorty argued in turn, "Memes are things like turns of speech, terms of aesthetic or moral praise, political slogans, proverbs, musical phrases, stereotypical icons, and the like." Upholding the political relevance of Dawkins's concept for a pragmatic conception of feminism, Rorty explained that "different batches of . . . memes are carried by different human social groups, and so the triumph of one such group amounts to the triumph of those . . . memes." Feminist memes can be understood as dominant clusters of public symbols that embody the political ideas and influence of the movement for women's liberation as a group from conditions of patriarchal oppression.[42]

The comparative analysis of her international reception at the turn of the twentieth century shows how Wollstonecraft came to be such a feminist meme. Sidney Tarrow has argued that political symbols are a vital part of any social movement. I build on his theory in conceptualizing memes as a highly visible type of political symbol, around which a social movement such as feminism can be organized. People latch onto the meme in their responses to the cause at hand, and thereby associate the cause with the meme. Such a potent symbol becomes shorthand for the movement at large and the ideas that drive it. Both negative and positive uses of the meme promote the growth of the movement by instigating debates, attracting attention to the cause, inspiring recruits to join, and endowing the group with an overarching sense of history and purpose.[43]

Wollstonecraft helped to fulfill these roles for the formation of modern feminism, by serving as a mimetic marker of the movement's philosophical origins, its social consequences, and its radical political aspirations. In their capacity as prominent feminist intellectuals, thinkers from Mott to Woolf utilized Wollstonecraft and her ideas as symbols in order to foster the authority, public appeal, and internal solidarity of their women's movements. The turn of the twentieth century was the pivotal juncture at which the term "feminism" began to be commonly used to describe women's movements around the globe. It is also the historical moment at which women's movements had evolved into highly sophisticated national and international-level organizations. In the early decades of the twentieth century, women's movements worldwide gained momentum toward realizing their reform agendas pertaining to women's rights to education, voluntary motherhood, property ownership, divorce, suffrage, and safe labor conditions.[44]

In this crucible of the development of what have retrospectively been labeled "first-wave" feminist movements, many intellectuals looked back to Wollstonecraft and her ideas to help ignite and unite each of their causes. There was a pattern of feminist interest in Wollstonecraft as a prescient model for independent womanhood, female sexual freedom, and egalitarian marriage as part of the broader culture of the women's movement from 1900 to 1930, as shown in famous essays by the Russian émigré anarchist Emma Goldman, the American anthropologist Ruth Benedict, and the British modernist novelist Woolf. Although they made multiple memes of their common icon to fit their particular national and political contexts, feminist intellectuals deployed their respective images of Wollstonecraft in similar ways for similar reasons. In using Wollstonecraft's persona and philosophy to both ground their movements in a historical starting point and orient them toward common political goals, they gave these movements an overarching structure—a beginning, a middle, and an end. Just as Wollstonecraft used literature as a sympathetic mode for human rights advocacy, her first-wave feminist followers appealed to her as a prophet, martyr, and dissenting voice of reason to craft an emotionally compelling narrative structure, or practical grounding and purpose, for their burgeoning reform movements.[45]

"My strongest incitement": The Millian Marital Model

Mill also wrote a kind of feminist narrative that could serve as a practical and emotional grounding, or motivation, for women's human rights advocacy. Like Wollstonecraft's, his feminist narrative

was an (auto)biography about his self-development through the experience of charting a new path in love, outside the bounds of patriarchal marriage. This (auto)biography was as much about him as it
was about his spiritual marriage with Taylor. She played the role of
Diotima to his Socrates, by guiding him, he professed, to "enlarge
and exalt my conceptions of the highest worth of a human being."
As he put it in the 1859 dedication to *On Liberty*, his (extra)marital
relationship with Harriet was "my strongest incitement" to write not
only this great work of political philosophy, but to write his own life
down, to make his own life worth reading. She provided the necessary reason for writing at all. As he shared in an early draft of his
Autobiography: "The poetic elements of her character, which were
at the time the most ripened, were naturally those which impressed
me first, and those years were, in respect of my own development,
mainly years of poetic culture." His immersion in her "poetic culture" gave him the chance to achieve in his later years a "purely literary life . . . which continued to be occupied in a preeminent degree
with politics." With his posthumously published *Autobiography*, Mill
fully merged the literary life of the writer with the political life of
the public servant. Most significantly for his women's human rights
advocacy, he used the *Autobiography* and the dedication to *On Liberty*
to champion the example of his "friend and wife," who steered him
to see the importance of "giving full freedom to human nature to
expand itself in innumerable and conflicting directions."[46]

Mill's *Autobiography* and Taylor's few remaining private letters to
him recalled how they became acquainted, at a dinner party in her
home, in the winter of 1830–31. The two intellectuals faced a moral
crisis soon thereafter. Because they unexpectedly fell in love, the
question arose: What were their obligations to Harriet's husband,
John Taylor, and the three children she had borne in that still youthful marriage? In 1833, Harriet followed John Taylor's advice and
took a retreat from both relationships. During this separation, she
corresponded with Mill, imploring him to share more of his feelings,
and his deeper sense of self, with her. On 6 September 1833, she
sent a letter to him at the India House, where he worked: "The most

horrible feeling I ever know is when for moments the fear comes over me that <u>nothing</u> which you say of yourself [is to be] absolutely relied on. That you are not <u>sure</u> even of your strongest feelings. Tell me again this is <u>not</u>." This emotional imperative, for Mill to both know himself and share himself, found its philosophical parallel in the *Autobiography*'s portrait of her character at this critical juncture: "Her unselfishness was not that of a taught system of ethics, but of a heart which thoroughly identified itself with the feelings of others, and often went to excess in consideration for them, by imaginatively investing their feelings with the intensity of its own." In the moral allegory of the *Autobiography*, Taylor represented the virtues of love and sympathy, and their power to inspire "a lovingness ever ready to pour itself forth upon any or all human beings who were capable of giving the smallest feeling in return." Mill offered himself as a model of the latter, emotionally meager, kind of human being, whose capability for expressing feeling was enriched over time by reflecting on the virtues of the woman he called, in an early draft of the *Autobiography*, his "main instructor."[47]

The complex outcome of the twenty-six-year-old Harriet's meditation on the state of her marriage was to choose Mill with her heart but to remain Taylor's devoted wife, with all the propriety of a married woman in Victorian Britain. She established a residence separate from her husband, where she met privately with Mill on evenings and weekends. She and Mill also took long vacations together. She never let her extended family beyond her husband know of the details of this arrangement. She continued to raise her children with Taylor at their home. Yet she involved Mill in educating her daughter Helen, who often resided and traveled with her mother. After her mother's death in 1858, Helen took on Harriet's role as intellectual collaborator by substantially assisting Mill with the production of his *Autobiography* and *Subjection of Women* for publication.[48]

In this highly irregular familial arrangement, Harriet had her share of difficult choices. But each choice illuminated the moral primacy of love and sympathy for others within her practical and caring, not abstract and taught, "system of ethics." In March 1849,

Harriet wrote to her husband, John, to say that "nothing but a feeling of right would prevent my returning at once" to care for him in his terminal cancer. Yet it was precisely such a "feeling of right" that led her to choose to nurse her partner Mill, who was rendered blind by illness, for three weeks that winter. In a letter to Mill later that year, she confided how her hospice care for her husband was a salve to her conscience. This intensive and giving practice of marital love allowed Harriet to "set against extreme sadness & the constant acute sense of being in an <u>utterly</u> false position." The act of loving both men helped her to interpret her fidelity as both capacious and unquestionable: she could love Mill enough to nurse him in his time of need, while choosing to care for John when he and their family needed her most.[49]

Harriet Taylor took the time to instruct Mill in the sympathetic basis for ethics while at John's sickbed. After Mill made the blunt and thoughtless suggestion that she should think of someone other than her patient, she wrote back with force: "Good God sh[ould] you think it a relief to think of somebody else some acquaintance or what not while <u>I</u> was dying?" A modern and feminist Diotima, Harriet sought to teach Mill that real love (including their relationship) ought not to be selfishly focused on any particular person or set of people but rather be generously dispersed toward those who needed it. To cement this moral fact in Mill's mind, she wrote of her dying husband, John: "There is nothing on earth I would not do for him & there is nothing in earth which can be done / do not write." This last imperative—"do not write"—marked the sacredness of her bond with John alongside her loving commitment to Mill and the learning process of his self-development as a sympathetic human being.[50]

Taylor's encouragement of Mill to know, share, and critically interpret himself in the context of his relationships shaped both the content and the direction of his *Autobiography*. It became as much the story of his self-development as a biography of a large and complicated family. In 1854, Harriet wrote to Mill regarding his writing of "the Life": "Should there not be a summary of our relationship from its commencement in 1830—I mean given in a dozen lines—so as to preclude other and different versions of our lives." While she thought this (auto)biographical exercise would be an "edifying picture for those poor wretches who cannot conceive friendship but in sex," her ultimate "reason for wishing it done" was their right as a couple to tell their "own" story. Vindicating a basic human right to self-interpretation and self-expression, especially in matters of the heart, she argued that "every ground should be occupied by ourselves on our own subject." The subject of their own lives was the practical and emotional "ground" they ought to occupy as authors of "the Life" they wished to share as a moral example with others.[51]

Paying tribute to his wife's intersubjective methods, Mill wrote in his *Autobiography* that he "settled" into a "purely literary," yet nonetheless "practical" and robustly political, life after Harriet died of illness in 1858. With his 1859 dedication to *On Liberty*, he represented his magnum opus to the world as the philosophical product of their spiritual marriage and intellectual collaboration. In the *Autobiography* he reinforced his interpretation of the book's expected longevity and value for humanity by describing its origins in his complex and conflicted marriage: "The conjunction of her mind with mine has rendered it a kind of philosophic text-book of a single truth, which the changes progressively taking place in modern society tend to bring out into ever stronger relief: the importance, to man and society, of a large variety in types of character, and of giving full freedom to human nature to expand itself in innumerable and conflicting directions." Just as the "conjunction" of their minds led to their "fusion" into the material form of the book *On Liberty*, their nearly thirty-year (extra)marital relationship was the rich ethical site for the treatise's mandate of free, full, and "conflicting" directions for human self-development.[52]

In the *Autobiography*, Mill connected his grief for the "irreparable loss" of Harriet with his growing hunger for writing and other kinds of political action in his remaining years. One of his (or rather, "my") "earliest cares" in life without Harriet was to "print and publish" *On Liberty*, in order to "consecrate it to her memory." He credited Harriet with inspiring his "literary life" and, most important, his self-development into a human being who thought himself capable of independent, creative, caring, yet capaciously ethical thought. Their relationship(s) had taught him that he was much more than "an interpreter of original thinkers, and mediator between them and the public." He was in fact an original thinker, in ethical realms well beyond the comforting certainties of logic and science, whose writings had tremendous moral import for humanity's present and future. The posthumously published *Autobiography* became his literary tribute to Harriet and their relationships' shaping of his self-understanding as an author of a political kind of literature. As with Wollstonecraft's, the influence of Mill's political literature was vast. The *Autobiography*, but perhaps even more effectively his world-renowned dedication to *On Liberty*, pointed to the deep familial roots of the global problem of patriarchy. The power of these texts lay in their proposal of a practical yet imaginative and intensely empathetic solution to patriarchy: a new model of marriage, based on "the Life" itself.[53]

Millian Marriage Goes Global

Mill's dedication to *On Liberty* begins: "To the beloved and deplored memory of her who was the inspirer, and in part the author, of all that is best in my writings." The instant global success of *On Liberty* made this tribute matter almost everywhere. By Mill's death in 1873, the book had appeared in multiple English editions plus German, Polish, French, Dutch, Russian, and Japanese translations. The treatise's strikingly personal inscription consequently became Mill's most important (auto)biographical tribute to Harriet and their marriage to be published during his lifetime.[54]

According to the dedication, it was in Harriet's roles as Mill's "friend and wife" that she modeled to him an "exalted sense of truth." The author marked the absolute loss of her death alongside the enduring meaning of her life with a triumphant triple negative: he was left bereft yet grateful, as he found himself alone, "unprompted and unassisted" by her "all but unrivalled wisdom." *On Liberty* thus had to be the best political work he could have hoped to write, because its muse was "buried in her grave." This paratext to *On Liberty* claimed Taylor to be its author as much as Mill.[55]

By legitimating Taylor as the true and complete partner of Mill, the dedication resurrected her and their collaborative marriage as feminist political symbols for a broad and gender-inclusive audience. By emphasizing his debt to his "friend and wife," Mill challenged his fellow male intellectuals to sympathetically reflect on this marital model as clearing a path in the wilderness for personal and public liberty and happiness. His female readers, on the other hand, could find in his depiction of Taylor the promise of a new kind of marriage in which women would be first moral and intellectual equals alongside men and secondly wives and mothers.[56]

Around the same time as writers from New York to Buenos Aires to Prague made Wollstonecraft into an international feminist meme, Mill (and his marriage) became a widespread literary model for a practical kind of feminist political philosophy. He built his 1873 *Autobiography* around his conception of himself as ethically and intellectually transformed by his relationship with Taylor. His (or their) "Life" was translated into at least seven languages before 1900. While the dedication of *On Liberty* strongly alluded to their marriage, the *Autobiography* fleshed out Harriet and John Taylor's "Life" in much of its messy complexity. The near-global issuing of *The Subjection of Women*, often with substantial biographical and philosophical introductions by indigenous intellectuals, also contributed to the internationalization of the Taylor-Mill marital model. Together, these three texts provided their readers and commentators further reason and inspiration to follow Mill in the symbolic appropriation of his relationship with Taylor for their own feminist philosophical and political projects.

The non–Western European reception of the Millian marital model shows how such symbolic representations of human relationships can pass a practical and emotional test of cultural translation. The rootedness of such ideas in a particular time, place, culture, and set of personal circumstances is not an intractable obstacle to their cross-cultural meanings. A comparison of more than a century's worth of Indian, Czech, Japanese, and Korean responses to the Millian marital model illustrates its value as a morally responsible motivation for women's human rights advocacy, then and now.

As we saw in chapter 4, Govind Vasudev Kanitkar was the colonial subjudge and Brahmin liberal reformer who translated *The Subjection of Women* into his native Marathi in 1902. His poorly educated child bride, Kashibai, was only nine, and he only sixteen, when they were betrothed according to the customs of their Hindu community in 1870. Although they were devoted to one another and a joint set of moral and political values, Kashibai and Govind's marriage was always clouded and troubled by its origins in the patriarchal power structures of their families. As one of the first women to publically advocate for reform of child marriage via the Age of Consent Bill in 1891, Kashibai became one of the most famous indigenous feminists in Indian history. Her *Autobiography* and other life writings are in one sense the mirror image of Mill's: they charted the complicated practice of a new model of companionate marriage, similarly hindered by patriarchal traditions, yet spoke from a woman's perspective of irrevocable personal loss as a result of such unjust social structures.[57]

In an undated essay on her early education, Kashibai wrote of how Govind pushed her to learn English by introducing the recently published ideas of Mill's *Subjection of Women* to her: "As far as English was concerned 'he' had explained to me John Stuart Mill's *On the Subjection of Women*. Although I became acquainted with the book, I had not studied it systematically. I could not even read it. Sometimes 'he' explained it to me and said, 'You are not destined to read this book. You will not learn enough English to read it in this lifetime.' At this time I made a vow that, in this very life, I would translate one page of this book without help." Kashibai impersonally, even coldly, used the third person to refer to her husband's role in her attainment of English literacy. Her even colder use of quotation marks ("he") belied the emotional difficulties that arose from the practical asymmetries in their arranged marriage. Yet she still credited him with teaching her how to write biographies in English, and with providing editorial and translation assistance as her literary career moved forward: "He is the sole reason I have acquired the ability to write a book now. Even if I shod him in shoes made of my own skin, and did so for the next seven lives, this debt would not be repaid." The high price of her education was dutiful domestic service and childrearing, or, as she gruesomely imagined: making shoes for her husband out of her own skin. The self-abnegation implicit in this dehumanizing metaphor suggests that Kashibai felt their relationship, however progressive by current Brahmin standards, never fully escaped the patterns of domination and disrespect that characterized patriarchal marriages of their time.[58]

Kashibai was painfully aware of her husband's preference for fair-skinned women, which her darker coloring never fitted. She was also beset by his projection of (white and British) Taylor as an ideal spouse. Govind framed his 1902 foreword to *The Subjection of Women* with praise of Mill and his collaboration with his "superb" wife. It promoted a Romantic-liberal vision of Indian women educated in the style of Taylor to become the intellectual companions of their husbands. Govind's conciliatory liberal approach to colonial reform allowed for Indian women to become chaste and domesticated Harriet Taylors, but not fully independent women with strong identities beyond their marital roles.[59]

Much like Govind, Kashibai perceived the value of life writing for political reform, especially among those colonized peoples who had reason to be cautious in their claims for change. Composing a biography of the first female Maharashtran medical doctor, Anandibai Joshee, led her to consider the practical limitations of using histories of exemplary women to promote the cause of women's human rights. Kashibai instead pragmatically theorized the value of flattering men in the process of celebrating great women for the sake of feminist reform: "Instead of lauding women who have been thus improved we should praise men who have improved the condition of such women. Women, just like men, possess capability and rationality. But their capability finds no outlet." Even as Kashibai insisted "a woman's biography be written by a woman," she realistically assessed the need for women to gain favor of the men in power who controlled access to education, literacy, and the press itself. At stake in this set of trade-offs was the future realization of women's "capability and rationality" via the granting and exercise of human rights to education and political participation. Her feminist utopian fantasy novel, *The Palanquin Tassel* (written between 1897 and 1928), envisioned such a future, in which an Indian female political leader established equal economic rights for the sexes in quasi-Millian fashion. The novel moved even further beyond Mill in proposing the justice of equal descriptive (gender-based) parliamentary representation.[60]

In the lived reality of their marriage, the practice of the principle of equal respect remained elusive for Kashibai and Govind. They were separated during the last few years before he died in 1918. Deep disputes and disturbing emotions drove them apart: her religious turn to Theosophy against his wishes, and their mutual yet alienating grief over the devastating loss of a child. As the surviving spouse, Kashibai took a Millian path in serving as a leader in postcolonial Indian feminist-democratic politics. Also like Mill in his later "literary" and "political" years, Kashibai Kanitkar wrote her own post-humously published autobiography as a testament to the enduring meaning of her (and her husband's) own imperfect personal struggles toward realization of the "capability and rationality" of humankind.

Another prominent pair of married intellectuals, in turn-of-the-twentieth-century Prague, fared better than the Kanitkars in practicing the Millian marital model in their personal lives. Charlotte Garrigue Masaryk was the American wife of the Czech philosophy professor Tomáš Garrigue Masaryk. She translated and also likely penned the anonymous introduction to the 1890 Czech edition of Mill's *Subjection of Women*. The Masaryks had courted by reading *The Subjection of Women* together, so the introduction likely represented a collaborative synthesis of their feminist views, just as Mill's book was the product of decades of intellectual collaboration with his wife, Harriet. Tomáš became a noted Millian feminist lecturer in turn-of-the-century Prague. As the first president of Czechoslovakia in 1920, he proudly oversaw the political incorporation of women as equal citizens in the new republic.[61]

The Masaryks' appropriation of the Millian marital model appears to have been both privately happy for them and eventually publicly beneficial insofar as they led the battle for the enfranchisement of Czech women. As highly privileged, Western-educated members of the elite, however, they did not face the same obstacles to these goals as their contemporaries on another continent, the Kanitkars. Colonization and patriarchy were forces felt more in theory than in practice by the Masaryks. The Masaryks' international yet egalitarian marriage combined with Tomáš's Eastern European background likely aided their rooted cosmopolitan appropriation of Mill and Taylor for themselves and their national politics.

Charlotte's 1890 foreword emphasized the political relevance of Mill's book on women's rights for "Czech literature" and culture: "The translation of *Subjection of Women* is the introduction of Mill into our literature. With great joy we hope that this man's ideas, which so greatly influenced his contemporaries, will have the same beneficial effect also on us." Charlotte thus presented Mill as a highly salient philosophical source for rethinking and reforming women's status along egalitarian lines in the contemporary Czech context. Her foreword alluded to the significance of Mill's *Autobiography* for understanding the impact of his marriage for the writing of the arguments in *The Subjection of Women*. Taylor was more than a wife but rather someone with whom Mill had cultivated a lifelong "genuine friendship." "Mrs. Taylor" was a "great influence on his work" but especially "for the conception of the immense practical implications of the subjection of women." It was on the latter issue that Mill "drew upon his wife's guidance" in crafting his pivotal treatise on the topic.[62]

Charlotte Masaryk brought Mill into "Czech literature" via her translation of and biographical introduction to *The Subjection of Women* with the aim of "refreshing, relaxing, and uplifting" the "spirit" of the Czech people. Of all the texts by Mill she could have been the first to give to the Czechs, she chose the book that had most deeply shaped her as an individual and as a married woman. Mill's feminist liberalism, for the Masaryks, was a kind of practical philosophy to be lived out in love and politics, much as Harriet and John once had done.[63]

The 1921 Japanese introduction to *The Subjection of Women*, published in Tokyo in 1923, shows the growing non-Western salience of Wollstonecraft, Mill, and Taylor as personally compelling symbols for an international feminism. Ōuchi Hyōe (1888–1980) was the German-educated Japanese translator of this edition. Mill's political philosophy, especially his *On Liberty* but also his feminist ideas, had been robustly debated in Japan since the downfall of the Tokugawa shogunate and the transition to the Meiji regime in 1867. Ōuchi provided the first complete and literal translation of *The Subjection of Women* into his native language. His 1921 introduction underscored the emotional impact of the book on the rise of feminism worldwide: "Since its publication, it has been widely read in all the Western countries, and for a long time has been called 'the Bible of the Women's Suffrage Movement,' and it has served as source of spirit and power for those who have participated in the movement." Ōuchi mentioned Wollstonecraft's *Rights of Woman* as an important precursor to *The Subjection of Women*, then drew the conclusion that Mill's work "cannot hold the honor of being the origin of women's rights discourse, nor does it hold the special privilege of cornering the market on a perfect women's discourse." In 1957, he put the point more strongly in a new edition of *The Subjection of Women:* it was "because of people like Condorcet and Wollstonecraft" that other people, particularly in France and England, began to advocate "for women's equality." As important as Mill became for international feminism, the groundwork for Japanese and other non-Western feminisms had been laid down by the French revolutionary generation.[64]

Ōuchi's 1921 introduction dwelled on the significance of Mill's relationship with Taylor for cultivating the emotional power and persuasiveness of his feminist arguments. Indirectly referencing the *Autobiography*, Ōuchi described how Mill "expressed his sorrow at being separated from his wife, the object of his great passion; in death, she became the powerful motivating force that turned his lonely final years into prolific ones." Although he was skeptical of Mill's hagiographic treatment of his wife, Ōuchi conceded the psychological force of this rhetorical and narrative move. As an intellectual historian, he understood the subsequent intense concern with Taylor's impact on Mill as integral to the global spread of Millian feminism itself: "Thus, to return to his wife in the establishment of this work is not unreasonable, but in fact, is part of Mill's own exaggerated feeling that his wife was a greater thinker than himself—and at times even greater a poet than Carlyle or Shelley." The Taylor-Mill relationship was crucial for the "establishment" of *The Subjection of Women* as a canonical text for international feminism. The (auto)biographical depiction of this unusual marriage gave a Victorian British man's abstract work of political philosophy a compelling personal history and origin story that could both cross borders and bridge generations.[65]

Soon thereafter, Takahashi Hisanori took exactly this personal approach to writing his (auto)biographical introduction to the selected political writings of Mill in Japanese. Published in Tokyo in 1928, this edition contained translations of *On Liberty, Utilitarianism*, and *The Subjection of Women*, alongside some of Jeremy Bentham's works. Takahashi's translator's introduction to *On Liberty* was inserted between Mill's dedication to Taylor and chapter 1 of the book itself. Takahashi's introduction, like Mill's dedication, functioned as a paratext that dictated the authority and authorship of *On Liberty*. Takahashi understood his authority as a translator as stemming from his rescuing of Mill's meaning from loose and inaccurate Meiji-era translations in Japan after 1867. He represented this experience of literal translation as philosophically meaningful for himself as an empirically oriented and logical thinker: "Mill bestowed on this translator a manner of inquiry for his everyday life." Takahashi reinforced the parallel between Mill's conception of himself as the translator of Taylor's ideas for the world and his own historic role as a literal translator of Mill's major political writings for modern Japanese culture, by treating the dedication to *On Liberty* as strong empirical evidence of Mill's intellectual debt to his wife: "The extent of her influence on Mill is evident in his dedication page to her in *On Liberty*." Takahashi's introduction revealed his attentive reading of Mill's *Autobiog-*

raphy. Much like both Ōuchi in his 1921 foreword to *The Subjection of Women* and Mill in the *Autobiography* itself, he portrayed the death of Taylor as a traumatic yet transformative psychological linchpin in Mill's development as a political writer and activist: "Mill's despair need not even be mentioned."[66]

Forty years after he began his own translation of *The Subjection of Women*, Ōuchi wrote a new introduction for a corrected version of his 1921 edition undertaken by his thirty-three-year-old daughter-in-law, the Tokyo University–educated economist Ōuchi Setsuko. In his 1957 introduction Ōuchi Hyōe was at once more biographical and more autobiographical. On the autobiographical side, he revealed his intellectual partnership with his daughter-in-law Setsuko—a relationship much like that of Mill and his stepdaughter Helen Taylor, who together had produced *The Subjection of Women* in the 1860s after Harriet's death. He also provided a personal context for their reissuing of *The Subjection of Women* in Japanese: the devastating Great Kantō Earthquake of 1923 had destroyed most of the copies of his original edition. This national and personal tragedy gave them reason to publish a revised edition several decades later.

Ōuchi also discussed the broader intellectual context of his initial reception of *The Subjection of Women* into Japanese after World War I: "At the time, I was a bureaucrat in the Ministry of Finance and being in such a position I could not but feel the waves of the democratic movements that were taking place in Japan in response to shifts in international intellectual circles. Thus, I joined those young economics students who had gathered under the tutelage of Takano Iwasaburō at Tokyo University and discussed such matters with them." Each member of this group of young male intellectuals decided to "translate a classic work of the West." Preoccupied with the growth of capitalism, the group focused on economic texts. Ōuchi had been trained in Millian classical economics but chose to translate *The Subjection of Women* because of the emergence of a formal Japanese women's movement for suffrage after World War I. Also, he was interested in Mill as an immanent and progressive critic of "global capitalist economics," because "he had at times questioned . . . the limits of capitalism," especially for social justice for women and the poor.[67]

On the biographical side, the 1957 introduction placed even greater emphasis on the nearly mythological story of the Mill-Taylor marriage and its cross-cultural meaning for Japanese feminism: "From long ago, there are many tales of the meeting of the genius and the beauty. Even when the women's movement occurred in Japan, a number of such stories were told. Above all, however, this tale was about the nineteenth century's greatest economist on the one hand, and on the other an exceptional woman of London high society. That is why their romance remains a topic of interest among intellectual historians." After citing F. A. Hayek's 1951 book on Taylor and Mill, Ōuchi mentioned his own essay on their "romance" that he had published long ago in the January 1920 issue of the Japanese journal *Warera* (Us). He then implored his current readers to go back to neither of these commentaries but rather to Mill's *Autobiography* itself, in order to understand the marriage's literary significance for Mill's political thought.[68]

As with his 1921 foreword and Takahashi's 1928 translator's introduction, Ōuchi in 1957 foregrounded the emotional impact of Taylor's death on Mill's later years as a writer: "Needless to say, Mill's grief was great. He bought a small home in Avignon, in the south of France, where Mrs. Taylor died while traveling, and spent most of his remaining life there honoring her memory. *The Liberation of Women* came to fruition in this place, at such a time, and was organized into its present form and sent out into the world." Ōuchi's optimistic, forward-looking translation of the title of Mill's 1869 treatise (*The Liberation of Women*) fitted into his biographical thesis that the loss of Taylor was not total for Mill but rather a tipping point toward the reconstruction of himself and the emergent international feminist movement. As Ōuchi theorized in the spirit of chapter 4 of *The Subjection of Women*, "The liberation of women is the liberation of humanity. Human beings will be liberated as the great obstacle that thwarts the character development of half of their members is removed." Writing eleven years after the formal granting of equal rights to the sexes in the 1946 Japanese constitution, Ōuchi pushed his recently independent democracy to fully implement in culture the egalitarian principles implicit in its post–World War II (and postoccupation) legal and political order.[69] In another Asian country shaken by decades of war and Western occupation, a Korean edition of *The Subjection of Women* did not appear until 1986 in Seoul. As with several non–Western European readings of the text before it, the translator Ye-suk Kim's introduction used the relationship of Mill and Taylor as a concrete basis for cultivating cross-cultural understanding of the treatise. Mill not only philosophically defended but also practiced in his personal life a "unisex mindset" or "harmonious mind" that incorporated "intellect, which was viewed as men's virtue, and emotion, which was viewed as women's virtue." Building on Alice Rossi's classic biography of Mill and Taylor, Kim judged this androgynous style of thought to "probably" arise from "his equal and productive relationship with Taylor, which was ahead of its time."[70]

Pyŏng-hun Sŏ's introduction to the 2006 Seoul edition of *The Subjection of Women* shored up the translation's relevance for contemporary Korean feminist activism by way of a political reading of Mill's *Autobiography*. After discussing Mill's life and especially his relationship with Taylor, Sŏ upheld Mill as a model of personal authenticity. This authenticity, moreover, served as an affective basis for effective social and political reform: "The reader of this book will easily sympathize with Mill's authenticity. It is impressive how Mill stood against the society which regarded subjugation of women natural, and demonstrated his belief bravely and with confidence." Speaking to contemporary readers in South Korea, the translator encouraged them to "sympathize" with Mill on the grounds that he challenged entrenched gender norms in his traditionalistic society. His late-life activism, propelled by his enduring love of his dead wife, was all the more courageous for its refusal to accept his society's limiting, patriarchal views of propriety and the public-private distinction. Writing from within a twenty-first-century South Korean society with persistent patriarchal norms, Sŏ annotated *The Subjection of Women* in order to encourage contemporary Korean feminists to take inspiration from Mill's "authentic" approach to women's human rights advocacy as much as to urge a broader Korean readership to recognize this book as "the authoritative classic of feminism" worldwide. Perhaps with a silent nod to Mill's collaboration with his stepdaughter, Helen Taylor, on the composition of *The Subjection of Women*, Sŏ's analysis of the treatise concluded with a personal disclosure: "I am glad that my daughter Ji-Eun, who just started an undergraduate degree in her university, read this book."[71]

In the School of Wollstonecraft and Mill

As one of the most prominent intellectuals to face death threats, persecution, and exile for his writing on human rights issues, the British Indian novelist and memoirist Salman Rushdie has defended a political conception of literary traditions. As he puts it in his recent third-person memoir of his years in hiding under the alias Joseph Anton: literature "encouraged understanding, sympathy, and identification with people not like oneself" when "the world was pushing everyone in the opposite direction." For Rushdie, as for Wollstonecraft and Mill before him, literature and especially (auto)biographical writing had the power to elicit a sense of solidarity among people. This solidarity could serve as an emotional motive for a rooted yet responsible human rights ethic.[72]

Wollstonecraft's rational theology and Mill's secular liberal utilitarianism represent two, if not the two most influential, philosophical foundations for justifying women's human rights. Yet Wollstonecraft, Mill, and their international followers saw the practical insufficiency of such abstract rational justifications for persuading people to join their moral and political cause. An affective basis for women's human rights claims was necessary if people were to be moved to carry the claims forward into their cultures and laws. Rational justifications for women's human rights may productively work in tandem with emotional motivations for the same cause. Through their international reception, Wollstonecraft's and Mill's (auto)biographical writings gave diverse readers the right motives to write themselves and their peoples into the literature of human rights. Learning from this history, as well as from contemporary feminist theory, philosophers and other writers may find further ways to reconcile "rational" and "sentimental" approaches to defending and alleging the rights of humans.[73]

In his 1993 Oxford Amnesty lectures, Rorty made a plea for "long, sad, sentimental" stories to be seen as the most effective tools for teaching the powerful that the powerless also deserve human rights. His primary example was Harriet Beecher Stowe's 1852 novel *Uncle Tom's Cabin*, which persuaded many white Americans to care about the antislavery cause in the antebellum United States. I offer two addendums to this important point, one historical and the other philosophical. First, Wollstonecraft, Mill, and other feminist thinkers to the present day have successfully used both rational philosophical justifications and sentimental literary narratives to argue for the recognition of universal human rights. Second, feminist philosophers are rightly sensitive to the fact that women have often been denied status as human beings because of their supposed lack of reason. To dismiss rational approaches to justifying women's human rights in favor of purely "sentimental" modes of persuasion may perniciously reinforce the gender prejudices that feminist philosophy seeks to undercut in the first place. Finding ways of balancing appeals to reason and emotion in women's human rights advocacy is thus a defining practical task and tradition of feminist philosophy.[74]

Feeling passionate deliveries of arguments for human rights, audiences gain the power to use their imaginations to draw, from these wrongs of the past, a set of reasons for establishing rights for women and other humans in the present and future. The relationship between speaker and audience generates a dialogical and narrative framework for women's human rights advocacy. In the beginning, there are the wrongs done to women. In the middle, there is the allegation of a human right not to suffer such wrongs, and the hearing of and response to that voice in the wilderness. In the end, there is the psychological, cultural, and legal realization of a universal human rights ethic that recognizes the equalities as much as the differences between the sexes.[75]

Spivak argued that such a communal rewrite of the conditions for social justice depends on a "transaction between the speaker and the listener." Otherwise, the subaltern cannot speak (in voice or any other action), because they have not yet been heard. Spivak made an ethical distinction between speaking and talking. Speaking requires a dialogical relationship in which one is heard; talking may be mere utterance. Speaking need not be vocal but may be any kind of action (writing, leadership) that elicits a hearing or response from others. In her stirring reflection on the ancient religious practice of satī (the self-immolation of grieving widows) in her native India, Spivak used the example of these self-sacrificing women to illustrate the complexity of the problem of oppression. She did not aim to speak for these widows but rather to convey the difficulty of their struggle within colonial and patriarchal social structures. In so doing she rewrote the story of her fellow Indian women's suffering in a new postcolonial frame, which has since inspired others to better hear and respond to the voices of the subaltern in general.[76]

To make ethical claims for women's human rights requires a serious concern with the context for the claims themselves. The feminist advocate must train her eye like a good novelist, getting a sense of the social setting for patterns of injustice toward women. With this setting described in detail, the feminist advocate may endow even the most radical and risible claims for the rights of women with an inner, and richly literary, logic: as allegations based on the past, made in the present, and oriented toward the future, they at least can be understood as having a beginning, a middle, and an end. This narrative structure also endows these claims with the rhetorical potential to pose what Amartya Sen calls "wrathful" and "rational" arguments. From Wollstonecraft to MacKinnon, we hear moral outrage that emotionally reinforces what is rationally graspable as right for all humans. Wollstonecraft cried out against the sexual exploitation of women in the patriarchal marriages of her time as destructive to humanity as such. MacKinnon begs us to confront the atrocity of the genocidal rape of women as a crime against humanity itself. In each case, their wrathful reasoning pushed others in power, often men like Mill, to reform domestic and international laws and other cultural norms as a step toward institutionalizing women's human rights to not be raped in marriage and to not be raped in war.[77]

Given that many people do not respect others, and have been socialized not to respect those who are different or less powerful than them, feminist ethicists such as Nussbaum have hypothesized the moral preferences that human beings would have if they in lived in respect-enhancing social conditions. With these ideal moral preferences in mind—such as appreciation of the equal dignity of human beings—theorists in the "women's rights are human rights" movement have articulated the ethical conditions for developing the sense of solidarity necessary to support and grow the cause. This idea of a global feminist solidarity challenges the binaries and barriers between North and South, East and West while encouraging attention to the differences that give rise to internationally recognized women's human rights. Hirschmann has put it simply and clearly: the differences between women are the occasion for the theoretical argumentation of their rights. Listening, narration, questioning, and free discussion are a set of discursive practices that push people toward mutual respect of both their moral equality and their bodily/social differences.[78]

Joining the chorus of those interested in proceeding from the fact of difference and inequality, social scientists have demonstrated that there are many practical asymmetries between the sexes that are verifiably bad for women. Sen's landmark economic studies of the systematic malnutrition of girls and women and the widespread practice of female-selective abortion have given grave examples of objectively bad practices of sexual discrimination. Although economics and political science have done much to identify these issues and propose effective strategies for "removing manifest causes of injustice," part of the task of addressing unjust inequalities is not scientific but moral.[79]

The moral virtue of courage is often demanded of those who confront, in social and political reality, injustice toward girls and women.

In the same year as the 220th anniversary of the *Rights of Woman*, the Taliban shot fourteen-year-old Malala Yousafzai of Pakistan in the head for her public advocacy of the right of girls to education. Malala bravely chose to symbolically situate herself, via Internet videos and blogging, as a living example of the right of girls to primary and secondary schooling despite the dominant views of a violent and patriarchal religious group. UNESCO has reported that in her home country "over three million girls" are "out of school" and "nearly half of all rural females have never attended school." As she has recovered and recommitted herself to her political activism, Malala is a highly visible reminder of the fact that girls and women continue to need the institutionalization of the rights that their arguments seek to allege, defend, and extend. Before the United Nations in July 2013, she beseeched children around the world, "Let us pick up our books and our pens, they are our most powerful weapons" in the ongoing fight for the universal right to "free, mandatory" basic education. Her heroism in fighting for the right to education for all children was recognized in 2014, when she became the youngest person ever to win the Nobel Peace Prize.[80]

Malala's courage is extraordinary, but she is also just another girl, with flaws like any other person. Her strong positioning of her politics against the Taliban introduced a strain of antifundamentalist rhetoric to her speeches and writings, which angered her enemies. She risked losing her hard-won image as a peacemaker who seeks to reconcile her Muslim faith with feminism, especially among fundamentalist followers of Islam. Even as it is read around the world, her autobiography has been banned in private girls' and boys' schools in Pakistan. Malala's personal yet political predicament shows both the enduring promise and the real difficulties of women's human rights advocacy. In the school of Wollstonecraft and Mill, one learns by personal trial as much as by human error, but ultimately one learns to better defend the human rights of women.[81]

NOTES

Introduction

1. Mary Wollstonecraft, *A Vindication of the Rights of Woman*, in *The Works of Mary Wollstonecraft*, ed. Janet Todd and Marilyn Butler (New York: New York University Press, 1989), vol. 5, 69 (hereafter cited as *Rights of Woman* and *Works*); John Stuart Mill, *The Subjection of Women*, in *The Collected Works of John Stuart Mill*, ed. John M. Robson et al. (Toronto: University of Toronto Press, 1963–91), vol. 21, 299. *Collected Works* hereafter cited as *CW*. All quotes maintain the spelling, punctuation, and other literary qualities of the original.

2. Mary Ann Glendon, *A World Made New: Eleanor Roosevelt and the Universal Declaration of Human Rights* (New York: Random House, 2001), 311–12; Betty Friedan, "The National Organization for Women's 1966 Statement of Purpose" (1966). Accessed 3 July 2013 at http://www.now.org/history/purpos66.html

3. Charlotte Bunch, "Women's Rights as Human Rights: Toward a Re-Vision of Human Rights," *Human Rights Quarterly* 12:4 (November 1990), 486–98, especially 488, 496–97.

4. United Nations General Assembly, *Vienna Declaration and Programme of Action, 20 Years Working for Your Rights*, 1993 World Conference on Human Rights (United Nations, 2013), 37–39. Accessed 27 September 2013 at http://www.ohchr.org/Documents/Events/OHCHR20/VDPA_booklet_English.pdf

5. Ibid., 22.

6. Ibid., 37.

7. Thirty-five percent of women worldwide have been the victim of sexual violence. Department of Reproductive Health and Research, World Health Organization, "Global and Regional Estimates of Violence against Women: Prevalence and Health Effects of Intimate Partner Violence and Non-Partner Sexual Violence" (2013), 2. Accessed 27 September 2013 at http://apps.who.int/iris/bitstream/10665/85239/1/9789241564625_eng.pdf

8. Glendon, *A World Made New*, 310.

9. Jack Donnelly, *Universal Human Rights in Theory and Practice*, second edition (Ithaca: Cornell University Press, 2003), 7; Charles Beitz, *The Idea of Human Rights* (Oxford: Oxford University Press, 2009), 14.

10. Wollstonecraft, *Rights of Woman*, in *Works*, vol. 5, 153, 157, 249; Thomas Paine, *Political Writings*, ed. Bruce Kuklick (Cambridge: Cambridge University Press, 1997), 176; Joan Wallach Scott, *Only Paradoxes to Offer: French Feminists and the Rights of Man* (Cambridge, MA: Harvard University Press, 1996), 8, 20; Barbara Brandon Schnorrenberg, "The Eighteenth-Century Englishwoman," in *The Women of England from Anglo-Saxon Times to the Present*, ed. Barbara Kanner (Hamden, CT: Archon Books, 1979), 183–228, especially 201–3; Eileen Hunt Botting, "Wollstonecraft in Europe, 1792–1904: A Revisionist Reception History," *History of European Ideas* 39:4 (May 2013), 503–27.

11. John Rawls, *The Law of Peoples with "The Idea of Public Reason Revisited"* (Cambridge, MA: Harvard University Press, [1999] 2002), 109–11, 156–64; Susan M. Okin, "John Stuart Mill's Feminism: The Subjection of Women and the Improvement of Mankind," *New Zealand Journal of History* 7 (1973), 105–27; Susan M. Okin, *Women in Western Political Thought* (Princeton: Princeton University Press, 1979), 197–232; Susan M. Okin, "Gender Inequality and Cultural Differences," *Political Theory* 22:1 (February 1994), 12; Martha C. Nussbaum, *Sex and Social Justice* (Oxford: Oxford University Press, 1999), 10, 64; Martha C. Nussbaum, *Women and Human Development* (Cambridge: Cambridge University Press, 2000), 67–68, 140–42, 162; Martha C. Nussbaum, "Mill on Happiness: The Enduring Value of a Complex Critique," in *Utilitarianism and Empire*, ed. Bart Schultz and Georgios Varouxakis (Lanham, MD: Lexington Books, 2005), 107–24, especially 107–8; Martha C. Nussbaum, *Creating Capabilities: The Human Development Approach* (Cambridge, MA: Harvard University Press, 2011), 141–42; Eileen Hunt Botting, "Making an American Feminist Icon: Mary Wollstonecraft's Reception in U.S. Newspapers, 1800–1869," *History of Political Thought* 34:2 (Spring 2013), 273–95; Botting, "Wollstonecraft in Europe"; Eileen Hunt Botting and Sean Kronewitter, "Westernization and Women's Rights: Non-Western European Responses to Mill's *Subjection of Women*, 1869–1908," *Political Theory* 40:4 (August 2012), 464–94.

12. Amy P. Baeher, "Toward a New Feminist Liberalism: Okin, Rawls, and Habermas," *Hypatia* 11:1 (Winter 1996), 49–66; Nancy J. Hirschmann, "Difference as an Occasion for Rights: A Feminist Rethinking of Rights,

Liberalism, and Difference," *Critical Review of International Social and Political Philosophy* 2:1 (1999), 27–55, especially 37. By the term "feminism" and its variants, I follow Karen M. Offen in meaning arguments or forms of activism that criticize patriarchy and male privilege on behalf of the well-being of women as a group, in any epoch or culture. By organized feminism, I mean formal, public, and collective women's movements, often oriented toward political rights such as suffrage in the nineteenth century but also directed toward other economic or social goals such as education or work opportunities. These formal women's movements emerged in the mid- to late nineteenth century, first in the 1840s in the United States, then in Western Europe and Britain, and quickly grew in other regions of the world in the mid- to late nineteenth century. As Offen has shown, the term "feminist" was not used to describe such movements until 1870s France, whence it spread quickly around the globe. In past scholarship, I distinguished between Wollstonecraft, Mill, and other proto-feminists, and the self-identified feminists of the late nineteenth century and beyond. I have since abandoned this distinction in favor of the general use of the term "feminist" as a historiographical and hermeneutical concept that can be fruitfully applied to the analysis of arguments and activism concerning the betterment of women's social status in different historical contexts. Within this general category of analysis, I distinguish between the different historical manifestations of feminist arguments and activism that have developed in past texts and contexts. See Bonnie S. Anderson, *Joyous Greetings: The First International Women's Movement, 1830–1860* (Oxford: Oxford University Press, 2000); Lori Ginzberg, *Untidy Origins: A Story of Women's Rights in Antebellum New York* (Chapel Hill: University of North Carolina Press, 2005); Karen M. Offen, *European Feminisms, 1700–1950: A Political History* (Stanford: Stanford University Press, 2000), 19–20; Karen M. Offen, ed., *Globalizing Feminisms, 1789–1945* (London: Routledge, 2010), xxix–xxxiv.

13. Ruth Abbey, *The Return of Feminist Liberalism* (Montreal: McGill-Queens University Press, 2011), 10; Zillah R. Eisenstein, *The Radical Future of Liberal Feminism* (New York: Longman, 1981), 104; Elizabeth Fox-Genovese, *Feminism without Illusions: A Critique of Individualism* (Chapel Hill: University of North Carolina Press, 1992), 41.

14. Martha C. Nussbaum, *Sex and Social Justice* (Oxford: Oxford University Press, 1999), 57.

15. Susan M. Okin, "Feminism, Women's Human Rights, and Cultural Differences," *Hypatia* 13:2 (May 1998), 32–52, especially 34; Mill, *Subjection of Women*, in *CW*, vol. 21, 261–63.

16. Inderpal Grewal, "'Women's Rights as Human Rights': Feminist Practices, Global Feminism, and Human Rights Regimes in Transnationality," *Citizenship Studies* 3:3 (1999), 337–54, especially 337–38.

17. Amartya Sen, *The Idea of Justice* (Cambridge, MA: Harvard University Press, 2009), 7, 9, 21, 115–22, 161, 206–7, 392; Martha C. Nussbaum, *Frontiers of Justice: Disability, Nationality, Species Membership* (Cambridge, MA: Harvard University Press, 2006), 405–7; Rawls, *The Law of Peoples*, 3–4; Amartya Sen, *Development as Freedom* (New York: Anchor Books, [1999] 2000), 189.

18. Fred Dallmayr, "Cosmopolitanism: Moral and Political," *Political Theory* 31:3 (June 2003), 421–42, especially 433–34; Amartya Sen, "Consequentialist Evaluation and Practical Reason," *Journal of Philosophy* 97:9 (September 2000), 477–502, especially 497; Bunch, "Women's Rights as Human Rights," 496–97; Sen, *Development as Freedom*, 189. For the use of the term "aspirational" rights, see Onora O'Neill, "The Dark Side of Human Rights," *International Affairs* 81:2 (2005), 427–39, especially 429–30.

19. Agustín Fuentes, "Get Over It: Men and Women Are from the Same Planet," *Scientific American Blog*, 20 January 2012. Accessed 25 January 2012 at http://blogs.scientificamerican.com/guest-blog/2012/01/20/get-over-it-men-and-women-are-from-the-same-planet/. In chapter 3, I engage in greater detail the differences between postmodern theories of gender inspired by Judith Butler and the social scientific distinction between sex and gender, and align the latter approach more closely with the philosophical schools of Wollstonecraft and Mill.

20. Wollstonecraft, *Rights of Woman*, in *Works*, vol. 5, 112–13; Mill, *Subjection of Women*, in *CW*, vol. 21, 264, 269.

21. Marnie S. Anderson, *A Place in Public: Women's Rights in Meiji Japan* (Cambridge, MA: Harvard University Press, 2010), 10, 51, 60, 65, 156; Rebecca L. Copeland, *Lost Leaves: Women Writers of Meiji Japan* (Honolulu: University of Hawai'i Press, 2000), 163–64; Patricia Grimshaw, *Women's Suffrage in New Zealand* (Auckland: Auckland University Press, [1972] 1987), 15, 26, 33, 38, 41, 109; Asunción Lavrin, *Women, Feminism, and Social Change in Argentina, Chile, and Uruguay, 1890–1940* (Lincoln: University of Nebraska Press, 1995), 16, 32, 199; Glendon, *A World Made New*.

22. Brooke Ackerly, *Political Theory and Feminist Social Criticism* (Cambridge: Cambridge University Press, 2000), 152–61.

23. Nussbaum, *Women and Human Development*, 167–240.

24. John Rawls, *Political Liberalism*, expanded edition (New York: Columbia University Press, [1993] 2005), 64–65; Pablo Gilabert, "Humanist and Political Perspectives on Human Rights," *Political Theory* 39:4 (May 2011), 439–67.

25. Beitz, *The Idea of Human Rights*, 49; Mill, *On Liberty*, in *CW*, vol. 18, 224.

26. Rawls, *Political Liberalism*, 145; Alasdair MacIntyre, *After Virtue: A Study in Moral Theory* (Notre Dame: University of Notre Dame Press, [1981] 1984), 217; Beitz, *The Idea of Human Rights*, 49.

27. Roberto M. Dainotto, *Europe (in Theory)* (Durham: Duke University Press, 2007), 52–86.

28. Edward W. Said, *Orientalism* (New York: Vintage, [1979] 1994), 202–10; Thomas Nagel, "Appiah's Rooted Cosmopolitanism," in *Secular Philosophy and the Religious Temperament: Essays 2002–2008* (Oxford: Oxford University Press, 2010), 101–8.

29. Elizabeth Robins Pennell, *Mary Wollstonecraft Godwin* (London: W. H. Allen, [1884] 1885), 90.

30. Richard Rorty, "Human Rights, Rationality, and Sentimentality," in *The Rorty Reader*, ed. Christopher J. Voparil and Richard J. Bernstein (Oxford: Blackwell, 2010), 351–65.

31. Ackerly, *Political Theory and Feminist Social Criticism*, 2–4; Niamh Reilly, *Women's Human Rights: Seeking Gender Justice in a Globalizing Age* (Cambridge: Polity, 2009), 6–18; Chandra Talpade Mohanty, "Under Western Eyes: Feminist Scholarship and Colonial Discourses," *Feminist Review* 30 (Autumn 1988), 61–88; Chandra Talpade Mohanty, "Under Western Eyes Revisited," *Signs* 28:2 (Winter 2003), 499–535; Chandra Talpade Mohanty, *Feminism without Borders: Decolonizing Theory, Practicing Solidarity* (Durham: Duke University Press, 2003), 43–84.

Chapter One. A Philosophical Genealogy of Women's Human Rights

1. Jorge Luis Borges, "The Library of Babel," in *Labyrinths: Selected Stories and Other Writings*, tr. William Gibson (New York: New Directions, 1964), 51–58. For example, see Donnelly, *Universal Human Rights in Theory and Practice*, 58; Lynn Hunt, *Inventing Human Rights: A History* (New York: W. W. Norton, 2008), 1–34.

2. Donnelly, *Universal Human Rights in Theory and Practice*, 58; Richard Tuck, *Natural Rights Theories: Their Origin and Development* (Cam-

bridge: Cambridge University Press, 1981), 5–31; Brian Tierney, *The Idea of Natural Rights: Studies on Natural Rights, Natural Law, and Church Law, 1150–1625* (Grand Rapids, MI: Eerdmans, [1997] 2001), 43–77; Annabel Brett, *Liberty, Right, and Nature: Individual Rights in Later Scholastic Thought* (Cambridge: Cambridge University Press, [1997] 2003), 49–87. John Rawls rooted the rise of liberalism in the debates over rights and religion in the wars of sixteenth- and seventeenth-century England and Europe; see Rawls, *Political Liberalism*, xxiii–xxvii. For a more complex historical look at the evolution of rights discourse in the seventeenth and eighteenth centuries in the British Isles and its relevance for contemporary debates on liberalism, see Gordon J. Schochet, "Why Should History Matter? Political Theory and the History of Discourse," in *Varieties of British Political Thought, 1500–1800*, ed. J. G. A. Pocock, with Gordon J. Schochet and Lois G. Schwoerer (Cambridge: Cambridge University Press, [1993] 1996), 321–53, especially 321–36.

3. Donnelly, *Universal Human Rights in Theory and Practice*, 75, 81, 84; Micheline R. Ishay, *The History of Human Rights: From Ancient Times to the Globalization Era* (Berkeley: University of California Press, [2004] 2008), 1–61; Paul Gordon Lauren, *The Evolution of International Human Rights: Visions Seen*, third edition (Philadelphia: University of Pennsylvania Press, 2011), 5–42; Mary Ann Glendon, "Foundations of Human Rights: The Unfinished Business," *American Journal of Jurisprudence* 44:1 (1999), 1–14, especially 14; George Kateb, *Human Dignity* (Cambridge, MA: Belknap Press of Harvard University Press, 2011), ix–xiii; Nussbaum, *Women and Human Development*, 34–110; Sen, *Development as Freedom*, 227–48. For the idea of an overlapping consensus on human rights that connects liberal and decent peoples, and includes Western and non-Western religions and cultures, see Rawls, *The Law of Peoples*. Kateb's cosmopolitan ethic orients around a defense of the dignity of the human species, while Sen and Nussbaum elaborate an intercultural consensus on the universal human values that undergird claims to dignity, capability, and rights. Glendon, on the other hand, appeals to dignity as a background moral concept that might spur "world religions" to inspire their members to "respect the dignity of fellow members of the human family."

4. Nussbaum, *Women and Human Development*, 96–100; Sen, *Development as Freedom*, 3, 10, 35–53; for the natural law approach to deriving human rights, see John Finnis, *Natural Law and Natural Rights* (Oxford:

Clarendon Press, 1980). For a recent pragmatic approach to defining human rights in the context of the practices of international law, see Beitz, *The Idea of Human Rights*, 102.

5. Steven B. Smith, "What Is 'Right' in Hegel's *Philosophy of Right?*" *American Political Science Review* 83:1 (March 1989), 3–18, especially 6; ibid.

6. Beitz, *The Idea of Human Rights*, 59–68; Ian Shapiro, *The Evolution of Rights in Liberal Theory* (Cambridge: Cambridge University Press, 1986), 29–69. Samuel Moyn has recently revised this narrative of the origins of human rights by showing that the term "human rights" did not come to be strongly associated with international law and an international social movement until the 1970s. He acknowledges that rights discourse, activism, and philosophies had long preceded the 1970s, but he challenges the view that we can historically locate the "origins" of human rights in early modern Europe. Moyn, *The Last Utopia: Human Rights in History* (Cambridge, MA: Belknap Press of Harvard University Press, 2010), 1–43, plus appendix 1. Amartya Sen, "Human Rights and Asian Values," *New Republic*, July 14, 1997, 217:2/3, 33–40; William Theodore de Bary, "Introduction," in *Confucianism and Human Rights*, ed. William Theodore de Bary and Tu Weiming (New York: Columbia University Press, 1998), 6.

7. For two different approaches to tracing the global turn in political thought of the turn of the nineteenth century, both internationalist and imperial, see David Armitage, *Foundations of Modern International Thought* (Cambridge: Cambridge University Press, 2013), 135–232; Jennifer Pitts, *A Turn to Empire: The Rise of Imperial Liberalism in Britain and France* (Princeton: Princeton University Press, 2005). For international histories of feminism, see Ellen Carol DuBois, *Woman Suffrage and Women's Rights* (New York: New York University Press, 1998), 20; Anderson, *Joyous Greetings;* Offen, *European Feminisms;* Offen, ed., *Globalizing Feminisms;* Sen, *The Idea of Justice*, 116.

8. See Sarah Gwyneth Ross, *The Birth of Feminism: Woman as Intellect in Renaissance Italy and England* (Cambridge, MA: Harvard University Press, 2009); Nancy E. Van Deusen, ed. and tr., *The Souls of Purgatory: The Spiritual Diary of a Seventeenth-Century Afro-Peruvian Mystic, Ursula de Jesús* (Albuquerque: New Mexico University Press, 2004); Sophia, a Person of Quality, *Woman not inferior to man: or, A short and modest Vindication of the natural Right of the Fair-Sex to a perfect Equality of Power, Dignity, and Esteem, with the Men* (London, 1739), 37.

9. Schnorrenberg, "The Eighteenth-Century Englishwoman," 201–3; Charlotte Hammond Matthews, "Between 'Founding Text' and 'Literary Prank': Reasoning the Roots of Nísia Floresta's *Direitos das Mulheres e Injustiça dos Homens*," *Ellipsis* 8 (2010), 9–36; Marilyn Butler, ed., *Burke, Paine, Godwin and the Revolution Controversy* (Cambridge: Cambridge University Press, 1984), 72–80; Miriam Brody, "Editor's Introduction," in Mary Wollstonecraft, *A Vindication of the Rights of Woman* (New York: Penguin, 1985), 7–72; Wollstonecraft, *Rights of Woman*, in *Works*, vol. 5, 67, 91.

10. For the idea of a fraternal social contract geared toward the protection of the rights of males in modern republics, see Carole Pateman's *The Sexual Contract* (Stanford: Stanford University Press, 1988). For rights as powers and freedoms, see Thomas Hobbes's *Leviathan* (1651) and John Locke's *Second Treatise of Government* (1690). For rights as wants, see Edmund Burke, *Reflections on the Revolution in France* (1790). For rights as needs or entitlements that ought to be recognized in law, see Wollstonecraft, *Rights of Woman* (1792) and Thomas Paine, *Agrarian Justice* (1797).

11. Lois Schwoerer, *The Declaration of Rights of 1689* (Baltimore: Johns Hopkins University Press, 1981), 299–300. Locke's *A Letter concerning Toleration* (1689) set up an influential philosophical model for understanding religious liberty in terms of a dialectic between individual rights (to freedom of conscience) and duties (to respect other individuals' freedom of conscience).

12. Alan F. P. Snell, *Philosophy, Dissent, and Nonconformity, 1689–1920* (Cambridge: James Clark, 2004), 94–97; Immanuel Kant, *Toward Perpetual Peace and Other Writings on Politics, Peace, and History*, ed. Pauline Kleingeld (New Haven: Yale University Press, 2006), 37–59; Jean Hampton, *The Intrinsic Worth of Persons: Contractarianism in Moral and Political Philosophy*, ed. Daniel Farnham (Cambridge: Cambridge University Press, 2007), 13, 22; Onora O'Neill, "Justice, Capabilities, and Vulnerabilities," in *Women, Culture, and Development: A Study of Human Capabilities*, ed. Martha Nussbaum and Jonathan Glover (Oxford: Oxford University Press, 1995), 140–52.

13. Sharon Krause, *Civil Passions: Moral Sentiment and Democratic Deliberation* (Princeton: Princeton University Press, 2008), 77–110.

14. Tuck, *Natural Rights Theories*; William of Ockham, *A Short Discourse on the Tyrannical Government* (Cambridge: Cambridge University Press, 1992), 87–95, 110–17; John Duns Scotus, "Positive Law and Civil Au-

thority," in *Duns Scotus on the Will and Morality*, ed. Alan B. Wolter and William A. Frank (Washington: Catholic University of America Press, 1986), 311–17; Ockham, *Short Discourse*, 88; ibid., 90.

15. Tuck, *Natural Rights Theories*, 53–58; Francisco Suárez, "The Laws of God and the Lawgiver, Book III," in *From Irenaeus to Grotius: A Sourcebook in Christian Political Thought*, eds. Oliver O'Donovan and Joan Lockwood O'Donovan (Grand Rapids, MI: Eerdmans, 1999), 723–42; Tierney, *The Idea of Natural Rights*, 313. Nussbaum conceptualizes the human right to freedom from sexual coercion as derivative of the human capability for bodily integrity. See *Women and Human Development*, 78. For background on women's health during the Renaissance, see Judith C. Brown, "Everyday Life, Longevity, and Nuns in Early Modern Florence," in *Renaissance Culture and the Everyday*, ed. Patricia Fumerton and Simon Hunt (Philadelphia: University of Pennsylvania Press, 1999), 115–38; Nicholas Terpstra, *Lost Girls: Sex and Death in Renaissance Florence* (Baltimore: Johns Hopkins University Press, 2010).

16. Christopher Brooke, *Philosophic Pride: Stoicism and Political Thought from Lipsius to Rousseau* (Princeton: Princeton University Press, 2012), 40; Tierney, *The Idea of Natural Rights*, 326–27; Hugo Grotius, *The Rights of War and Peace*, vol. 2 (Indianapolis: Liberty Fund, 2005), 402, 947.

17. Grotius, *The Rights of War and Peace*, vol. 2, 451, 513–20, 709, 961, 1009, 1104.

18. Thomas Hobbes, *On the Citizen*, ed. Richard Tuck (Cambridge University Press, 1998), 107–10; Thomas Hobbes, *Leviathan*, ed. Richard Tuck (Cambridge: Cambridge University Press, 1997), 140; Gordon J. Schochet, *Patriarchalism in Political Thought: The Authoritarian Family and Political Speculation and Attitudes Especially in Seventeenth-Century England* (New York: Basic Books, 1975), 230; Hobbes, *Leviathan*, 62, 145; ibid., 140.

19. C. B. MacPherson, *The Political Theory of Possessive Individualism: Hobbes to Locke* (Oxford: Clarendon Press, 1962).

20. John Locke, *Second Treatise of Government*, in *Two Treatises of Government*, ed. Peter Laslett (Cambridge: Cambridge University Press, 1991), 381.

21. Ruth Grant, "John Locke on Women and the Family," in John Locke, *Two Treatises of Government and A Letter concerning Toleration*, ed. Ian Shapiro (New Haven: Yale University Press, 2003), 286–308; Okin, *Women in Western Political Thought*, 73, 233.

22. Linda Kerber, "The Republican Mother: Women and the Enlightenment—An American Perspective," *American Quarterly* 28:2 (1976), 187–205; Nathan Tarcov and Ruth Grant, "Introduction," in *Some Thoughts concerning Education*, ed. Nathan Tarcov and Ruth Grant (Indianapolis: Hackett, 1996), vii–xx, especially xi.

23. Immanuel Kant, *Observations on the Feeling of the Beautiful and the Sublime*, tr. John T. Goldthwait (Berkeley: University of California Press, [1960] 2003), 81; Kant, *Toward Perpetual Peace*, 114.

24. Schochet, *Patriarchalism*, 43–47, 151 note 48, 218.

25. Ibid., 276. For variations of this argument, see Kerber, "The Republican Mother"; Okin, *Women in Western Political Thought*; Pateman, *The Sexual Contract*.

26. Boyd Hilton, "1807 and All That: Why Britain Abolished Her Slave Trade," in *Abolitionism and Imperialism in Britain, Africa, and the Atlantic*, ed. Derek Peterson (Athens: Ohio State University Press, 2010), 63–83; Virginia Sapiro, "Wollstonecraft, Feminism, and Democracy: 'Being Bastilled,'" in *Feminist Interpretations of Mary Wollstonecraft*, ed. Maria J. Falco (University Park: Penn State University Press, 1996), 33–45. Kerber, "The Republican Mother"; Okin, *Women in Western Political Thought*, 341; Okin, "Feminism, Women's Human Rights, and Cultural Differences," 34.

27. Letter from Abigail Adams to John Adams, 31 March–5 April 1776; Letter from John Adams to Abigail Adams, 14 April 1776 (electronic edition), *Adams Family Papers: An Electronic Archive*, Massachusetts Historical Society. http://www.masshist.org/digitaladams/. One of the best examples of Rousseau's worries about women's sexual power over men is found in his demand for social segregation of the sexes in public events such as the theater in his *Letter to d'Alembert* (1758). Letter from John Adams to Abigail Adams, 14 April 1776 (electronic edition), *Adams Family Papers: An Electronic Archive*, Massachusetts Historical Society. http://www.masshist.org/digitaladams/

28. Pateman, *The Sexual Contract*, 9, 97–99.

29. Brooke, *Philosophic Pride*, 189; Jean-Jacques Rousseau, *Julie, or the New Heloise*, tr. Philip Stewart and Jean Vaché (Dartmouth: University of New England Press, 1997), 279.

30. Wollstonecraft, *Rights of Men*, in *Works*, vol. 5, 33.

31. Scott, *Only Paradoxes to Offer*, 4–12; Charles Maurice Talleyrand-Périgord, *Rapport sur l'instruction publique* (Paris: de l'imprimerie na-

tionale, 1791). As quoted in Wollstonecraft, *Rights of Woman*, in *Works*, vol. 5, 67.

32. Anonymous, "Défense des droits des femmes, suivie de quelques considérations sur des sujets politiques et moraux, ouvrage traduit de l'anglais, de Marie Wollstonecraft," *Almanach littéraire ou Etrennes d'Apollon* (Paris, 1793), 218–19; G. W. F. Hegel, *Elements of the Philosophy of Right*, ed. Allen Wood (Cambridge: Cambridge University Press, 1991), 23.

33. Janet Todd, *Mary Wollstonecraft: A Revolutionary Life* (Columbia: Columbia University Press, 2000), 185; Susan Branson, *These Fiery Frenchified Dames: Women and Political Culture in Early National Philadelphia* (Philadelphia: University of Pennsylvania Press, 2001), 38; David Lundberg and Henry F. May, "The Enlightened Reader in America," *American Quarterly* 28 (Spring 1976), 14; Sally Ann Kitts, "Mary Wollstonecraft's 'A Vindication of the Rights of Woman': A Judicious Response from Eighteenth-Century Spain," *Modern Language Review* 89:2 (April 1994), 351–59; John Windle, *Mary Wollstonecraft Godwin, 1759–1797: A Bibliography of the First and Early Editions, with Briefer Notes on Later Editions and Translations* (New Castle, DE: Oak Knoll Press, 2000).

34. Kitts, "Wollstonecraft's 'A Vindication of the Rights of Woman,'" 356; ibid., 358–59; Sally Ann Kitts, *The Debate on the Nature, Role, and Influence of Women in Eighteenth-Century Spain* (London: Edwin Mellen Press, 1995), 226; Heikki Lempa, "Patriarchalism and Meritocracy: Evaluating Students in Late Eighteenth-Century Schnepfanthal," *Paedagogica Historica* 42:6 (December 2006), 742–43; C. G. Salzmann, "Vorrede," in *Rettung der Rechte des Weibes mit Bermerkungen über politische und moralische Gegenstände* (Schnepfenthal, 1793–94), vol. 1, xviii–xix; C. G. Salzmann, "Anmerkungen," in *Rettung der Rechte des Weibes mit Bermerkungen über politische und moralische Gegenstände* (Schnepfenthal, 1793–94), vol. 2, 117; Laura Kirkley, "Feminism in Translation: Re-Writing the Rights of Woman," in *Crossing Cultures: Nineteenth-Century Anglophone Culture in the Low Countries*, ed. Tom Toremans and Walter Verschueren (Leuven: Leuven University Press, 2009), 190; Carol Gold, *Educating Middle-Class Daughters: Private Girls Schools in Copenhagen, 1790–1820* (Copenhagen: Museum Tusculanum Press, 1996), 202 note 19.

35. Mary Kelley, *Learning to Stand and Speak: Women, Education, and Public Life in America's Republic* (Chapel Hill: University of North Carolina Press, 2006), 47; Marcelle Thiébaux, "Mary Wollstonecraft in Federalist

America, 1791–1802," in *The Evidence of Imagination: Studies of Interactions between Life and Art in English Romantic Literature*, ed. D. H. Reiman, M. C. Jaye, and B. T. Bennett (New York, 1978), 195–228, especially 197; Elias Boudinot, "An Oration Delivered at Elizabeth-Town, New-Jersey: Agreeably to the Resolution of the State Society of Cincinnati on the Fourth of July" (Elizabethtown, NJ: Shepard Kollock, 1793), 24; Rosemarie Zagarri, *Revolutionary Backlash: Women and Politics in the Early American Republic* (Philadelphia: University of Pennsylvania Press, 2007), 42.

36. Anonymous, "To a Young Lady, who sent to the author for 'The Rights of Man,' written by Mr. Paine," in *United States Chronicle* 8:412 (Providence, RI: Bennett Wheeler, 24 November 1791), 4. The heading for the poem states that it was reprinted "from the *New-York Daily Advertiser*." Thomas Taylor, *A Vindication of the Rights of Brutes* (London, 1792), 77–78; Anonymous, *A Sketch of the Rights of Boys and Girls. By Launcelot Light, of Westminster School; and Laetitia Lookabout of Queen's Square, Bloomsbury* (London: J. Bew, 1792), 5, 14; "Susannah Staunch," "The Rights of Woman," *Supplement to Dunlap's American Daily Advertiser*, No. 4280 (13 October 1792), 4; ibid.

37. Charles Taylor, *Modern Social Imaginaries* (Durham: Duke University Press, 2004), 156–58; Vincent P. Muñoz, *God and the Founders* (Cambridge: Cambridge University Press, 2009), 210; Bernard Bailyn, *The Ideological Origins of the American Revolution* [1967] 1992), 43–44.

38. Eileen Hunt Botting, *Family Feuds: Wollstonecraft, Burke, and Rousseau on the Transformation of the Family* (Albany: State University of New York Press, 2006), 158; Lyndall Gordon, *Vindication: A Life of Mary Wollstonecraft* (New York: HarperCollins, 2005), 12–18, 46.

39. Virginia Sapiro, *A Vindication of Political Virtue: The Political Theory of Mary Wollstonecraft* (Chicago: University of Chicago Press, 1992), 171–72; Richard Vernon, *Friends, Citizens, Strangers: Essays on Where We Belong* (Toronto: University of Toronto Press, 2005), 58–80; Wollstonecraft, *Rights of Men*, in *Works*, vol. 5, 7, 11, 34, 51; Wollstonecraft, *Rights of Woman*, in *Works*, vol. 5, 65, 67, 82, 266.

40. Wollstonecraft, *Rights of Men*, in *Works*, vol. 5, 9, 24, 41; Wollstonecraft, *Rights of Woman*, in *Works*, vol. 5, 83, 245.

41. Wollstonecraft as "M.", "*Letters on Education: With Observations on Religious and Metaphysical Subjects. By Catharine Macaulay Graham*," in *Works*, vol. 7, 320; Wollstonecraft, *Rights of Woman*, in *Works*, vol. 5, 119; Vernon, *Friends, Citizens, Strangers*, 59–61.

42. Immanuel Kant, *Groundwork for the Metaphysics of Morals*, ed. Lara Denis (Peterborough: Broadview, 2005), 58–66, 83; Rousseau, *Julie*, 610; Wollstonecraft, *Rights of Woman*, in *Works*, vol. 5, 119.

43. Wollstonecraft, *Rights of Men*, in *Works*, vol. 5, 16; "Auxiliary, adj. and noun," *Oxford English Dictionary*, online edition, www.oed.com; Wollstonecraft, *Rights of Woman*, in *Works*, vol. 5, 180; Susan Khin Zaw, "The Reasonable Heart: Mary Wollstonecraft's View of the Relation between Reason and Feeling in Morality, Moral Psychology, and Moral Development," *Hypatia* 13:1 (Winter 1998), 78–117.

44. Wollstonecraft, *Rights of Woman*, in *Works*, vol. 5, 81–82, 115, 125, 217.

45. Botting, *Family Feuds*, 136–55; Gordon, *Vindication*, 40–79; Barbara Taylor, *Mary Wollstonecraft and the Feminist Imagination* (Cambridge: Cambridge University Press, 2003), 103–8; Sarah Hutton, "The Ethical Background of the Rights of Women," in *Philosophical Theory and the Universal Declaration of Human Rights*, ed. William Sweet (Ottawa: University of Ottawa Press, 2003), 27–40.

46. Botting, *Family Feuds*, 158–59.

47. Wollstonecraft's view of God as unitary remains stable, even as she moves toward her own creative formulation of a Romantic deism in her *Letters Written during a Short Residence in Sweden, Norway, and Denmark* (1796). See Botting, *Family Feuds*, 179. Wollstonecraft, *Rights of Men*, in *Works*, vol. 5, 61.

48. Wollstonecraft, *Rights of Men*, in *Works*, vol. 5, 61.

49. Ibid., 35.

50. Gordon, *Vindication*, 48; ibid.; Wollstonecraft, *Rights of Men*, in *Works*, vol. 5, 60; Richard Price, *Four Dissertations* (London: T. Cadell, [1767] 1777), 6; Wollstonecraft, *Rights of Woman*, in *Works*, vol. 5, 84, 153.

51. Wollstonecraft, *Rights of Men*, in *Works*, vol. 5, 52.

52. Taylor, *Mary Wollstonecraft and the Feminist Imagination*, 105.

53. Richard Price, "Observations on the Nature of Civil Liberty," in *Political Writings*, ed. D. O. Thomas (Cambridge: Cambridge University Press, 1991), 33; Price, "Observations," 23; ibid., 21–23.

54. James E. Crimmins, *Secular Utilitarianism: Social Science and the Critique of Religion in the Thought of Jeremy Bentham* (Oxford: Oxford University Press, 1990); Mill, *Autobiography*, in *CW*, vol. 1, 6, 41–45.

55. Jeremy Bentham, *Rights, Representation, and Reform: Nonsense upon Stilts and Other Writings on the French Revolution*, ed. Philip Schofield and Catherine Pease-Watkin (Oxford: Oxford University Press, 2002), xlvii,

317; Mill, *Utilitarianism*, in *CW*, vol. 10, 242, 247; Mill, *On Liberty*, in *CW*, vol. 18, 224.

56. Joseph Hamburger, *John Stuart Mill on Liberty and Control* (Princeton: Princeton University Press, 1999), 45; ibid.

57. Mill, *Autobiography*, in *CW*, vol. 1, 5; ibid., 41.

58. Ibid., 9; ibid., 11; ibid.; ibid.; ibid., 31.

59. Ibid., 41; ibid.; ibid., 45; ibid.

60. Ibid., 55; ibid., 49.

61. Ibid., 55; ibid., 67.

62. Ibid., 69; ibid., 137; ibid. Mill accepted Bentham's view that nonhuman animals should be included alongside humans in the calculation of utility because they were likewise sentient beings, capable of pain and pleasure. For his strongest defense of "the rights of animals" against those who would deny them any legal protection from suffering, see Mill, "Whewell on Moral Philosophy [1852]," in *CW*, vol. 10, 187. Although chapter 2 of *Utilitarianism* cited Epicurus as a precursor to modern utilitarianism, Mill focused on the project of revising Bentham rather than reclaiming ancient or modern Epicureanism. More to the point of this genealogy, he never appealed to Epicureanism or Stoicism as sources for his theory of moral rights. See Mill, *Utilitarianism*, in *CW*, vol. 10, 209–11.

63. Mill, *Autobiography*, in *CW*, vol. 1, 137; ibid., 139; ibid.

64. Ibid., 143; ibid.

65. Ibid., 145; ibid., 147; ibid., 153; ibid.; David Bromwich, "A Note on the Life and Thought of John Stuart Mill," in John Stuart Mill, *On Liberty*, ed. David Bromwich and George Kateb (New Haven: Yale University Press, 2003), 1–27, especially 7; William Wordsworth, "Preface," *Lyrical Ballads* (1801).

66. Mill, *On Liberty*, in *CW*, vol. 18, 261.

67. Mill, *Subjection of Women*, in *CW*, vol. 21, 326.

68. Mill, *On Liberty*, in *CW*, vol. 18, 223–24, 266; Mill, *Subjection of Women*, in *CW*, vol. 21, 266; Alan Ryan, *John Stuart Mill* (New York: Pantheon, 1970), 242–43, 252; Alan Ryan, "J. S. Mill on Education," *Oxford Review of Education* 37:5 (2011), 653–67.

69. Gregory Claeys, *Mill and Paternalism* (Cambridge: Cambridge University Press, 2013), 23; Mill, *Autobiography*, in *CW*, vol. 1, 107; ibid., 129; Windsor Daggett, *A Down-East Yankee from the District of Maine* (Portland, ME: A. J. Huston, 1920), 31–32.

70. Mill, *Autobiography*, in *CW*, vol. 1, 107; Arianne Chernock, *Men and the Making of Modern British Feminism* (Stanford: Stanford University Press, 2010), 114.

71. F. A. Hayek, *John Stuart Mill and Harriet Taylor: Their Correspondence and Subsequent Marriage* (London: Routledge and Kegan Paul, 1951); Alice S. Rossi, "Sentiment and Intellect: The Story of John Stuart Mill and Harriet Taylor Mill," in John Stuart Mill and Harriet Taylor Mill, *Essays on Sex Equality*, ed. Alice S. Rossi (Chicago: University of Chicago Press, 1970), 3–63, especially 22; ibid., 21.

72. Mill and Taylor, *Essays on Sex Equality*, 76; ibid., 84.

73. Ibid., 85; Wollstonecraft also referred to patriarchal marriage as a kind of "legal prostitution"; for example, *Rights of Men*, in *Works*, vol. 5, 22. Mill and Taylor, *Essays on Sex Equality*, 86.

74. Mill, *Autobiography*, in *CW*, vol. 1, 193–95.

75. John Stuart Mill and Auguste Comte, *The Correspondence of John Stuart Mill and Auguste Comte*, tr. and ed. Oscar A. Haac (New Brunswick, NJ: Transaction, 1995), 188; James P. Scanlan, "John Stuart Mill in Russia: A Bibliography," *Mill News Letter* 4:1 (Fall 1968), 2–11.

76. Mill and Comte, *Correspondence*, 180.

77. Ibid., 200; ibid., 202.

78. Jo Ellen Jacobs, "Introduction," in *The Complete Works of Harriet Taylor Mill*, ed. Jo Ellen Jacobs and Paula Harms Payne (Bloomington: Indiana University Press, 1998), xxviii (hereafter cited as *Complete Works*); Harriet Taylor Mill, "Enfranchisement of Women," in *CW*, vol. 21, 397; Harriet Taylor Mill and John Stuart Mill, "Women, Rights of," in *CW*, vol. 21, 386.

79. Barbara Caine, "Victorian Feminism and the Ghost of Mary Wollstonecraft," *Women's Writing* 4:2 (1997), 261–75.

Chapter Two. Foundations of Universal Human Rights

1. Wollstonecraft, *Rights of Woman*, in *Works*, vol. 5, 153, 157, 249; Ronald Dworkin, *Taking Rights Seriously* (London: Bloomsbury, [1977] 1997), 6; Bentham, *Rights, Representation, and Reform*, xlvii, 317.

2. John Rawls, *A Theory of Justice*, revised edition (Cambridge, MA: Belknap Press of Harvard University Press, [1971] 1999), 184–85.

3. Beitz, *The Idea of Human Rights*, 49. The place of virtue in Wollstonecraft's and Mill's moral and political philosophies is explored at length in chapter 3. Mill, *Auguste Comte and Positivism*, in *CW*, vol. 10, 267.

4. Rawls, *Political Liberalism* (1993). For nonfoundationalist approaches to justifying universal human rights in the tradition of Rawlsian political liberalism, see Rawls, *The Law of Peoples* (1999), Donnelly, *Universal Human Rights in Theory and Practice* (2003), and Beitz, *The Idea of Human Rights* (2009). Other nonfoundationalist schools of thought on human rights, such as Richard Rorty's, are not my concern in this chapter. Rorty's sentimentalist alternative to the Rawlsian approach is treated in chapter 5. See Rorty, "Human Rights, Rationality, and Sentimentality."

5. Donnelly, *Universal Human Rights in Theory and Practice*, 7–21.

6. Gilabert, "Humanist and Political Perspectives on Human Rights," 441; ibid.; Brooke Ackerly, "Human Rights Enjoyment in Theory and Activism," *Human Rights Review* 12 (2011), 221–39, especially 225; Sen, "Consequentialist Evaluation and Practical Reason," 497; Sen, *The Idea of Justice*, 362–63.

7. Thomas Banchoff and Robert Wuthnow, eds., *Religion and the Global Politics of Human Rights* (Oxford: Oxford University Press, 2011); Minky Worden, ed., *The Unfinished Revolution: Voices from the Global Fight for Women's Rights* (New York: Seven Stories Press, 2012); Glendon, *A World Made New*; Wendy Shalit, *A Return to Modesty: Discovering the Lost Virtue* (New York: Simon and Schuster, 2000), 111, 191.

8. Gilabert, "Humanist and Political Perspectives on Human Rights"; Mill, *Subjection of Women*, in *CW*, vol. 21, 340; Ian Shapiro, *Political Criticism* (Berkeley: University of California Press, 1990), 290–92; Ackerly, *Political Theory and Feminist Social Criticism*, 11–12.

9. Sapiro, *A Vindication of Political Virtue*, 74–76, 118–19; Lena Halldenius, "The Primacy of Right: On the Triad of Liberty, Equality and Virtue in Wollstonecraft's Political Thought," *British Journal for the History of Philosophy* 15:1 (2007), 75–99; Elizabeth Frazer, "Mary Wollstonecraft on Politics and Friendship," *Political Studies* 56:1 (March 2008), 237–56, especially 251; Ruth Abbey, "Are Women Human? Wollstonecraft's Defense of Rights for Women," in Mary Wollstonecraft, *A Vindication of the Rights of Woman*, ed. Eileen Hunt Botting (New Haven: Yale University Press, 2014), 229–45.

10. Wollstonecraft, *Rights of Woman*, in *Works*, vol. 5, 220, 124; Jane Duran, *Eight Women Philosophers: Theory, Politics, and Feminism* (Champaign: University of Illinois Press, 2006), 114–15; Mary Hawkesworth, *Political Worlds of Women: Activism, Advocacy, and Governance in the Twenty-First Century* (Boulder: Westview, 2012), 41.

11. For a reading of Price as a Kantian ethicist, see M. B. Smith, "Does Humanity Share a Common Moral Faculty?" *Journal of Moral Philosophy* 7:1 (2010), 37–53.

12. Immanuel Kant, *Groundwork for the Metaphysics of Morals*, ed. and tr. Allen W. Wood (New Haven: Yale University Press, 2002), 14–15.

13. Ibid., 3–5, 27.

14. Sapiro, *A Vindication of Political Virtue*, 49–51; Taylor, *Mary Wollstonecraft and the Feminist Imagination*, 12, 226; Botting, *Family Feuds*, 164–67; Natalie F. Taylor, *The Rights of Woman as Chimera: The Political Philosophy of Mary Wollstonecraft* (New York: Routledge, 2007), 182; Abbey, "Are Women Human? Wollstonecraft's Defense of Rights for Women," 235; Wollstonecraft, *Rights of Woman*, in *Works*, vol. 5, 84.

15. Wollstonecraft, *Rights of Woman*, in *Works*, vol. 5, 95; Sapiro, *A Vindication of Political Virtue*, 92.

16. Wollstonecraft, *Rights of Woman*, in *Works*, vol. 5, 266, 67.

17. Onora O'Neill, "Kantian Approaches to Some Famine Problems," in *Matters of Life and Death: New Introductory Essays in Moral Philosophy*, ed. Tom Regan (New York: McGraw Hill, 1980), 258–70; Onora O'Neill, *Constructions of Reason: Explorations of Kant's Practical Philosophy* (Cambridge: Cambridge University Press, 1989), 75–77, 188; Jean Hampton, *The Intrinsic Worth of Persons: Contractarianism in Moral and Political Philosophy*, ed. Daniel Farnham (Cambridge: Cambridge University Press, 2007), 13–25; Wollstonecraft, *Rights of Woman*, in *Works*, vol. 5, 266. For a helpful summary of Kant's misogynistic biases, see Lara Denis, "From Friendship to Marriage: Revising Kant," *Philosophy and Phenomenological Research* 63:1 (2001), 1–28.

18. Wollstonecraft, *Rights of Woman*, in *Works*, vol. 5, 114; ibid., 216.

19. Kant, *Groundwork for the Metaphysics of Morals* (tr. Wood), 46–48. One version of Kant's philosophical anthropology is found in *The Critique of Judgment* (1790). Wollstonecraft referenced this book by "Mr. Kant" in *Hints*, in *Works*, vol. 5, 267. See also Kant, selections from "Critique of Judgment," in *Perpetual Peace*, 37–43. O'Neill, "Kantian Approaches to Some Famine Problems"; Wollstonecraft, *Rights of Men*, in *Works*, vol. 5, 16; ibid.

20. Wollstonecraft, *Rights of Woman*, in *Works*, vol. 5, 131.

21. Wollstonecraft, *Rights of Men*, in *Works*, vol. 5, 34.

22. Onora O'Neill, "Justice, Gender, and International Boundaries," *British Journal of Political Science* 20:4 (October 1990), 439–59; Wollstonecraft, *Rights of Woman*, in *Works*, vol. 5, 222.

23. Botting, *Family Feuds*, 163–66.
24. Lisa Isherwood, *Introducing Feminist Christologies* (New York: Continuum, 2001), 52–53.
25. Wollstonecraft, *Rights of Woman*, in *Works*, vol. 5, 101, 121; Wollstonecraft, *Maria, or the Wrongs of Woman*, in *Works*, vol. 1, 108, 111, 174.
26. Wollstonecraft, *Rights of Woman*, in *Works*, vol. 5, 110. In this interpretation of Wollstonecraft's conception of human development, I use some of the terms found in Martha Nussbaum's list of the ten central human capabilities, such as bodily integrity and play. See *Women and Human Development*, 78–80.
27. Wollstonecraft, *Rights of Woman*, in *Works*, vol. 5, 229.
28. Ibid., 266; ibid.
29. Sen, "Consequentialist Evaluation and Practical Reason," 497; Sen, *Development as Freedom*, 227–48.
30. Hamburger, *John Stuart Mill on Liberty and Control*, xiii.
31. Mill, *On Liberty*, in *CW*, vol. 18, 223; Mill, *Utilitarianism*, in *CW*, vol. 10, 210.
32. Mary Ann Glendon, *Rights Talk: The Impoverishment of Political Discourse* (New York: Simon and Schuster, 1991); Mill, *On Liberty*, in *CW*, vol. 18, 261; ibid., 267.
33. Mill, *Utilitarianism*, in *CW*, vol. 10, 207; J. O. Urmson, "The Interpretation of the Moral Philosophy of J. S. Mill," in *Mill's Utilitarianism: Critical Essays*, ed. David Lyons (New York: Rowman and Littlefield, 1997), 1–8, especially 7.
34. Mill, *On Liberty*, in *CW*, vol. 18, 224; Mill, *Utilitarianism*, in *CW*, vol. 10, 214; Mill, *On Liberty*, in *CW*, vol. 18, 224; John M. Robson, *The Improvement of Mankind: The Social and Political Thought of John Stuart Mill* (London: Routledge and Kegan Paul, 1968), 150; Mill, "Whewell on Moral Philosophy [1852]," in *CW*, vol. 10, 187.
35. Mill, *Utilitarianism*, in *CW*, vol. 10, 210; ibid.; ibid.; Mill, *On Liberty*, in *CW*, vol. 18, 224; ibid., 270; ibid.
36. Mill, *Utilitarianism*, in *CW*, vol. 10, 212–13.
37. Ibid., 214; ibid., 213; ibid., 214.
38. Rawls, *A Theory of Justice*, 184–85.
39. Mill, *Utilitarianism*, in *CW*, vol. 10, 255; ibid., 251.
40. D. G. Brown, "Mill's Act-Utilitarianism," in *Mill's Utilitarianism*, ed. Lyons, 25–28; Gerald J. Postema, "Bentham's Utilitarianism," in *The Blackwell Guide to Mill's Utilitarianism*, ed. Henry R. West (Oxford: Blackwell,

2006), 26–44, especially 28; L. W. Sumner, "Mill's Theory of Rights," in *The Blackwell Guide to Mill's Utilitarianism*, 184–98; Derek Parfit, *Reasons and Persons* (New York: Oxford University Press, 1984), 387.

41. Mill, *On Liberty*, in *CW*, vol. 18, 261; ibid., 270; ibid., 223.

42. Nancy J. Hirschmann, *Gender, Class, and Freedom in Modern Political Theory* (Princeton: Princeton University Press, 2008), 216–23, 266.

43. Urmson, "The Moral Philosophy of J. S. Mill," 3; David Lyons, "Human Rights and the General Welfare," in *Mill's Utilitarianism*, ed. Lyons, 29–43, especially 36; Mill, *Utilitarianism*, in *CW*, vol. 10, 256; ibid., 259; J. B. Schneewind, *Sidgwick's Ethics and Victorian Moral Philosophy* (Oxford: Oxford University Press, 1977), 336–37.

44. Lyons, "Human Rights and the General Welfare," 33.

45. Mill, *On Liberty*, in *CW*, vol. 18, 224; Mill, *Utilitarianism*, in *CW*, vol. 10, 215; Mill, *Autobiography*, in *CW*, vol. 1, 153. For Mill's critique of coverture, see *Subjection of Women*, in *CW*, vol. 21, 283–86.

46. Susan Leigh Anderson, "Mill's Life," in *The Blackwell Guide to Mill's Utilitarianism*, 22.

47. Mill, *Utilitarianism*, in *CW*, vol. 10, 242, 247.

48. Mill, *On Liberty*, in *CW*, vol. 18, 270; ibid., 269.

49. Rawls, *Political Liberalism*, xxvii; Rawls, *The Law of Peoples*, 18.

50. Mill, *Utilitarianism*, in *CW*, vol. 10, 247; ibid., 255. On the latter passage in chapter 5 of *Utilitarianism*, Georgios Varouxakis points out that Mill's broader distinction between the perfect obligations of justice (providing rights) and the imperfect obligations of morality (giving charity) means that Mill is not like some contemporary "cosmopolitan" theorists who treat these obligations identically. Rather, for Mill, justice is technically a part of morality but not "coextensive" with it. While agreeing with Varouxakis that Mill does not conflate perfect and imperfect obligations of morality, I make a case in chapter 5 for why Mill's literary writings model a "rooted cosmopolitan" approach to theorizing global justice, in which the direct or vicarious experience of loving and respectful relationships motivates people to be moral as well as just toward human beings (and sentient life) in general. Georgios Varouxakis, *Liberty Abroad: J. S. Mill on International Relations* (Cambridge: Cambridge University Press, 2013), 42–43.

51. Mill, *Subjection of Women*, in *CW*, vol. 21, 287–88; ibid., 300.

52. "CEDAW 2014." Accessed 15 December 2014 at http://www.women streaty.org/index.php/about-cedaw/cedaw-by-the-numbers

53. Wollstonecraft may have found her way to Forster via Cookson, as she quoted virtually the same passages on polygamy from Forster's voyage as Cookson. See Johann Reinhold Forster, *Observations Made during a Voyage round the World* (London: G. Robinson, 1778), 428; James Cookson, *Thoughts on Polygamy, Suggested by the Dictates of Scripture, Nature, Reason, and Common-Sense* (Winchester, England: J. Wilkes, 1782), 333; Wollstonecraft, *Rights of Woman*, in *Works*, vol. 5, 139. For an extended study of Enlightenment-era liberal critiques of polygamy, see John Witte Jr., *The Western Case for Monogamy over Polygamy* (Cambridge: Cambridge University Press, 2015), chapter 9.

54. Lara Denis has argued that a revised Kantian feminist conception of marriage would indeed be this kind of higher friendship. Denis, "From Friendship to Marriage: Revising Kant." See also Ruth Abbey, "Back to the Future: Marriage as Friendship in the Thought of Mary Wollstonecraft," *Hypatia* 14:3 (1999), 78–95.

55. Taylor, *The Rights of Woman as Chimera*, 180; Frazer, "Mary Wollstonecraft on Politics and Friendship"; Wollstonecraft, *Lessons*, in *Works*, vol. 4, 270; Botting, *Family Feuds*, 185–86. In the *Rights of Woman*, Wollstonecraft tellingly eliminates one line from her quote of Forster that Cookson left in, regarding the ordination of monogamy for Europe by divine particular providence: "Here, no doubt, providence has enforced the necessity of monogamy." See Forster, *Observations Made during a Voyage round the World*, 428; Cookson, *Thoughts on Polygamy*, 333; Wollstonecraft, *Rights of Woman*, in *Works*, vol. 5, 139.

56. Shirin Ebadi, "Islamic Law and the Revolution against Women," in *The Unfinished Revolution*, ed. Worden, 55–56; Wollstonecraft, *Rights of Woman*, in *Works*, vol. 5, 108.

57. Lily Munir as quoted in Katherine Robinson, "Islamic Cosmopolitics, Human Rights, and Anti-Violence Strategies in Indonesia," in *Anthropology and the New Cosmopolitanism: Rooted, Feminist, and Vernacular Perspectives*, ed. Pnina Werbner (New York: Berg, 2008), 121; Ebadi, "Islamic Law and the Revolution against Women," 55–56; ibid.; ibid.

58. Mill, *On Liberty*, in *CW*, vol. 18, 290; Mill, *Subjection of Women*, in *CW*, vol. 21, 336.

59. Mill, *On Liberty*, in *CW*, vol. 18, 290; ibid., 291.

60. Ibid., 291.

61. Ibid.

62. "Encouraging to Women," *Woman's Exponent* 2:22 (15 April 1874), 175; Carol Cornwall Madsen, "Emmeline B. Wells: Romantic Rebel," in

Supporting Saints: Life Stories of Nineteenth-Century Mormons, ed. Donald Q. Cannon and David J. Whittaker (Provo, UT: Brigham Young University, Religious Studies Center, 1985), 305–41; ibid.; Bruce Baum, "Feminism, Liberalism, and Cultural Pluralism: J. S. Mill on Mormon Polygamy," *Journal of Political Philosophy* 5:3 (1997), 230–53, especially 238.

63. Baum, "Feminism, Liberalism and Cultural Pluralism," 230; Madsen, "Emmeline B. Wells: Romantic Rebel"; Barbara Caine, "Elizabeth Cady Stanton, John Stuart Mill, and the Nature of Feminist Thought," in *Elizabeth Cady Stanton, Feminist as Thinker: A Reader in Documents and Essays*, ed. Ellen Carol DuBois and Richard C. Smith (New York: New York University Press, 2007), 50–65.

64. Madsen, "Emmeline B. Wells: Romantic Rebel."

65. Robert Putnam and David Campbell, *American Grace: How Religion Divides and Unites Us* (New York: Simon and Schuster, [2010] 2012), 241; Rawls, *Political Liberalism*, 36–37.

66. Ebadi, "Islamic Law and the Revolution against Women," 58.

Chapter Three. Theories of Human Development

1. Mill, *On Liberty*, in *CW*, vol. 18, 302. In addition to basic human rights to food and education, Mill addressed the right to security, or to be free from "personal violence" (a right that had special salience for women in abusive marriages). See *Subjection of Women*, in *CW*, vol. 21, 284. Wollstonecraft, following Rousseau, argued that "self-preservation" is the "first law of nature" and entails rights to sustenance and security. See *Rights of Men*, in *Works*, vol. 5, 16; *Rights of Woman*, in *Works*, vol. 5, 110. For Wollstonecraft's extended defense of education as a fundamental human right of girls and boys, see chapter 12 of the *Rights of Woman*.

2. Wollstonecraft, *Rights of Woman*, in *Works*, vol. 5, 75; Mill, *Autobiography*, in *CW*, vol. 1, 153; Mill, *On Liberty*, in *CW*, vol. 18, 266. For contemporary liberal theories of virtue ethics, see Stephen Macedo, *Liberal Virtues: Citizenship, Virtue, and Community in Liberal Constitutionalism* (Oxford: Clarendon, 1990); Peter Berkowitz, *Virtue and the Making of Modern Liberalism* (Princeton: Princeton University Press, 1999).

3. Nussbaum, "Mill on Happiness," 114–17.

4. Although Nussbaum and others, such as Natalie Taylor, have argued that Aristotle's ethics may be read as applying to all people, his examples of virtue typically draw on elite men's roles in his ancient Athenian society. Taylor has read his views on marriage to mean that he thought women

were capable of the same virtues as men. Even if we grant Aristotle such a generous egalitarian reading of his ethics, nowhere will a reader find evidence of his concern with egalitarian political ideas such as universal human rights or universal primary education that only fully emerged in the late eighteenth century. Nussbaum, "Mill on Happiness," 114–17; Taylor, *The Rights of Woman as Chimera*, 148–70; Wollstonecraft, *Rights of Men*, in *Works*, vol. 5, 20 note 4; Wollstonecraft, *Rights of Woman*, in *Works*, vol. 5, 81, 108. For Wollstonecraft's theory of democracy, see Daniel I. O'Neill, *The Burke-Wollstonecraft Debate: Savagery, Civilization, and Democracy* (University Park: Pennsylvania State University Press, 2007), chapter 7. While it is undisputed that Mill had extensively read Aristotle's corpus, the context for Wollstonecraft's exposure to Aristotelian ideas still remains unknown. Wollstonecraft appears to have been directly familiar with the *Politics* and at least indirectly indebted to the *Nicomachean Ethics*. See Taylor, *The Rights of Woman as Chimera*, 8. Although scholars have yet to establish how Wollstonecraft was at least indirectly exposed to the ideas of Aristotle's *Ethics*, the most likely and immediate historical source (and filter) was her rational Christian moral theology, which served as the metaphysical basis of her ethical system.

5. Sapiro, *A Vindication of Political Virtue*. For Wollstonecraft as a virtue ethicist, see Abbey, "Are Women Human?" (2014); Sandrine Berges, *The Routledge Guidebook to Wollstonecraft's A Vindication of the Rights of Woman* (London: Routledge, 2013), especially the conclusion; Frazer, "Mary Wollstonecraft on Politics and Friendship" (2008); and Taylor, *The Rights of Woman as Chimera* (2007). For Mill as a virtue ethicist, see Marcia Baron, "Virtue Ethics in Relation to Kantian Ethics: An Opinionated Overview and Commentary," in *Perfecting Virtue: New Essays on Kantian Ethics and Virtue Ethics*, ed. Lawrence Jost and Julian Wuerth (Cambridge: Cambridge University Press, 2011), 8–37; Samuel Clark, "Love, Poetry, and the Good Life: Mill's *Autobiography* and Perfectionist Ethics," *Inquiry* 53:6 (December 2010), 565–78; Robert Devigne, *Reforming Liberalism: J. S. Mill's Use of Ancient, Religious, Liberal, and Romantic Moralities* (New Haven: Yale University Press, 2006), 55–56; Wendy Donner, "John Stuart Mill on Education and Democracy," in *J. S. Mill's Political Thought: A Bicentennial Reassessment*, ed. Nadia Urbinati and Alex Zakaras (Cambridge: Cambridge University Press, 2007), 250–74; Nussbaum, "Mill on Happiness." Frederick Rosen has pointed out that the tradition of reading Mill's feminism in light of his

concern with "character" or "ethology" dates to Alan Ryan's *J. S. Mill* (London: Routledge and Kegan Paul, 1974), 156. See Frederick Rosen, *Mill: Founders of Modern Social and Political Thought* (Oxford: Oxford University Press, 2013), 252. For Mill as primarily a theorist of freedom as nondomination, see Maria Morales, "Rational Freedom in John Stuart Mill's Feminism," in *J. S. Mill's Political Thought*, ed. Urbinati and Zakaras, 43–66. For Wollstonecraft as primarily a theorist of virtue, see Taylor, *The Rights of Woman as Chimera*.

6. Alan Ryan, "J. S. Mill on Education," *Oxford Review of Education* 37:5 (2011), 653–67, especially 657; Mill, "Inaugural Address Delivered to the University of St. Andrews," in *CW*, vol. 21, 217–18; Sen, *The Idea of Justice*, 269–90; Nussbaum, *Creating Capabilities*, 17–45.

7. Mill, *Autobiography*, in *CW*, vol. 1, 153; Hamburger, *John Stuart Mill on Liberty and Control*, 20–21, 135–39, 150–51, 226–29.

8. Alan M. S. J. Coffee, "Mary Wollstonecraft, Freedom, and the Enduring Power of Social Domination," *European Journal of Political Theory* 12:2 (April 2013), 116–35; Lena Halldenius, "The Political Conditions of Free Agency: The Case of Mary Wollstonecraft," in *Freedom and the Construction of Europe*, ed. Quentin Skinner and Martin van Gelderen (Cambridge: Cambridge University Press, 2013), vol. 2, 227–46, especially 234; Wollstonecraft, *Rights of Woman*, in *Works*, vol. 5, 120; ibid., 131.

9. Martha C. Nussbaum, "Nature, Function, and Capability: Aristotle on Political Distribution," in *Wider Working Papers 31* (Helsinki, December 1987), 1–50; Amartya Sen, *Inequality Reexamined* (Cambridge, MA: Harvard University Press, [1992] 1995), 90–91. See also MacIntyre, *After Virtue*, xv. Nussbaum, *Creating Capabilities*, 17–45; Sen, "Consequentialist Evaluation and Practical Reason," 477–502, especially 497.

10. Wollstonecraft, *Rights of Woman*, in *Works*, vol. 5, 266; Mill, *Subjection of Women*, in *CW*, vol. 21, 278.

11. Wollstonecraft, *Rights of Men*, in *Works*, vol. 5, 9.

12. Wollstonecraft, *Rights of Woman*, in *Works*, vol. 5, 121.

13. *Oxford English Dictionary*, online edition, "Gender, noun." The *American Journal of Psychology* in 1945 published the first social scientific use of "gender" to mean the "socialized obverse of sex." Wollstonecraft, *Rights of Woman*, in *Works*, vol. 5, 88.

14. Wollstonecraft, *Rights of Woman*, in *Works*, vol. 5, 88.

15. Ibid., 216; ibid., 93; ibid., 30; ibid., 130, 186.

16. Mill, *Subjection of Women*, in *CW*, vol. 21, 269; ibid., 261, 269.

17. Mill, "Letter to Carlyle, 5 October 1833," in *CW*, vol. 12, 184; Nadia Urbinati, "John Stuart Mill on Androgyny and Ideal Marriage," in *Mill's The Subjection of Women: Critical Essays*, ed. Maria H. Morales (Lanham, MD: Rowman and Littlefield, 2005), 157–82, especially 157.

18. Mill, "On Marriage," in *CW*, vol. 21, 41.

19. Mill and Taylor, "Women, Rights of," in *CW*, vol. 21, 387–88; Mill, *Considerations on Representative Government*, in *CW*, vol. 19, 479.

20. Mill, *Logic*, in *CW*, vol. 7, 85.

21. Rosen, *Mill*, 252–55.

22. Mill, "Speech on the Admission of Women to the Electoral Franchise, 20 May 1867," in *CW*, vol. 28, chap. 55, 152.

23. Urbinati, "John Stuart Mill on Androgyny," 175 note 8.

24. Wollstonecraft, *Rights of Woman*, in *Works*, vol. 5, 75; "John Stuart Mill on Woman Suffrage," *New York Times*, 21 July 1867. Reprinted from the *Topeka Record*.

25. Jean Elshtain, *Meditations on Modern Political Thought: Masculine/Feminine Themes from Luther to Arendt* (University Park: Penn State University Press, [1986] 1992), 40; Susan Mendus, "The Marriage of True Minds: The Ideal of Marriage in the Philosophy of John Stuart Mill," in *Mill's The Subjection of Women*, ed. Morales, 135–56.

26. Wollstonecraft, *Rights of Woman*, in *Works*, vol. 5, 193; ibid., 140; Jeremy Waldron, "Mill on Liberty and the Contagious Diseases Acts," in *J. S. Mill's Political Thought*, ed. Urbinati and Zakaras, 11–42, especially 30–32.

27. Mill, *Subjection of Women*, in *CW*, vol. 21, 298; Urbinati, "John Stuart Mill on Androgyny"; Okin, *Women in Western Political Thought*, 226–27.

28. Mill, *Subjection of Women*, in *CW*, vol. 21, 297; Torben Iversen and Frances Rosenbluth, *Women, Work, and Politics: The Political Economy of Gender Equality* (New Haven: Yale University Press, 2010), vii–xv, 81–109.

29. Wollstonecraft, *Rights of Woman*, in *Works*, vol. 5, 114; Urbinati, "John Stuart Mill on Androgyny."

30. Claudia Johnson, *Equivocal Beings: Politics, Gender, and Sentimentality in the 1790s: Wollstonecraft, Radcliffe, Burney, Austen* (Chicago: University of Chicago Press, 1995), 11; Wollstonecraft, *Rights of Woman*, in *Works*, vol. 5, 146, 208; Johnson, *Equivocal Beings*. Lyndall Gordon has suggested that Wollstonecraft was more than tolerant, indeed protective,

of her close friend Joseph Johnson's homosexuality. Gordon, *Vindication*, 387. Wollstonecraft playfully praised the transvestite Madame d'Eon as an example of a "woman" with a "masculine" education in the *Rights of Woman* (*Works*, vol. 5, 146). Louis Crompton, "Jeremy Bentham's Essay on Paederasty," *Journal of Homosexuality* 3:4 (1978), 389–405; Claeys, *Mill and Paternalism*, 204–6.

31. Judith Butler, *Gender Trouble: Feminism and the Subversion of Identity* (New York: Routledge, 1990); Martha C. Nussbaum, "The Professor of Parody," *New Republic*, 22 February 1999, 37–45.

32. Mill, "Inaugural Address," in *CW*, vol. 21, 217, 222, 253–55.

33. Wollstonecraft, *Rights of Woman*, in *Works*, vol. 5, 89; Mill, *Subjection of Women*, in *CW*, vol. 21, 271.

34. Amartya Sen, *Commodities and Capabilities* (New York: North-Holland, 1985), 21–22; Nussbaum, *Women and Human Development*, chapter 2.

35. Wendy Gunther-Canada, *Rebel Writer: Mary Wollstonecraft and Enlightenment Politics* (DeKalb: Northern Illinois University Press, 2001), 43–50; Taylor, *Mary Wollstonecraft and the Feminist Imagination*, 238–44; Wollstonecraft, *Wrongs of Woman*, in *Works*, vol. 1, 113.

36. Mill, *Subjection of Women*, in *CW*, vol. 21, 270; ibid.; ibid.; ibid., 272; ibid., 271.

37. Sandrine Berges, "Why Women Hug Their Chains: Wollstonecraft and Adaptive Preferences," *Utilitas* 23:1 (2011), 72–87; Jennifer Saul, "Implicit Bias, Stereotype Threat, and Women in Philosophy," in *Women in Philosophy: What Needs to Change?* ed. Katrina Hutchison and Fiona Jenkins (Oxford: Oxford University Press, 2013), 39–60, especially 42.

38. Berges, "Why Women Hug Their Chains," 87; Nussbaum, *Women and Human Development*, 111–66; Susan Gubar, "Feminist Misogyny: Mary Wollstonecraft and the Paradox of 'It Takes One to Know One,'" *Feminist Studies* 20:3 (Autumn 1994), 452–73.

39. Berges, "Why Women Hug Their Chains," 82–84; Mill, *Subjection of Women*, in *CW*, vol. 21, 269; ibid.

40. Mill, *Subjection of Women*, in *CW*, vol. 21, 272; ibid.; Iversen and Rosenbluth, *Women, Work, and Politics*.

41. Mill, *Subjection of Women*, in *CW*, vol. 21, 305; Mozaffar Qizilbash, "Capability, Happiness and Adaptation in Sen and J. S. Mill," *Utilitas* 18:1 (2006), 20–32.

42. Wollstonecraft, *Rights of Woman*, in *Works*, vol. 5, 240; ibid.; ibid. For the Millennium Development Goals, see http://www.un.org/millenniumgoals/

43. John Mason, "Scottish Charity Schools of the Eighteenth Century," *Scottish Historical Review* 33:115 (April 1954), 1–13, especially 11–13.

44. Sylvana Tomaselli, "Biographical Directory," in Mary Wollstonecraft, *A Vindication of the Rights of Men and A Vindication of the Rights of Woman*, ed. Sylvana Tomaselli (Cambridge: Cambridge University Press, 1995), 320; William J. Reese, "The Origins of Progressive Education," *History of Education Quarterly* 41:1 (Spring 2001), 1–24, especially 10–13.

45. Johann N. Neem, *Creating a Nation of Joiners: Democracy and Civil Society in Early National Massachusetts* (Cambridge, MA: Harvard University Press, 2008), 28; Marion Rust, *Prodigal Daughters: Susanna Rowson's Early American Women* (Chapel Hill: University of North Carolina Press, 2008), 86–91; Eileen Hunt Botting and Sarah L. Houser, "'Drawing the Line of Equality': Hannah Mather Crocker on Women's Rights," *American Political Science Review* 100:2 (2006), 265–78; Robert W. T. Martin, "Between Consensus and Conflict: Habermas, Post-Modern Conflict, and the Early American Public Sphere," *Polity* 37:3 (July 2005), 365–88, especially 385.

46. Wollstonecraft, *Rights of Woman*, in *Works*, vol. 5, 240; ibid., 230.

47. Ibid., 246.

48. Ibid., 241.

49. Ibid., 236; ibid., 245; Jean-Jacques Rousseau, *Discourse on the Origin of Inequality* (1755), in *The Social Contract and the First and Second Discourses*, ed. and tr. Susan Dunn (New Haven: Yale University Press, 2002), 84–85; Wollstonecraft, *Rights of Woman*, in *Works*, vol. 5, 245.

50. Wollstonecraft, *Rights of Woman*, in *Works*, vol. 5, 237; ibid., 246.

51. Ibid., 240; Ryan, "J. S. Mill on Education," 666 note 15.

52. Stephen Broadberry, "Human Capital and Skills," in *The Cambridge Economic History of Modern Britain*, vol. 2, ed. Roderick Floud and Paul Johnson (Cambridge: Cambridge University Press, 2004), 56–73, especially 57; Henry Reeves, *John Stuart Mill: Victorian Firebrand* (London: Atlantic, 2007), 455; Mill, "Sarah Austin's Translation of Cousin," in *CW*, vol. 23, 729–30. See also Mill, "Prospects of France," in *CW*, vol. 22, 641–44; "Reform in Education," in *CW*, vol. 21, 61–74; Reeves, *John Stuart Mill*, 455; Hamburger, *John Stuart Mill on Liberty and Control*, 10.

53. Mill, *On Liberty*, in *CW*, vol. 18, 303; Mill, "Inaugural Address," in *CW*, vol. 21, 248.

54. Mill, "Letter to the Rev. Leopold John Bernays, 8 January 1868," in *CW*, vol. 16, 1347–48.

55. Mill, *On Liberty*, in *CW*, vol. 18, 266; ibid., 262.

56. Mill, "Inaugural Address," in *CW*, vol. 21, 224; ibid., 218; ibid., 219.

57. Andrew Valls, "Self-Development and the Liberal State: The Cases of John Stuart Mill and Wilhelm von Humboldt," *Review of Politics* 61:2 (Spring 1999), 251–74; Mill, *On Liberty*, in *CW*, vol. 18, 264; Mill, *Utilitarianism*, in *CW*, vol. 10, 213.

58. Mill, *Utilitarianism*, in *CW*, 236–37; Nussbaum, "Mill on Happiness," 110–17; Mill, "Wordsworth and Byron 30 January, 1829," in *CW*, vol. 26, 441–42; Ryan, "J. S. Mill on Education," 655.

59. Mill, *Principles of Political Economy*, in *CW*, vol. 2, 208.

60. Ryan, "J. S. Mill on Education," 657; Mill, "Inaugural Address," in *CW*, vol. 21, 221; Mill, *Subjection of Women*, in *CW*, vol. 21, 308.

61. Hollie Mann and Jeff Spinner-Halev, "John Stuart Mill's Feminism: On Progress, the State, and the Path to Justice," *Polity* 42:2 (2010), 244–70.

62. Mill, *On Liberty*, in *CW*, vol. 18, 224.

63. Wollstonecraft, *Rights of Woman*, in *Works*, vol. 5, 220; Wollstonecraft, *Rights of Men*, in *Works*, vol. 5, 46.

64. Wollstonecraft, *Rights of Woman*, in *Works*, vol. 5, 250; ibid.

65. Mill, *Principles of Political Economy*, in *CW*, vol. 2, 206, 208–9; Mill, *Autobiography*, in *CW*, vol. 1, 239; Mill, *Subjection of Women*, in *CW*, vol. 21, chap. 4.

66. Hirschmann, *Gender, Class, and Freedom*, 238–39; Mill, *Subjection of Women*, in *CW*, vol. 21, 326.

67. United Nations, "We Can End Poverty: Millennium Development Goals and Beyond 2015 Fact Sheet" (2013). Accessed 24 December 2013 at http://www.un.org/millenniumgoals/pdf/Goal_2_fs.pdf; U.N. Women, "The Unfinished Agenda: Balance Sheet of Progress and Backlogs on Gender Equality" (2012). Accessed 24 December 2013, at http://www.unifem.org/attachments/products/MDGsAndGenderEquality_2_UnfinishedAgenda.pdf

68. Mill, "Inaugural Address," in *CW*, vol. 21, 257.

Chapter Four. The Problem of Cultural Bias

1. Michel Foucault, *Discipline and Punish: The Birth of the Prison* (New York: Vintage, [1975] 1995); Carol Gilligan, *In a Different Voice: Psychological Theory and Women's Development* (Cambridge, MA: Harvard University Press, [1982] 1993); Charles Taylor, *Sources of the Self: The Making of the Modern Identity* (Cambridge: Cambridge University Press, 1989), especially 40–42.

2. Jürgen Habermas, *The Inclusion of the Other: Studies in Political Theory*, ed. Ciaran Cronin and Pablo De Greiff (Cambridge, MA: MIT Press, 1998); Rawls, *The Law of Peoples*.

3. Anthony Pagden, "Human Rights, Natural Rights, and Europe's Imperial Legacy," *Political Theory* 31:2 (April 2003), 171–99; Clare Midgley, *Feminism and Empire: Women Activists in Imperial Britain, 1790–1865* (New York: Routledge, 2007), 13–20; Javed Majeed, "James Mill's *The History of British India*," in *Utilitarianism and Empire*, ed. Schultz and Varouxakis, 93–106; Pitts, *A Turn to Empire*, 123–62; Karuna Mantena, "Mill and the Imperial Predicament," in *J. S. Mill's Political Thought*, ed. Urbinati and Zakaras, 298–318.

4. Jane Rendall, "'The grand causes which combine to carry mankind forward': Wollstonecraft, History, and Revolution," *Women's Writing* 4:2 (1997), 155–72; O'Neill, *The Burke-Wollstonecraft Debate*, 37–41; Charles W. Mills, *The Racial Contract* (Ithaca: Cornell University Press, 1997), 13. Thomas McCarthy's *Race, Empire, and the Idea of Human Development* (Cambridge: Cambridge University Press, 2009) follows Mills in offering an insightful and critical focus on the problematic racial and racist dimensions of modern theories of human development.

5. Jean-Jacques Rousseau, *The Discourses and Other Early Political Writings*, ed. Victor Gourevitch (Cambridge: Cambridge University Press, 1997), 6, 9; Botting, *Family Feuds*, 42–43, 62–63.

6. Karen O'Brien, *Women and Enlightenment in Eighteenth-Century Britain* (Cambridge: Cambridge University Press, 2009), 78–79; O'Neill, *The Burke-Wollstonecraft Debate*, 117–18; Rendall, "'The grand causes which combine to carry mankind forward'"; Wollstonecraft, "Review of Samuel Stanhope Smith, An Essay on the Causes of the Variety of Complexion and Figure in the Human Species. To which are added, Strictures on Lord Kaims's Discourse on the original Diversity of Mankind," in *Works*, vol. 7, 54; Scott Juengel, "Countenancing History: Mary Wollstonecraft, Samuel Stanhope Smith, and Enlightenment Racial Science," *ELH* 68:4 (Winter 2001), 897–927; Lord Kames, *Sketches of the History of Man*, third edition (Dublin: James Williams, 1779), vol. 1, 339.

7. James Mill, *The History of British India* (London: Baldwin, Cradock, and Joy, 1817), vol. 1, xv.

8. Pitts, *A Turn to Empire*, 123–62; Mantena, "Imperial Predicament," 298–318; Alan Ryan, "Bureaucracy, Democracy, Liberty: Some Un-

answered Questions in Mill's Politics," in *J. S. Mill's Political Thought*, 148; Edward W. Said, *Orientalism* (New York: Vintage, [1979] 1994), 202–10; Margaret Kohn and Keally McBride, *Political Theories of Decolonization: Postcolonialism and the Problem of Foundations* (Oxford: Oxford University Press, 2011), 5; Nadia Urbinati, "The Many Heads of the Hydra: J. S. Mill on Despotism," in *J. S. Mill's Political Thought*, ed. Urbinati and Zakaras, 66–98; Holmes, "Making Sense of Liberal Imperialism," in *J. S. Mill's Political Thought*, ed. Urbinati and Zakaras, 319–46; Mill, *Subjection of Women*, in *CW*, vol. 21, 264.

9. Joyce Zonana, "The Sultan and the Slave: Feminist Orientalism and the Structure of *Jane Eyre*," *Signs* 18:3 (Spring 1993), 592–617; Antoinette M. Burton, *Burdens of History: British Feminists, Indian Women, and Imperial Culture, 1865–1915* (Chapel Hill: University of North Carolina Press, 1994), 39, 75–76, 110; Moira Ferguson, *Colonialism and Gender Relations from Mary Wollstonecraft to Jamaica Kincaid: East Caribbean Connections* (New York: Columbia University Press, 1994); Midgley, *Feminism and Empire*.

10. Said, *Orientalism*, 202–10. Worldcat and interlibrary loan enabled this survey of the global publication of Mill's *Subjection of Women*.

11. Said, *Orientalism*, 202–10; Mohanty, "Under Western Eyes: Feminist Scholarship and Colonial Discourses," 61–88; Mohanty, "Under Western Eyes Revisited," 499–535.

12. Bertrand Badie, *The Imported State: The Westernization of the Political Order*, tr. Claudia Royal (Stanford: Stanford University Press, 2000), 2, 7–9, 11.

13. Offen, *European Feminisms*, 19–20; Offen, "Introduction," in *Globalizing Feminisms*, xxix–xxxiv; Nagel, "Appiah's Rooted Cosmopolitanism."

14. Wollstonecraft, *Rights of Woman*, in *Works*, vol. 5, 82, 183–84.

15. Ibid., 183; Gilligan, "Letter to Readers, 1993," in *In a Different Voice*, xxiii.

16. Wollstonecraft, *Rights of Woman*, in *Works*, vol. 5, 186–87.

17. David Hume, "Of the Association of Ideas," in *Enquiry concerning Human Understanding* (1748), section 3.

18. Annette C. Baier, *Moral Prejudices: Essays on Ethics* (Cambridge, MA: Harvard University Press, 1995), 51–94; Wollstonecraft, *Rights of Woman*, in *Works*, vol. 5, 187.

19. Wollstonecraft, *Rights of Woman*, in *Works*, vol. 5, 187; Moya Lloyd, "A Feminist Mapping of Foucauldian Politics," in *Feminist Interpretations*

of Michel Foucault, ed. Susan Heckman (University Park: Pennsylvania State University Press, 1996), 241–64; Wollstonecraft, *Rights of Woman*, in *Works*, vol. 5, 113.

20. Wollstonecraft, *Rights of Woman*, in *Works*, vol. 5, 116; Thomas Nagel, *The View from Nowhere* (Oxford: Oxford University Press), 63.

21. Charles Taylor, "Foucault on Freedom and Truth," *Political Theory* 12:2 (May 1984), 152–83; Susan Heckman, "Editor's Introduction," *Feminist Interpretations of Michel Foucault*, ed. Susan Heckman (University Park: Pennsylvania State University Press, 1996), 2.

22. For example, Wollstonecraft, *Rights of Woman*, in *Works*, vol. 5, 74, 76, 232, 266. For analysis of Montesquieu's and Voltaire's polarization of northern and southern European cultures, see Dainotto, *Europe (in Theory)*, 52–86, 94–95. Similarly, Adam Smith referred to the parts of Europe "south of Cape Finisterre" (in northwest Spain) as nonmanufacturing cultures. In Smith's theory of development, the economic drain of the Roman Catholic Church hierarchy reduced the intellectual output and other forms of productivity in southern Europe in comparison to Protestant Western Europe. See Smith, *The Wealth of Nations* (G. Bell, 1908), especially 87–88, 311, 336–37. Price, *Discourse on the Love of Our Country*, in *Political Writings*, 179.

23. In the *Rights of Woman*, Wollstonecraft referred to Portugal as one of the "most uncivilized European states." *Works*, vol. 5, 167. In *Letters Written during a Short Residence in Sweden, Norway, and Denmark*, she negatively judged the Swedes against the "well-bred French." *Works*, vol. 6, 251. For example, Wollstonecraft, *Rights of Woman*, in *Works*, vol. 5, 109, 111, 113, 187, 266, 232, 271; *Letters Written during a Short Residence in Sweden, Norway, and Denmark*, in *Works*, vol. 6, 244, 257–58.

24. Lady Wortley Montagu, *Letters of the Right Honourable Lady Mary Wortley Montagu written during her travels in Europe, Asia, and Africa Which contain, among other curious relations, accounts of the policy and manners of the Turks drawn from sources that have been inaccessible to other travellers* (London: T. Becket, 1763); Zonana, "The Sultan and the Slave," 600; Ruth Bernard Yeazell, *Harems of the Mind* (New Haven: Yale University Press, 2000), 272.

25. Wollstonecraft, *Rights of Woman*, in *Works*, vol. 5, 74, 76, 266.

26. For example, Marilyn Butler and Janet Todd, eds., in Wollstonecraft, *Works*, vol. 5, 113†b, 155†b; Eugene F. Provenzo Jr., "Time Exposures," *Educational Studies* (2010), 145–46.

27. Wollstonecraft, *Rights of Woman*, in *Works*, vol. 5, 109.

28. Antje Bernstein, *Women of Pleasure: Prostitution in Eighteenth-Century London* (Norderstedt, Germany: GRIN, 2005), 12.

29. Wollstonecraft, *Rights of Woman*, in *Works*, vol. 5, 115.

30. Wollstonecraft, *Rights of Men*, in *Works*, vol. 5, 14; Pitts, *A Turn to Empire*.

31. Inderpal Grewal, *Home and Harem: Nation, Gender, Empire, and the Cultures of Travel* (Durham: Duke University Press, 1996), 54; Zonana, "The Sultan and the Slave," 602.

32. Wollstonecraft, *Rights of Woman*, in *Works*, vol. 5, 98; Hirschmann, *The Subject of Liberty*, 170–98.

33. Samara Cahill, "Powers of the Soul: Wollstonecraft, Islam, and Historical Progress," *Assuming Gender* 1:2 (Autumn 2010), 22–43.

34. Wollstonecraft, *Rights of Woman*, in *Works*, vol. 5, 88; Wollstonecraft, *Rights of Men*, in *Works*, vol. 5, 45; Wollstonecraft, *Rights of Woman*, in Works, vol. 5, 159; ibid., 84.

35. Zonana, "The Sultan and the Slave"; Burton, *Burdens of History*, 66; Grewal, *Home and Harem*, 83; Midgley, *Feminism and Empire*, 20; Grewal, *Home and Harem*, 54.

36. Zonana, "The Sultan and the Slave," 602.

37. Letter from Abigail Adams to John Adams, 4 January 1795 (electronic edition), *Adams Family Papers: An Electronic Archive*, Massachusetts Historical Society. http://www.masshist.org/digitaladams/; Wollstonecraft, *Rights of Woman*, in *Works*, vol. 5, 187.

38. Gordon, *Vindication*, 53–54; Price, "A Future Period of Improvement," in *Political Writings*, 170; Helen Thomas, *Romanticism and Slave Narratives: Transatlantic Testimonies* (Cambridge: Cambridge University Press, 2000), 221; Peter A. Dorsey, *Common Bondage: Slavery as Metaphor in Revolutionary America* (Knoxville: University of Tennessee Press, 2009), 32, 137.

39. Letter from Abigail Adams to John Adams, 4 January 1795 (electronic edition), *Adams Family Papers: An Electronic Archive*, Massachusetts Historical Society. http://www.masshist.org/digitaladams/

40. Zonana, "The Sultan and the Slave," 600; Hannah Mather Crocker, *Observations on the Real Rights of Women* (Boston: John Eliot, 1818), 23.

41. Sarah Grimké, *Letters on the Equality of the Sexes* (Boston: I. Knapp, 1838), 34–35; Grewal, "Women's Human Rights," 351.

42. Grewal, "Women's Human Rights."

43. Mohanty, "Under Western Eyes," 61–88; Mohanty, "Under Western Eyes Revisited," 499–535.

44. Mill, *Subjection of Women*, in *CW*, vol. 21, 264; ibid., 275; ibid. On Mill's private views on the transcendence of religion, see Hamburger, *John Stuart Mill on Liberty and Control*, 65–85.

45. Mill, *Subjection of Women*, in *CW*, vol. 21, 267; Ryan, "Bureaucracy," 149–51; Mill, *Subjection of Women*, in *CW*, vol. 21, 296; see also 275 and 288; Mark Tunick, "Tolerant Imperialism: John Stuart Mill's Defense of British Rule in India," *Review of Politics* 68:4 (2006), 586–611; Mantena, "Imperial Predicament," 305–6.

46. Mill, *Subjection of Women*, in *CW*, vol. 21, 336, 288.

47. Ibid., 282; Said, *Orientalism*, 3; Mill, *Subjection of Women*, in *CW*, vol. 21, 282; Provenzo, "Time Exposures"; Said, *Orientalism*, 206–7. See, for example, Jean Auguste Dominique Ingres's painting *La grande odalisque* (1814).

48. Said, *Orientalism*, 209; Mill, *Subjection of Women*, in *CW*, vol. 21, 290; ibid., 324; ibid., 321.

49. Mill, *Subjection of Women*, in *CW*, vol. 21, 310; ibid.; Said, *Orientalism*, 207.

50. Mill, *Subjection of Women*, in *CW*, vol. 21, 303 note 1; ibid.; Tunick, "Tolerant Imperialism," 605; Mill, *Subjection of Women*, in *CW*, vol. 21, 316.

51. Mill, *Subjection of Women*, in *CW*, vol. 21, 326; ibid., 340; Lynn Zastoupil, *John Stuart Mill and India* (Stanford: Stanford University Press, 1994), 169–207; Margaret Kohn and Daniel I. O'Neill, "A Tale of Two Indias: Burke and Mill on Empire and Slavery in the West Indies and America," *Political Theory* 34:2 (April 2006), 192–228.

52. Mill, *Subjection of Women*, in *CW*, vol. 21, 261–63; Hirschmann, *Gender, Class, and Freedom*, 238; Elizabeth S. Smith, "John Stuart Mill's 'The Subjection of Women': A Re-examination," *Polity* 34:2 (Winter 2001), 181–203; Mill, *Subjection of Women*, in *CW*, vol. 21, 340.

53. James P. Scanlan, "John Stuart Mill in Russia: A Bibliography," *Mill News Letter* 4:1 (Fall 1968), 2–11; Douglas Howland, *Personal Liberty and Public Good: The Introduction of John Stuart Mill to Japan and China* (Toronto: University of Toronto Press, 2005); Okin, "John Stuart Mill's Feminism: The Subjection of Women and the Improvement of Mankind," 105–27; Richard Stites, *The Women's Liberation Movement in Russia: Feminism, Nihilism, and Bolshevism, 1860–1930* (Princeton: Princeton University Press, [1978] 1991), 73–74; Lavrin, *Women, Feminism and Social Change*, 16, 32, 199; Barbara Caine, *English Feminism, 1780–1980* (Oxford: Oxford University Press, 1997), 107; Offen, *Euro-*

pean Feminisms, 139–41; Smith, "John Stuart Mill's 'The Subjection of Women,'" 181–203; Caine, "Elizabeth Cady Stanton, John Stuart Mill, and the Nature of Feminist Thought," 50–65.

54. Stites, *Women's Liberation*, 30, 68–69, 73–75, 89–92. An 1869 translation by Mark Vovchak was reprinted in 1870 with a foreword by Maria Tsebrikova (Marie Zebrikoff). An 1869 edition, reprinted in 1870 and 1896, was translated and introduced by Grigory Blagosvetlov. Plus, there was an 1869 edition by Nikolai Mikhailovsky, reprinted in 1870 and 1906. Scanlan, "Mill in Russia," 4, 7; Stites, *Women's Liberation*, 74 note 20. Stites missed Mikhailovsky's edition, and Scanlan missed Vovchack/Tsebrikova's edition.

55. Isaiah Berlin, *Russian Thinkers* (New York: Penguin, [1978] 2008), 6; Andrzej Walicki, *A History of Russian Thought from the Enlightenment to Marxism* (Oxford: Clarendon Press, 1988), 60, 350–52; Stites, *Women's Liberation*, 44; ibid., 73. For a comparative study of the three early Russian forewords to the *Subjection of Women*, see Botting and Kronewitter, "Westernization and Women's Rights."

56. S. A. Vengerov, ed., "Grigory Blagosvetlov," *Russian Books with Biographical Facts about the Authors and Translators* (St. Petersburg: A. E. Bineke, 1898), vol. 2, 415; ibid.; Andrzej Walicki, *Russian Social Thought: An Introduction to the Intellectual History of Nineteenth-Century Russia* (Goleta, CA: Russian Review, 1977), 7, 13, 15.

57. G. E. Blagosvetlov, "Foreword," in John Stuart Mill, *O Podchinenii zhenshchiny*, ed. G. E. Blagosvetlov (St. Petersburg: A. Morigerovsky, 1869), iii–xv, translation by Elena Rozina; ibid.; ibid.

58. Ibid.; ibid.; Walicki, *Russian Social Thought*, 6–15; Blagosvetlov, "Foreword," iii–xv; Mill, *Subjection of Women*, in *CW*, vol. 21, 282; Stites, *Women's Liberation*, 74.

59. Blagosvetlov, "Foreword," iii–xv; Mill, *Subjection of Women*, in *CW*, vol. 21, 326; Blagosvetlov, "Foreword," iii–xv.

60. Govind Vasudev Kanitkar, "Preface," in John Stuart Mill, *Striyāñcī paravaśatā* (Mumbaīnta: Bābājī Sakhārāma āṇi Kampanī, 1902), 1–28, Epilogue, 1–2, translation by Sarvottam Dhanorkar; Frantz Fanon, *The Wretched of the Earth*, tr. Richard Philcox (New York: Grove Atlantic [1963] 2004), 159; Jayanti K. Patel, "Indian Nationalism and Freedom Struggle: A Conceptual Framework," in *Regional Roots of Indian Nationalism: Gujarat, Maharashtra, and Rajasthan*, ed. Makrand Mehta (New Delhi: Criterion, 1990), 4; Edward Said, *Culture and Imperialism* (London: Chatto and Windus, 1993), 271–72.

61. Padma Anagol, *The Emergence of Feminism in India, 1850–1920* (Aldershot: Ashgate, 2005), 60; Rosalind O'Hanlan, "Introduction," in *A Comparison between Women and Men: Tarabai Shinde and the Critique of Gender Relations in Colonial India* (Madras: Oxford University Press, 1994), 14; Sisir Kumar Das, *A History of Indian Literature: 1800–1910. Western Impact: Indian Response* (New Delhi: Sahitya Akademi, 1991), 181; Prachi Deshpande, "Kanitkar, Kashibai," *Oxford Encyclopedia of Women in World History*, ed. Bonnie G. Smith (Oxford: Oxford University Press, 2008), vol. 1, 4–5; O'Hanlan, "Introduction," 15; ibid.; Anagol, *Feminism in India*, 60; Deshpande, "Kanitkar, Kashibai," 4–5; ibid.

62. Kanitkar, "Preface," Epilogue, 1; O'Hanlan, "Introduction," 41.

63. Kanitkar, "Preface," 10; ibid.; ibid., 13.

64. Ibid., 13; ibid., Epilogue, 1; ibid.; Frantz Fanon, *A Dying Colonialism* (New York: Grove, 1965), 42–46; Radhika Mohanram, *Black Body: Women, Colonialism, and Space* (Minneapolis: University of Minnesota Press, 1999), 72.

65. Kanitkar, "Preface," 13; ibid., 24; ibid., 25.

66. Ibid., 14; ibid.; ibid., 8; ibid., 24; ibid., 9.

67. Carolyn Burdett, "A Difficult Vindication: Olive Schreiner's Wollstonecraft Introduction," *History Workshop* 37 (Spring 1994), 177–87, especially 177.

68. Elizabeth van Heyningen, "Women and Gender in the South African War, 1899–1902," in *Women in South African History: They Remove Boulders and Cross Rivers*, ed. Nomboniso Gasa (Cape Town: Human Sciences Research Council, 2007), 115.

69. Olive Schreiner, "Introduction to the Life of Mary Wollstonecraft and the Rights of Woman" (1889), *History Workshop* 37 (Spring 1994), 188–93, especially 190; ibid.; ibid., 193; Carolyn Burdett, *Olive Schreiner and the Progress of Feminism: Evolution, Gender, Empire* (London: Palgrave, 2001), 175.

70. Schreiner, "Introduction," 193; ibid., 192.

71. Ibid., 193; Wollstonecraft, *Rights of Woman*, in *Works*, vol. 5, 131; Schreiner, "Introduction," 193.

72. Gayatri C. Spivak, "Can the Subaltern Speak for Themselves? [Revised Edition]," in *Can the Subaltern Speak for Themselves? Reflections on the History of an Idea*, ed. Rosalind C. Morris (New York: Columbia University Press, 2010), 21–40.

73. Olive Schreiner, *Woman and Labor* (Stokes, 1911), 108; ibid., 242; ibid., 243.

74. M. Tsebrikova, "Introduction," in John Stuart Mill, *Podchinenie zhenshchiny*, ed. Marko Vovchak (St. Petersburg: S. V. Zvonaryov, 1870), i–xxxvi, translation by Elena Rozina; Martina Barros Borgoño, "Prólogo," *La esclavitud de la mujer* (estudio crítico por Stuart Mill), *Revista de Santiago* (1872), 112–24, translation by Bryan Scoular.

75. Lavrin, *Women, Feminism and Social Change*, 300; Javiera Errázuriz Tagle, "Discourses on Women's Suffrage in Chile, 1865–1949," *Historia* 38:2 (December 2005), 257–86; Erika Maza Valenzuela, "Catholicism, Anticlericalism, and the Quest for Women's Suffrage in Chile," Working Paper 214, The Helen Kellogg Institute for International Studies (December 1995), 19–20; Erika Maza Valenzuela, "Liberals, Radicals, and Women's Citizenship in Chile, 1872–1930," Working Paper 245, The Helen Kellogg Institute for International Studies (November 1997), 9–10.

76. Walicki, *Russian Social Thought*, 5; P. Bykov, "Maria Tsebrikova," 1911. Accessed 8 June 2011 at http://az.lib.ru/b/bykow_p_w/text_0380 .shtml; Theodore Stanton, ed., *The Woman Question in Europe* (New York: G. P. Putnam, 1884), 390–423; Jaakoff Prelooker, *Heroes and Heroines of Russia* (London: Simpkin, 1908), 110; Adele Lindemeyer, "Maternalism and Child Welfare in Late Imperial Russia," *Journal of Women's History* 5:2 (Fall 1993), 117.

77. Tsebrikova, "Introduction," i–xxxvi; ibid.; ibid.; ibid.

78. Borgoño, "Prólogo," 112–24; ibid.; ibid.; ibid.; ibid.

79. Tsebrikova, "Introduction," i–xxxvi; ibid.

80. Borgoño, "Prólogo," 112–24; ibid.; Mill, *Subjection of Women*, in *CW*, vol. 21, 340.

81. Valenzuela, "Catholicism," 3; Valenzuela, "Liberals," 10; Borgoño, "Prólogo," 112–24; ibid.; Jadwiga E. Pieper Mooney, *The Politics of Motherhood: Maternity and Women's Rights in Twentieth-Century Chile* (Pittsburgh: University of Pittsburgh Press, 2009), 2; Valenzuela, "Catholicism," 3; Valenzuela, "Liberals," 10–12.

82. Prelooker, *Russian Heroes*, 99; Stanton, *Woman Question*, 390–423; Margaret McFadden, *Golden Cables of Sympathy: The Transatlantic Sources of Nineteenth-Century Feminism* (Lexington: University Press of Kentucky, 1999), 79, 85–106.

83. Tsebrikova, "Introduction," i–xxxvi.

84. Offen, *European Feminisms*, 19–20; Offen, *Globalizing Feminisms*, xxix–xxxiv; Nancy Cott, *The Grounding of Modern Feminism* (New Haven: Yale University Press, 1987), 14; Lavrin, *Women, Feminism, and Social Change*, 34; Elvira López, "El movimiento feminista," doctoral dissertation, Universidad de Buenos Aires, 1901, 168, translation by Andrea Veach.

85. López, "El movimiento feminista," 168.

86. Ibid., 168, 206.

87. Francine Masiello, *Between Civilization and Barbarism: Women, Nation, and Literary Culture in Modern Argentina* (Lincoln: University of Nebraska Press, 1992), 85.

88. Ackerly, *Political Theory and Feminist Social Criticism*, 2–4; Nussbaum, *Women and Human Development*, 301–3; Hirschmann, *The Subject of Liberty*, 197.

89. Abbey, *The Return of Feminist Liberalism*, 103. Here and elsewhere I follow Mohanty's use of the term "Two-Thirds World" to convey the vast scope of global poverty; a more regionally specific synonym is the "global South." See Mohanty, *Feminism without Borders*, 43–84, 226–28. Mill, *Subjection of Women*, in *CW*, vol. 21, 279. For example, Beitz, *The Idea of Human Rights*, 186–96; Sen, *The Idea of Justice*, 71–72, 115–17, 162–67, 374–75.

90. Martha C. Nussbaum, "Toward a Globally Sensitive Patriotism," *Daedalus* 137:3 (Summer 2008), 78–93; Kwame Anthony Appiah, *Cosmopolitanism: Ethics in a World of Strangers* (New York: W. W. Norton, 2007), xviii; Will Kymlicka and Kathryn Walker, "Introduction," *Rooted Cosmopolitanism: Canada and the World*, ed. Will Kymlicka and Kathryn Walker (Vancouver: University of British Columbia Press, 2012), 1.

91. For example, Diana J. Schaub, *Erotic Liberalism: Women and Revolution in Montesquieu's Persian Letters* (London: Rowman and Littlefield, 1995), 7; Michael Curtis, *Orientalism and Islam: European Thinkers on Oriental Despotism in the Middle East and India* (Cambridge: Cambridge University Press, 2009), 3–4, 8–9, 18–30, 51–52.

Chapter Five. Human Stories

1. A helpful overview of the international trend toward linking the narration of human stories with human rights advocacy since the Second World War, and especially in the aftermath of the Holocaust, is found in Kay Schaffer and Sidonie Smith, *Human Rights and Narrated Lives:*

The Ethics of Recognition (New York: Palgrave Macmillan, 2004), 13–34. I am pushing this history further back in time, showing that (auto)biographical human rights narratives in fact date to at least the late eighteenth century.

2. Wollstonecraft, *Rights of Woman*, in *Works*, vol. 5, 69, 73–74, 88, 101, 200.

3. Mill, *Autobiography*, in *CW*, vol. 1, 247.

4. David Comer Kidd and Emanuele Castano, "Reading Literary Fiction Improves Theory of Mind," *Science* 342:6156 (8 October 2013), 377–80.

5. Hunt, *Inventing Human Rights: A History*, 40–42, 68; Gordon Schochet, "Toleration, Liberty, and Rights: or What Hobbes Knew, Others Feared, and Hohfeld Figured Out," in *The Liberal-Republican Quandary in Israel, Europe, and the United States: Early Modern Thought Meets Current Affairs*, ed. Thomas Maissen and Fania Oz-Salzberger (Boston: Academic Studies Press, 2012), 115–32, especially 126.

6. Hunt, *Inventing Human Rights*, 68; Wollstonecraft, *Letters on the Management of Infants*, in *Works*, vol. 4, 460; Wollstonecraft, *Letters Written during a Short Residence in Sweden, Norway, and Denmark*, in *Works*, vol. 6, 280; Wollstonecraft, *Letters to Imlay*, in *Works*, vol. 6, 370. (*Letters to Imlay* was edited and published by Godwin in 1798, but we have no reason to believe that he made editorial additions to Wollstonecraft's original letters to her first husband.) Wollstonecraft, *Mary, a Fiction*, in *Works*, vol. 1, Advertisement; Wollstonecraft, *Maria, or the Wrongs of Woman*, in *Works*, vol. 1, 95.

7. Mill, "Attack on Literature," in *CW*, vol. 22, 320.

8. Catharine A. MacKinnon, *Are Women Human? And Other International Dialogues* (Cambridge, MA: Belknap Press of Harvard University Press, 2006), 23–24, 162, 175, 196–208; Nussbaum, *Women and Human Development*, 15–24; Abbey, *The Return of Feminist Liberalism*, 111–16, 139–41, 164–66, 270–71; Sen, *Development as Freedom*, 189; Brooke Ackerly, *Universal Human Rights in a World of Difference* (Cambridge: Cambridge University Press, 2008), 136.

9. For example, see Lee Siegel's critique of the 2006 postmodern novel by Dave Eggers, *What Is the What?* Eggers blurred fiction and fact, autobiography and biography, and author and subject by using first-person voice to tell the story of how Valentino Achak Deng survived the exodus from the civil wars in Sudan. Siegel, "The Niceness Racket," *New Republic*, online edition, 19 April 2007. Accessed 27 August 2012

at http://www.powells.com/review/2007_04_19.html. Ackerly, *Political Theory and Feminist Social Criticism*, 152–61.

10. Grewal, "'Women's Rights as Human Rights'"; Mohanty, *Feminism without Borders*, 226–28; Spivak, "Can the Subaltern Speak for Themselves?"

11. Brooke A. Ackerly and Jacqui True, *Doing Feminist Research in Political and Social Science* (New York: Palgrave, 2010), 129, 200–203; Hirschmann, *The Subject of Liberty*, 239 note 3.

12. Wollstonecraft, *Mary, a Fiction*, in *Works*, vol. 1, 7; Gordon, *Vindication*, 31–37.

13. Wollstonecraft, *Mary, a Fiction*, in *Works*, vol. 1, 18, 25.

14. Ibid., 33, 38, 55.

15. Wollstonecraft, *Mary, a Fiction*, 72, 73.

16. William Godwin, *Memoirs of the Author of A Vindication of the Rights of Woman*, ed. Pamela Clemit and Gina Luria Walker (Peterborough: Broadview, 2001), 95.

17. Wollstonecraft, *Letters Written during a Short Residence in Sweden, Norway, and Denmark*, in *Works*, vol. 6, 279.

18. Ibid.; Martha Nussbaum, *The Fragility of Goodness: Luck and Ethics in Greek Tragedy and Philosophy* (Cambridge: Cambridge University Press [1986] 2001).

19. David Hume, "Of Personal Identity," in *A Treatise of Human Nature* (London: John Noon, 1739), vol. 1, part 4, section 6.

20. Botting, "Wollstonecraft in Europe, 1792–1904: A Revisionist Reception History."

21. Ibid.; Roxanne Eberle, *Chastity and Transgression in Women's Writing, 1792–1897: Interrupting the Harlot's Progress* (New York: Palgrave, 2002), 58.

22. Gordon, *Vindication*, 61.

23. Ibid., 342; Shapiro, *Political Criticism*, 55, 290–91.

24. Wollstonecraft, *Maria, or the Wrongs of Woman*, in *Works*, vol. 1, 111, 120.

25. Ibid., 174, 184; Janet Todd, "Introduction," in Mary Wollstonecraft and Mary Shelley, *Mary, Maria, Matilda* (New York: Penguin, 1992), xxvi.

26. Janet Todd, *Mary Wollstonecraft: A Revolutionary Life* (New York: Columbia University Press, 2000), ix.

27. Wollstonecraft, *Rights of Woman*, 130; Wollstonecraft, *Maria*, 120; Jennifer Lorch, *Mary Wollstonecraft: The Making of a Radical Feminist* (Ox-

ford: Berg, 1990); Taylor, *Mary Wollstonecraft and the Feminist Imagination*, 238–39.

28. Annie Nathan Meyer, *Women's Work in America* (New York: Henry Holt, 1891), 150.

29. Stanton was the primary author of *The Woman's Bible* (1895), which gave a controversial feminist reading of the Judeo-Christian scriptures, debunking the moral authority of past patriarchal interpretations.

30. Rebecca Larson, *Daughters of Light: Quaker Women Preaching and Prophesying in the Colonies and Beyond* (New York: Alfred A. Knopf, 1999), 18; William M. Jackson, "Ignorance of the Bible—A Loss to Society," *Friends Intelligencer Supplement* (Philadelphia), 15 September 1906, 12 (a transcript of a speech made at the Friends General Conference, Maryland, 1906).

31. Lucretia Mott, *Lucretia Mott: Her Complete Speeches and Sermons*, ed. Dana Greene (New York: Edwin Mellen Press), 270; Eileen Hunt Botting and Christine Carey, "Wollstonecraft's Philosophical Impact on Nineteenth-Century American Women's Rights Advocates," *American Journal of Political Science* 48:4 (October 2004), 707–22, especially 712.

32. Elizabeth Cady Stanton, *Eighty Years and More (1815–1897): Reminiscences of Elizabeth Cady Stanton* (London: T. Fisher Unwin, 1898), 83; Elizabeth Cady Stanton, Susan B. Anthony, Matilda Joslyn Gage, *History of Woman Suffrage, Volume I, 1848–1861* (Rochester, NY: Charles Mann, 1889), 423–24.

33. Steven B. Smith, "How to Read Lincoln's Second Inaugural Address," in *The Writings of Abraham Lincoln*, ed. Steven B. Smith (New Haven: Yale University Press, 2012), 477.

34. Elizabeth Cady Stanton, *The Selected Papers of Elizabeth Cady Stanton and Susan B. Anthony, Volume II: Against an Aristocracy of Sex*, ed. Ann D. Gordon (New Brunswick, NJ: Rutgers University Press, 2000), 428.

35. Ellen Carol DuBois, *Feminism and Suffrage: The Emergence of an Independent Women's Movement in America, 1848–1869* (Ithaca: Cornell University Press, 1999), 188; Sue Davis, *The Political Thought of Elizabeth Cady Stanton: Women's Rights and the American Political Traditions* (New York: New York University Press, 2008), 128–56; Suzanne Marilley, *Woman Suffrage and the Origins of Liberal Feminism in the United States, 1820–1920* (Cambridge, MA: Harvard University Press, 1996), 165–69; Botting, "Making an American Feminist Icon: Mary Wollstonecraft's Reception in U.S. Newspapers, 1800–1869," 292–93.

36. "Among the Strong Minded," *Weekly Georgia Telegraph*, 7 May 1869, 7; Carrie Chapman Catt, "Then . . . and Now" (1939), 19, in "Speech Fragments," Papers of Carrie Chapman Catt Collection at the Library of Congress, Library of Congress, Washington; Susan B. Anthony, "Inscription" (1904), in Mary Wollstonecraft's *A Vindication of the Rights of Woman* (Boston: Thomas and Andrews, 1792), the Susan B. Anthony Special Collection, Rare Book/Special Collections, Library of Congress, Washington.

37. Pennell, *Mary Wollstonecraft Godwin*, 90; Bertha Pappenheim (as P. Berthold), "Einleitung," in Mary Wollstonecraft, *Die Verteidigung der Rechte der Frau*, tr. P. Berthold (Dresden and Leipzig: E. Pierion's, 1899), xiii, translation by Christine Carey Wilkerson.

38. J. S. Pederson, "Mary Wollstonecraft: A Life in Past and Present Times," *Women's History Review* 20:3 (2011), 423–36; Anna Holmová, "Předmluva," in Mary Wollstonecraft, *Obrana práv žen* (Otázky a názory, XII), tr. Anna Holmová (Prague, 1904), vi, xvi, translation by Irena Cajkova.

39. Mrs. Humphrey Ward, *The Testing of Diana Mallory*, in *Harper's Magazine* 116 (December 1907), 905; "A Voice in the Wilderness," *Votes for Women* 5 (29 March 1912), 212.

40. Jacob Bouten, *Mary Wollstonecraft and the Beginnings of Female Emancipation in France and England* (Philadelphia: Porcupine Press, [1922] 1975), 8; Raymond Birn, *Crisis, Absolutism, Revolution: Europe and the World, 1648–1789* (Toronto: University of Toronto Press, 2005), 389; Virginia Woolf, *The Second Common Reader* (New York: Houghton Mifflin Harcourt, [1932] 2003), 163.

41. Carl Schmitt, *Political Theology: Four Chapters on the Concept of Sovereignty*, tr. George Schwab (Chicago: University of Chicago Press, 1985), 36; James Darsey, *The Prophetic Tradition and Radical Rhetoric in America* (New York: New York University Press, 1997), 34.

42. Michelle Kort, "Ryan Gosling, Feminist Scholar," *Ms. Magazine Blog*, 14 October 2011. Accessed 3 January 2012 at http://msmagazine.com/blog/blog/2011/10/14/ryan-gosling-feminist-scholar/; Richard Dawkins, *The Selfish Gene* (Oxford: Oxford University Press, [1976] 2006), 192, 322; Richard Rorty, "Feminism and Pragmatism," in *Feminist Interpretations of Richard Rorty*, ed. Marianne Janack (University Park: Penn State University Press, 2010), 22; Offen, *European Feminisms*, 19–20; Offen, ed., *Globalizing Feminisms*, xxix–xxxiv.

43. Sidney Tarrow, *Power in Movement: Social Movements, Collective Action, and Politics* (Cambridge: Cambridge University Press, 1994), 118–34.

44. Cott, *The Grounding of Modern Feminism*, 3, 14; Offen, *European Feminisms*, 19, 144–81.

45. Clare Hemings, *Why Stories Matter: The Political Grammar of Feminist Theory* (Durham: Duke University Press, 2011), 33–34; Alice Wexler, "Emma Goldman on Mary Wollstonecraft," *Feminist Studies* 7:1 (Spring 1981), 113–33; Gordon, *Vindication*, 451. Following convention, I use the term "first-wave" to describe feminist arguments and activism prior to the post–World War II revival of the women's movement. For the origin of the term "first-wave feminism," see Marsha Lear, "The Second Feminist Wave," *New York Times Magazine*, 10 March 1968, 24.

46. Mill, *On Liberty*, in *CW*, vol. 18, 217; Mill, *Autobiography*, in *CW*, vol. 1, 198, 259, 264.

47. Taylor Mill, *Complete Works*, 328; Mill, *Autobiography*, in *CW*, vol. 1, 195–96.

48. Jo Ellen Jacobs and Paula Harms Payne, "Introduction" and "To John Stuart Mill," in Taylor Mill, *Complete Works*, 12–35, 320–23.

49. Taylor Mill, "To John Stuart Mill," in *Complete Works*, 355, 439.

50. Ibid., 360, 370.

51. Ibid., 375.

52. Mill, *Autobiography*, in *CW*, vol. 1, 264. For Mill, it would be a cosmic irony if indeed Harriet died of syphilis contracted from her husband John Taylor, who, like many middle-class men of his time, probably used prostitutes before his marriage at thirty to his eighteen-year-old wife. It would be doubly ironic if indeed the diagnosis of syphilis drove her away from John toward Mill, yet led her to prohibit sexual intercourse with either man. Near the end of his life, Mill defended the rights of prostitutes to bodily integrity against overweening legal and medical interventions for the sake of preventing the spread of venereal disease. For a discussion of the possible reasons for Harriet's illness and death, and their implications for her relationships, see Jacobs and Payne, "Introduction," xxxi. See also Jeremy Waldron, "Mill on Liberty and on the Contagious Diseases Acts," in *J. S. Mill's Political Thought*, ed. Urbinati and Zakaras, 11–42. Mill, *Autobiography*, in *CW*, vol. 1, 199, 259.

53. Mill, *Autobiography*, in *CW*, vol. 1, 252, 261.

54. Mill, *On Liberty*, in *CW*, vol. 18, 217.

55. Ibid.
56. Ibid.
57. Meera Kosambi, ed. and tr., *Feminist Vision or "Treason against Men"? Kashibai Kanitkar and the Engendering of Marathi Literature* (Ranikhet: Permanent Black, 2008), 4; Deshpande, "Kanitkar, Kashibai," 5.
58. Kosambi, *Feminist Vision*, 57, 61.
59. Deshpande, "Kanitkar, Kashibai," 4–5; Kanitkar, "Preface," 11.
60. Kosambi, *Feminist Vision*, 60, 66, 325–26. As Kashibai Kanitkar suggested, Mill's economic feminism may be read as necessitating equal economic opportunities for the sexes despite the fact that he did not always explicitly push his premises to this logical conclusion. Similarly, Nancy Hirschmann has made the case that Mill's economic feminism justifies pay for housewives' productive yet traditionally unpaid domestic labor. See Nancy J. Hirschmann, "Mill, Political Economy, and Women's Work," *American Political Science Review* 102:2 (May 2008), 199–213.
61. Melissa Feinberg, *Elusive Equality: Gender, Citizenship, and the Limits of Democracy in Czechoslovakia, 1918–1950* (Pittsburgh: University of Pittsburgh Press, 2006), 17.
62. Charlotte Garrigue Masaryk, "John Stuart Mill", in John Stuart Mill, *Poddanství žen*, tr. Charlotte Garrigue Masaryk (Prague, 1890), 171–75, especially 175, translation by Irena Cajkova.
63. Ibid.
64. Ōuchi Hyōe, "Translator's Introduction," in John Stuart Mill, *Fujin kaihō ron* (Tokyo: Dōjinsha Shoten, 1923), 1–7, translation by Mamiko Suzuki; Ōuchi Hyōe, "Analysis," in John Stuart Mill, *Josei no kaihō*, tr. Ōuchi Setsuko (Tokyo: Iwanami Shoten, 1957), 193–209, translation by Mamiko Suzuki; Howland, *Personal Liberty and Public Good*, 115.
65. Ōuchi, "Translator's Introduction," 1–7.
66. Takahashi Hisanori, "Translator's Introduction" and "John Stuart Mill and His Philosophy," in Jeremy Bentham and John Stuart Mill, *Kōriron* (Tokyo: Shunjūsha, 1928), 3–4, 5–12, translation by Mamiko Suzuki.
67. Ōuchi, "Analysis," 193–209.
68. Ibid.
69. Ibid.
70. Ye-suk Kim, "Word from Translator," in John Stuart Mill, *Yŏsŏng Ŭi Yesok*, tr. Ye-suk Kim (Seoul: Yihwa Yŏja Taehakkyo Ch'ulp'anbu, 1986), 5–8, translation by Min Jung Park.
71. Pyŏng-hun Sŏ, "Word from Translator" and "The Meaning and Limitation of *Subjection of Women*," in John Stuart Mill, *Yŏsŏng Ŭi Chong-*

sok, tr. Pyŏng-hun Sŏ (Seoul-si: Ch'aek Sesang, 2006), 5–9, 194–215, translation by Min Jung Park.

72. Salman Rushdie, *Joseph Anton: A Memoir* (New York: Random House, 2012), 626 (Kindle edition).

73. Rorty, "Human Rights, Rationality, and Sentimentality," 364–65.

74. Ibid.

75. For a contemporary defense of the derivation of rights from wrongs, see Alan Dershowitz, *Rights from Wrongs: A Secular Theory of the Origin of Rights* (New York: Basic Books, 2004).

76. Gayatri Spivak, "Subaltern Talk: Interview with the Editors," in *The Spivak Reader: Selected Works of Gayatri Chakravorty Spivak*, ed. Donna Landry and Gerald MacLean (New York: Routledge, 1996), 287–308, especially 291.

77. Sen, *The Idea of Justice*, 392.

78. Nussbaum, *Creating Capabilities*, 82–83; Mohanty, *Feminism without Borders;* Reilly, *Women's Human Rights*, 13; Hirschmann, "Difference as an Occasion for Rights."

79. Amartya Sen, "India's Women: The Mixed Truth," *New York Review of Books* 60:15 (October 10, 2013). Accessed 4 January 2014 at http://www.nybooks.com/articles/archives/2013/oct/10/indias-women-mixed-truth/?insrc=toc; Sen, *The Idea of Justice*, 70.

80. Declan Walsh, "Taliban Gun Down Girl Who Spoke Up for Rights," *New York Times*, 9 October 2012. Accessed 26 November 2012 at http://www.nytimes.com/2012/10/10/world/asia/teen-school-activist-malala-yousafzai-survives-hit-by-pakistani-taliban.html; Seema Jilani, "The Forgotten Malala," *New York Times*, 12 March 2013. Accessed 29 December 2013 at http://kristof.blogs.nytimes.com/2013/03/12/the-other-malala/; Adam B. Ellick, "Documenting a Pakistani Girl's Transformation," *New York Times*, 7 October 2013. Accessed 29 December 2013 at http://www.nytimes.com/2013/10/08/world/asia/the-making-of-Malala.html.

81. Malala Yousafzai, with Christina Lamb, *I Am Malala: The Girl Who Stood Up for Education and Was Shot by the Taliban* (New York: Little Brown, 2013); Zofeen T. Ebrahim, "Pakistan: Debate Rages over Malala Book Ban," in "Xindex: The Voice of Free Expression," 15 November 2013. Accessed on 29 December 2013 at http://www.indexcensorship.org/2013/11/malalas-book-banned-in-pakistan/

INDEX